THE CASE OF
THE BODIES
IN THE CUPBOARD...

▼

"Christie, a bald-headed, bespectacled hypochondriac, suffered from problems of sexual impotence that led him to prefer his victims to be unconscious or dead. He achieved this by an ingenious arrangement which enabled him to bubble coal gas through a mixture of Friar's Balsam, designed to clear the sinuses.... Women were lured to his shabby flat in Rillington Place and persuaded to sit in a chair with their heads covered with a cloth, breathing in the steam of Friar's Balsam mixed with coal gas; when they were unconscious, they were raped and strangled. The first victim was lured back to the flat in September 1943, when Christie's wife was away visiting relatives; she was buried in the back garden. So was a woman from his place of work, three months later. For the next nine years there were no more victims; then, in December 1952, Christie strangled his wife, Ethel, and placed her body under the floorboards in the front room. After this, he seemed to lose all control and murdered three more women in the course of a few weeks, placing their half-naked bodies in a large kitchen cupboard..."

▼

"A sprawling history of the evolution of forensic science.... A writer who has spent so much time pondering violent crime is well placed to celebrate the meticulous scientific sleuths who help bring criminals to book."

—*The Observer*

WRITTEN IN BLOOD

THE CRIMINAL MIND & METHOD

COLIN WILSON

WARNER BOOKS

A Time Warner Company

This work is volume three in a trilogy
first published in hardcover in Great Britain
entitled WRITTEN IN BLOOD.

WARNER BOOKS EDITION

Copyright © 1989 by Colin Wilson
All rights reserved.

Cover design by Don Puckey
Cover photos by AP/Wide World and Popperphoto

This Warner Books Edition is published by arrangement with
Thorsons UK, Denington Estate, Wellingborough, Northants NN8 2RQ,
England

Warner Books, Inc.
666 Fifth Avenue
New York, N.Y. 10103

 A Time Warner Company

Printed in the United States of America

First Warner Books Printing: January, 1992

10 9 8 7 6 5 4 3 2 1

For John Kennedy Melling

ACKNOWLEDGMENTS

This book owes an immense debt of gratitude to two friends: John Kennedy Melling and Stuart Kind, both of whom have provided me with so much material that they are virtually the co-authors. I was also fortunate enough to secure the cooperation of many other experts in various fields, including Dr. Mike Sayce, Dr. Alf Faragher, Dr. Denis Hocking, and Candice Skrapec, one of America's leading authorities on serial killers. Other American friends who provided information are June O'Shea, Stephen Spickard, Dennis Stacy, Denis Rickard, Michael Flanagin, and Ann Rule. As usual, access to the immense library of my friend Joe Gaute was invaluable, as was the help of the crime-specialist bookseller Camille Wolfe. Two skilled crime writers, Brian Marriner and John Dunning, also provided invaluable information on many cases. Others to whom I owe a debt of gratitude are Paul Williams, Donald Rumbelow (both of the Metropolitan Police), Robin Odell, James Rentoul, D. J. Werrett, and Ian Kimber.

ANALYTICAL TABLE
OF
CONTENTS

Fredric Wertham and the Oedipus murder case. Yochelson and Samenow are converted from "liberalism." Dan MacDougald and the "faulty blocking mechanism." The FBI Psychological Profiling team. The psychology of a sex killer. The Boston Strangler. Son of Sam. The case of Gerald Stano. Lombroso invents the lie detector. August Vollmer is appointed Marshall of Berkeley. Larson and the lie detector. The kidnapping of Father Heslin. Gerald Thompson fools the lie detector. Chris Gugas and the actor accused of indecent exposure. The Petroklos murder case. Hypnosis as a tool of detection. The murder of Ruth Downing. Avery and Aurbeck learn hypnosis. Can a man be hypnotized to kill?: the Hardrup case. The murders of Carl Gregory. The new menace: the "random killer." Dean Corll. The Freeway Killer. John Wayne Gacy. Pedro Lopez, Ecuador's mass murderer of girls. Dennis Nilsen, the Muswell Hill murderer. Daniel Barbosa. The case of Henry Lee Lucas. Lucas murders his mother. Released from jail. His career as a serial killer. Joel Norris on serial killers. The case of Ted Bundy. The vanishing girls. Bundy's escape. The Tallahassee killings. Bundy is convicted. What turned Bundy into a killer? The "hunchback." A new criminology. Van Vogt's "Right Man" theory. "The decision to be out of control." All serial killers have Right Man characteristics. Charles Manson. The case of Leonard Lake. "Sex slaves." Maslow on "dominance." The Moors Murder case—Brady and Hindley. The 'criminal history of mankind." Wells on "jostling crowds." Murderous tyrants. The "golden age of crime detection." The solution of the problem of serial killers? "A diagnostic or prediction instrument." VICAP—the Violent Criminal Apprehension Program. Use of genetic fingerprinting. Conclusions.

Postscript   263

1

The Power of Poison

For more than 2,000 years, poison was the favorite weapon of the assassin. The reason was simple: it was practically undetectable. There was not a single doctor in the ancient world who could have distinguished between sudden death due to poison and sudden death due to heart attack or stroke. In Rome at the time of Jesus, death from strychnine, aconite, belladonna, arsenic, mercury, lead, and poisonous fungi was as common as death by gunshot wounds in Al Capone's Chicago.

The most notorious *cause célèbre* to come down to us from the ancient world was a case involving multiple poisoning, as well as various other forms of murder, and it provides a remarkable insight into the depravity that prevailed even in the Rome of Julius Caesar, before Tiberius, Caligula, Nero and the rest embarked on their careers of mass murder.

The accused was a man named Cluentius, who was suspected of killing his stepfather by poison. But the reason he was on trial, in 66 B.C., was that he was accused of his stepfather's "judicial murder". Eight years earlier, Cluentius had accused his stepfather, a man called Oppianicus, of trying to have him poisoned. The resulting trial was particularly disgraceful because it was widely rumored that the judges had been bribed—probably by both sides. At all events, Oppianicus had been found guilty, and sentenced to exile. And it was while in exile that he had died with an unexpectedness that gave rise to suspicions of poisoning.

The great Roman orator Cicero was engaged to defend Cluentius. Cicero was weak, vain, and boastful, but his brilliance in public argument was unparalleled. He made no attempt to prove his client innocent, or even to prove Oppianicus guilty; instead, he poured out a list of Oppianicus's supposed crimes that left the judges stunned and shattered. If even a half of it is true, then Oppianicus deserves to rank with the most notorious mass murderers in history.

Oppianicus lived in the small town of Larinum, about 125 miles from Rome, and around 80 B.C. he decided to marry a rich matron named Sassia. This lady was apparently a nymphomaniac who had seduced her own daughter's husband, Melinus, then persuaded him to divorce the daughter and marry herself. So Oppianicus found himself confronting a preliminary obstacle in the form of Sassia's young husband. He overcame this by having Melinus poisoned, after which he lost no time in proposing to the rich widow. But Sassia was unhappy—not about the death of her husband, but about the fact that Oppianicus already had two young children by two recent wives. (One wife had died, and he had divorced the other.) If she married him, part of her own fortune would descend to these children. Oppianicus also, according to Cicero, solved this problem with characteristic simplicity. He invited the son of his divorced wife to come and stay with him; within an hour of arriving, the boy was dead. Ten days later, the other child—a baby—was also dead. In ancient Rome, such deaths, due to cholera or the plague, were common. Sassia now saw no obstacle to the marriage, so she and Oppianicus quickly became husband and wife.

Her motives may have been fear as well as self-interest. Oppianicus was not a man to be crossed with impunity, as he had shown a few years earlier. His mother-in-law in those days was a woman called Dinaea, who had lost all her three sons—which meant, of course, that her fortune would in due course descend to her daughter, Oppianicus's wife. Then, suddenly, Dinaea heard that one of her sons was still alive; he had not been killed in battle, as she thought, but was being held prisoner of war. She begged her relatives to try and find him, and Oppianicus was among those who agreed to help. But he had no intention of keeping his promise; an additional heir would prevent his wife inheriting. Dinaea died suddenly and unexpectedly; and when the other relatives tried to locate the missing heir, he had vanished. Oppianicus had arranged to have him kidnapped and murdered. The relatives denounced Oppianicus as a murderer; the citizens of Larinum rose up against him, and Oppianicus had to flee for his life. But he had no intention of staying in exile. The whole country was in ferment, due to civil war, and Oppianicus had no difficulty raising an army of mercenaries. He descended on Larinum, deposed its rulers, and proceeded to execute all his enemies, claiming that the victorious General Sulla (later dictator) had authorized him to do so.

According to Cicero, Oppianicus had poisoned at least one of his previous wives, as well as his brother Gaius and his brother's wife, who was pregnant at the time. But his career of crime began to falter when he murdered a rich young man called Asuvius. It was a brilliantly ingenious plot. Asuvius had decided to go to Rome for a week of debauchery. Oppianicus invited himself along too, taking also a local scoundrel named Avillius. And one night, when Asuvius was safely in bed with a prostitute, Oppianicus rushed around to various acquaintances and claimed that his friend Asuvius was seriously ill, and wanted to make his will. In fact, the man who was lying in bed and pretending to be ill was the scoundrel Avillius. And when the fake Asuvius had made his will, and it had been duly signed and witnessed, the real Asuvius was taken for a walk and murdered; his body was then buried in a sandpit.

It looked like the perfect crime; Oppianicus only had to wait for the statutory time, then claim the dead man's fortune. But things began to go wrong. Friends of the dead man made inquiries, and found that he had last been seen in company with Avillius. Dragged in front of the commissioner of police, Avillius broke down and confessed. Oppianicus was promptly arrested. But his power was great, and his fortune even greater. The commissioner of police was well bribed, and the case abandoned "for lack of evidence".

But now the master villain finally overreached himself. He decided that his next victim should be his stepson Cluentius who, ever since the scandal of the seduced son-in-law, had not been on speaking terms with his mother, Sassia. Cluentius was unwell, and was being treated by a doctor. The doctor's slave, Diogenes, was approached and asked to slip poison into Cluentius's medicine. The slave said he would think about it, and went and told his master. The doctor passed on the information to Cluentius, who immediately realized that fate was offering him the opportunity to bring his stepfather to justice. But he had to act with extreme caution. His first step was to buy the slave Diogenes, so he could be relied upon to cooperate. Next, Diogenes had to apparently agree to the murder plot. The intermediary— the man who had tried to bribe Diogenes—was a swindler and confidence man named Fabricius. When Diogenes told him he was willing to cooperate, the trap was set. The poison and the money were to be handed over to Diogenes by a servant called Scamander. And at the crucial moment, a group of Cluentius's friends leapt out of hiding and seized Scamander, as well as the poison and the money.

Even now, Cluentius had to proceed with caution. Unless Scamander implicated Fabricius, and Fabricius implicated Oppianicus, then he was no better off than before. So first he prosecuted Scamander and, when the court found Scamander guilty, went on to prosecute Fabricius, who was obviously responsible for his servant's actions. Only when Fabricius was also found guilty of attempted poisoning did he go on to prosecute Oppianicus for being behind the whole plot. And, as we have already seen, the judges sentenced Oppianicus to exile, where two years later, he suddenly died . . .

It sounds as if justice had finally triumphed. But this would undoubtedly be a naïve assumption. There can be little doubt that Oppianicus was a multiple murderer; but it is doubtful whether Cluentius was as innocent as Cicero insisted. It seems highly likely that he had his stepfather poisoned. Cicero dismisses this with the comment that Cluentius had no reason to hate Oppianicus, for Oppianicus was already a ruined man, "whose lot was so wretched that death would have been a happy release". This is obvious nonsense. Oppianicus was a wealthy man and his wife was a wealthy woman; in exile or not, he could still plot revenge.

Oppianicus died in 72 B.C. His son, Oppianicus Jr., brought the case against Cluentius six years later. Why such a long wait? The answer can be found in Cicero's defense speech. Cluentius was also accused of trying to poison Oppianicus Jr. It happened at the wedding of Oppianicus Jr., when someone passed him a cup of honeyed wine. It was intercepted by one of his friends, who drank it and fell down dead. Again, Cicero dismisses the accusation as absurd; why, he asks, should Cluentius want to poison his half-brother? But the answer is obvious: because their mother Sassia was a highly dangerous woman, who would never cease to urge Oppianicus Jr. to avenge his father's death. This is, of course, precisely what happened when Oppianicus Jr. accused Cluentius of judicial murder. So, far from being innocent, it seems reasonably certain that Cluentius was guilty of murder and attempted murder, as well as of bribing the judges.

Cicero himself emerges from the case without much credit. He later boasted that he had pulled the wool over the eyes of the judges. What he meant is not clear, but the likeliest assumption is that he knew Cluentius was guilty of murder, attempted murder, and bribery. He also had to explain why he himself had been, at one time, the tool of the mass murderer Oppianicus. When the servant Scamander was accused of attempting to murder Cluentius, it was Cicero who appeared in Scamander's defense. He insisted, with shocked sincerity, that he had no idea of the strength of the evidence against Scamander. But it is unlikely that a lawyer as experienced as Cicero took on a case without knowing exactly what he was doing. The truth is that Cicero was a brilliant weakling, who changed his allegiance as often as it suited him. It is satisfying to record that he finally changed it once too often. When his old friend Julius Caesar was murdered, Cicero took the side of the murderers. When the assassins were defeated, Mark Antony ordered Cicero's death; the executioner caught up with him at his villa at Capetae, and cut off his hands and his head.

2

It seems strange that a criminal as enterprising as Oppianicus should not have achieved greater notoriety in the annals of mass murder. The answer is that he was far from unique. In the first century B.C., Rome was full of poisoners and assassins. There were undoubtedly dozens of other cases that have been forgotten because the advocate was less celebrated than Cicero. Yet Rome was not always a criminals' paradise. As Michael Grant notes in his introduction to Cicero's murder trials: "Murder first became a conspicuous feature of the public life of Rome in 133 B.C., when the aristocratic but radical and reformist *(popularis)* tribune of the people Tiberius Sempronius Gracchus was clubbed to death by the senators he had defied, and by their friends." Before that time, Rome seems to have been a fairly law-abiding place. It was the murder of Gracchus that unleashed a tide of criminality, so that Rome in 70 B.C. had much the same problem as London in A.D. 1770.

The cause was also much the same. As Henry Fielding pointed out, London's "crime explosion" was due to the extreme misery of the poor and the conspicuous consumption of the rich. Rome had been familiar with the problem for centuries—the first strike in history occurred in 494 B.C., when the poor (or plebians) all marched out of Rome, and threatened to go and found their own city unless they were given their rights. The patricians were forced to concede them their own representatives (tribunes), and from then on, Rome became a textbook example of Karl Marx's class struggle. But the struggle turned into a landslide of murder only after the killing of Tiberius Gracchus in 133 B.C., and of his brother Gaius 11 years later. Tiberius was stunned by a blow from the leg of a bench dealt by a fellow senator, then beaten to death by others. Three hundred of his friends and followers were also murdered. A few years later, the class struggle surfaced again, in the bloody confrontation between the left-wing Marius and the right-wing Sulla. Each retained power for a time; each murdered his enemies by the dozen. Once murder has been justified as a political expedient, it can turn into a habit, then a disease. For the next five centuries, the history of ancient Rome is a story of continuous murder.

During that time, poisoning developed into a fine art; experts in its use could prepare poisons that would kill instantly, or take months. The Roman historian Tacitus tells us about a professional poisoner called Locusta, who had been condemned to death, then reprieved to work for the rich, and how she prepared a poison for the emperor Claudius, which was administered in a dish of mushrooms. When it took too long to work, the emperor's physician Xenophon persuaded him that he needed to vomit, and inserted a poisoned feather down his throat, whereupon Claudius finally succumbed. His successor Nero was so delighted that he often used to make a joke about mushrooms being a dish fit for the gods (Claudius having been proclaimed a god). He also made use of Locusta to get rid of Claudius's son Britannicus. His first attempt was a failure—the poison only gave the 14-year-old youth diarrhea—so Nero made Locusta prepare the poison in front of his own eyes. When she finally made a poison that killed a pig on the spot, he hastened off to the dining-room, where the boy was eating. A taster had to try every mouthful of food and drink before Britannicus tasted it, but the boy was handed a drink so hot that it scalded his mouth. Thereupon he took a drink from a glass of cold water, which contained the poison, and fell down dead. Nero shook his head sadly, and remarked that such attacks often carried off epileptics. The other guests decided that it was better to show no surprise, and resumed their dinner.

The skill of the Italians in the art of poisoning became a legend; but, like most legends, it lacked a solid foundation. During the Middle Ages and the Renaissance, there were incredible stories of poisons that could be smeared on a letter or the pages of a book, and that would kill the reader through the pores of the skin; in fact, no such poison was known. The same is true of the "venom" that the Borgias are supposed to have concealed in a spiked ring, so they could kill by merely shaking hands. No such deadly venom existed—most snakes have to inject a fairly large quantity of poison to kill their prey. It is also one of the disappointing facts of history that Lucrezia Borgia, whose name has become synonymous with poison, never killed anyone in her life (she was a mild, gentle girl) by "venom" or any other means. Her murderous brother Cesare, who undoubtedly had dozens of killings to his credit, usually preferred stabbing or strangling.

But by the beginning of the sixteenth century, the virtues of poison as an easy and undetectable way of removing enemies had become widely recognized in Europe, particularly in Rome and Venice. The most powerful men in Venice belonged to the secret Council of Ten, which dealt with conspiracy, treason and offenses against morals, and there is a record of their proceedings dealing with various proposed assassinations, with the word "Factum" written at the side of the assassinations that had been carried out. On December 15, 1543, a Franciscan monk called John of Ragusa offered the council a selection of poisons, and stated his terms for killing various eminent personages: 500 ducats for the Great Sultan, 150 for the King of Spain, 60 for the Duke of Milan, 50 for the Marquis of Mantua and 100 for the Pope. In the following year this offer was accepted, but the records do not detail the results.

The first member of this "Italian school of poisoners" whose name has come down to us is a Sicilian woman called Tofania di Adamo, born about 1640, who moved to Naples in 1659 and marketed a brand of poison that became known as Acqua Tofana. It seems to have been a clear liquid compounded mainly from arsenic and, since this can be used for the complexion, it was sold quite openly, sometimes under the name of "Elixir of St. Nicholas of Bari" (Bari being a town whose water had healing qualities). The chronicles indicate that Tofania became a kind of consultant poisoner—like certain of her Parisian contemporaries who became notorious in the "Affair of the Poisons". She also, apparently, achieved enough influence to become a successful actress. Eventually, alerted by large numbers of sudden deaths, the police decided to arrest her, whereupon she fled and took refuge in a convent. Her pursuers tried psychological warfare, and spread rumors that she had poisoned the city's water supply; this alarmed the nuns, who allowed her arrest. Under torture, she confessed to being responsible for about 600 deaths, including two popes. In 1709 she was strangled and thrown into the courtyard of the convent in which she had taken refuge.

There are also records of a secret society of poisoners, consisting mainly of bored wives, that flourished in Rome during the pontificate of Alexander VII in the 1660s. They gathered about a fortune-teller named Hieronyma Spara, who trained them in the art of poisoning. She was eventually arrested by the Papal police and tortured on the rack. She refused to confess, but one of her acolytes showed less endurance. La Spara and a dozen other women were hanged, and many others whipped through the streets.

A curious glimpse of the state of medical knowledge about poisons can be obtained from an account of the inquest of the Earl of Atholl in 1579. Atholl died after attending a banquet given by the unpopular regent Morton, and poison was suspected. Six doctors were present when the body was opened, and most seemed to agree that he had died from "venom". But the only one who made any attempt to test the verdict was a doctor who dipped his finger into the contents of the stomach, and then tasted it. A contemporary account says he became ill within an hour or so. In 1611, a similar method was used at the inquest on George Home, Earl of Dunbar; it was suspected that a poison had been administered to him in tablets of sugar by Queen Elizabeth's chief minister Robert Cecil. The doctor named Martin Souqir tried a popular method of testing for poison—laying his finger on the dead man's heart, then touching the finger to his tongue. The record stated that Souqir died within a few days, but it seems clear that, if this was so, it was certainly not as a result of the poison administered to Dunbar.

By 1530, the poison legend had taken root in England. When a cook named Rose, a member of the household of the Bishop of Rochester, was accused of poisoning a sauce-pan of porridge and causing two deaths, an Act of Poisoning was hastily passed, on the grounds that "unless it was severely punished, no man would in the future have any security against death by such means". The penalty was to be boiled to death, and this was the punishment that was meted out to the cook in Smithfield. Sixty-four years later, Queen Elizabeth's physician, Dr. Ruy Lopez, was castrated, disemboweled and quartered on a mere suspicion (which we now know to be unfounded) that he was plotting to poison the queen. And a yeoman named Edward Squyer suffered the same fate after he had placed his hand on the pommel of the queen's saddle, crying "God save the queen!" The charge was that he had used this opportunity to smear a deadly poison, obtained from Spain, on the saddle, a poison of such a strength that the queen would have died if she had merely touched it. Squyer may have been guilty as charged—at this distance in time there is no way to assess the evidence—but one thing is certain: that at that time, there was no poison that could kill from mere skin contact.

By this time, chemistry was beginning to develop into a science. For centuries it had been merely another name for alchemy: the search for the Philosopher's Stone that would turn base metals into gold and prolong life. But an increasing number of doctors began to study chemistry simply to discover the secrets of healing. Most of them still accepted the notion (derived from Aristotle) that everything was composed of the four elements—earth, air, fire, and water. In the sixteenth century the great Paracelsus had caused a revolution by rejecting that notion—but in favor of the equally dubious idea that the basic elements are mercury, sulphur, and salt. The greatest seventeenth-century chemist Van Helmont rejected the three elements of Paracelsus in favor of water and air. But in spite of this muddle, chemists were becoming skilled in the practical business of learning the medical properties of various chemicals—so the German Glauber gave his name to a powerful laxative called Glauber's Salt (sodium sulphate), which he preferred to call miracle salt *(sal-mirabile)*. And Franciscus Sylvius, as we have already seen, made the even more interesting discovery of the spirit called Geneva or gin.

In the first decade of the seventeenth century there lived in London an undistinguished apothecary named James Franklin and, towards the end of April 1613, he was approached by a brothel-keeper named Mother Turner with a request for undetectable poisons. (A few poisons caused obvious effects, such as turning the eyeballs yellow, causing the hair to fall out, and so on.) Its purpose was to do away with a brilliant homosexual poet and courtier, Sir Thomas Overbury, who had been thrown into the Tower of London on the orders of the king, James I. Overbury was a victim of a plot hatched by his former lover Robert Carr, and Carr's vindictive mistress Frances, a girl with the face of a juvenile delinquent and the temperament of a young Lady Macbeth. Carr had become the king's favorite, and Overbury was his secretary. But Overbury had made no secret of his detestation of Carr's concubine, Lady Frances Howard, and did his unsuccessful best to dissuade him from marriage. Carr himself was getting tired of Overbury's sulks and tempers, and had no difficulty in persuading the king that a few months in the Tower would improve his manners. But Lady

Frances had an even better idea—that Overbury should
waste away gently in the Tower, so his death would be
ascribed to the dampness of the dungeons.

James Franklin had no difficulty recommending a number
of slow poisons. Overbury was in an ideal situation for a
poisoner, at the mercy of a jailer—Lady Frances had con-
trived the dismissal of the governor of the Tower, Sir
William Wood, and his replacement by one of her own
friends, Sir Gervase Elwes. Another servant of the countess,
Richard Weston, was appointed Overbury's personal attendant—
and poisoner. Mother Turner handed Weston vials of white
arsenic, corrosive sublimate (mercuric chloride), powdered
diamonds (probably powdered glass for which Franklin
charged the price of diamonds), cantharides (Spanish fly)
and something called Great Spiders, and for the next three
months, Overbury ingested these regularly with his meals,
until he was hardly more than a skeleton. In September, he
died of exhaustion. A jury declared that his death was due
to natural causes (mercuric chloride produces the symptoms
of syphilis) and he was hastily buried.

Carr and Lady Frances now went ahead with their marriage. All seemed well until, two years later, the chemist's
assistant who had prepared the poisons for James Franklin
lay on his deathbed, and confessed to a priest. If Carr (now
the Earl of Rochester) had still been the king's favorite, the
confession would undoubtedly have been ignored. But the
king had found a new lover, George Villiers, and Carr was
making scenes. James ordered the affair to be investigated:
the result was the arrest of everyone concerned: Robert and
Frances Carr, Mother Turner, Richard Weston, Sir Gervase
Elwes, and James Franklin. All were sentenced to death, but
the king had promised Carr that he would not be executed;
instead, he and Lady Frances—who now hated one another—
spent six years in the Tower. They were then allowed to
retire to their country home, where Lady Frances died of
cancer of the womb at the age of 39.

3

A few decades later, another chemist, rather more eminent than Franklin, found himself in a court of law charged with providing poisons. He was Christoph Glaser, a Swiss from Basle, and he was famous in his time for his method of making "glaserite" (potassium sulphate) much used as a fertilizer, as well as for his celebrated treatise on chemistry. Glaser was thrown into the Bastille after being charged with aiding the infamous Marquise de Brinvilliers, the most notorious poisoner of her day.

The Marquise—born Marie Madeleine d'Aubray in July 1630—was not beautiful, but since she was petite, with blue eyes and blonde hair, she was exceedingly attractive. She was also a nymphomaniac; in her later confession she admits that sexual experimentation with her brothers began at the age of 7 and included sodomy. At the age of 21, Marie married a gambler and womanizer, the Marquis de Brinvilliers, the colonel of a regiment. Around 1660, he became acquainted with a handsome young captain, the Chevalier Godin de Sainte-Croix, whom he liked so much that he introduced him into his home, and Ste-Croix and the lively marquise were soon lovers. The husband, apparently, found nothing disagreeable in this situation, since most ladies of the aristocracy had their *cavalier*, but her father took an altogether less relaxed view, and induced the king, Louis XIV, to grant him a *lettre de cachet*, enabling him to have the cavalier arrested and thrown in the Bastille. This act was to have unfortunate consequences for the Viscount d'Aubray and his family, for Ste-Croix found himself sharing a cell with a well-known poisoner named Exili, whose first name seems to be unrecorded. Exili had apparently learned his craft in Italy—one chronicler makes him a pupil of a La Toffana—and had worked for Olimpia Maidalchina, sister-in-law of Pope Innocent the Tenth and unofficial queen of Rome. Queen Christina of Sweden had met the poisoner in Rome, and he is supposed to have entered her service. When he arrived in France, after her abdication, his reputation was so unsavory that he was thrown into the Bastille. Exili recognized Ste-Croix's value as a patron, and proceeded to teach him the fundamentals of the art of making poison. We are told that one of these was *venin de crapaud*—toad venom, made by injecting a toad with arsenic, allowing it to decay, and distilling the flesh. But this notion sounds as preposterous as a formula attributed to the Borgias—poisoning a bear with arsenic, suspending it upside down, and collecting the froth that dribbles from its mouth. It is far more probable that Exili taught Ste-Croix how to administer poisons like arsenic and mercuric chloride in quantities that could not be detected.

When Ste-Croix came out of prison, after seven weeks, he succeeded in procuring the release of Exili. The latter was promptly deported to London, but soon succeeded in slipping back into France, and went to live in Ste-Croix's house, where the lessons in toxicology continued.

Yet when Ste-Croix and his mistress decided to poison her father, in order to expedite her inheritance, they decided against using one of Exili's concoctions; instead they turned to Christoph Glaser, the king's Apothecary-in-Ordinary. It was Glaser who provided them with a poison that was guaranteed undetectable. They began by trying it out on the maidservant Françoise in a dish of gooseberries. It gave her severe stomach pains and permanently impaired her health, but she recovered; Marie and her lover therefore requested a stronger brew from Glaser.

It was now three years since Ste-Croix had been in prison, and the Viscount d'Aubray was reconciled to his daughter, believing that she had broken off relations with her lover. In Whitsun 1666, he invited her and her children to visit him at his estate in Offémont. There, after eating a bowl of soup, he began to suffer stomach pains. His daughter insisted on sending for a doctor, who diagnosed indigestion. She nursed her father devotedly throughout a six-month illness, during which he had many recoveries and many relapses; finally, in September 1666, he died.

Marie now proceeded to take a series of lovers, including her husband's cousin, the Marquis de Nadaillac, and her own cousin, by whom she had a child. (She had two children by Ste-Croix.) She also seduced the tutor of her children, a young man named Briancourt. But by 1670, both she and her husband were urgently in need of money. The greater part of her father's fortune had been inherited by her two brothers. The solution was obvious . . .

But first, it was necessary to conduct further experiments to make sure the poison was undetectable. Marie began to pay visits to a hospital run by Sisters of Mercy, the Hôtel-Dieu, carrying biscuits and preserved fruits. The doctors were puzzled when some of their patients began to suffer from an unknown disease whose chief symptom was fatigue, followed by a gradual wasting away. Marie called several times to follow the progress of these unfortunates, and showed the appropriate distress when they finally expired. (It is only fair to add that Voltaire, in his book on Louis XIV, dismissed this whole story as the invention of a sensational chronicler.)

Marie's two brothers were, respectively, a Civil Lieutenant and a Court Councillor; the elder, Antoine d'Aubray d'Offémont, was married; the younger brother, who was unmarried, lived with them. Impatient at the slowness of the poison, Marie hired two assassins to stab one brother to death when he was on the road, but they bungled it. After that failure, she reverted to the more reliable method. A valet called Jean Hamelin, known as La Chausée, was hired, and accompanied Marie on a visit to her brothers. The elder brother became suspicious one day when some wine tasted too acidic and smelt of vitriol; but La Chausée—explained apologetically that he had left some medicine in the bottom of the glass, and this was accepted. Three months later, in April 1670, La Chausée accompanied the brothers to Villequoy, in Beauce. After a meal of pigeon pie, seven people were overcome with vomiting. Five days

later, the brothers returned to Paris, where the illness of the
elder puzzled the doctors. He died on June 17, 1670. In
September, the younger brother died of the same illness.
Doctors who performed a post-mortem suspected poison,
but were not sufficiently certain to pursue the charge. La
Chausée received a bequest of 100 crowns for his devoted
service.

Ste-Croix and La Chausée now began to blackmail her,
and part of the servant's price was Marie's sexual favors—a
secretary calling one day found them in a compromising
position. And, incredibly, Marie told her young lover Briancourt
about the poisoning of her brothers. When Ste-Croix tried to
force her to disgorge the 55,000 livres she had promised to
pay for his help, she made a scene and took poison. Warm
milk made her vomit and counteracted the poison, but she
was ill for several months. And Ste-Croix continued to
blackmail her, threatening her with a certain box that he
kept in his laboratory, which contained some compromising
letters. It seems that she decided that one solution would be
to poison her husband and marry Ste-Croix, and proceeded
to administer small quantities of poison to the penniless
gambler. Ste-Croix had no wish to marry her, and is said to
have administered antidotes, so the unfortunate man's health
swung like a pendulum between extremes. For whatever
reasons, the baron survived her.

Constant need for money led her to decide to poison the
two remaining relatives who stood in the way of the family
inheritance: her sister-in-law, Marie Thérèse Mangot, and
her sister, a nun, also called Thérèse. And she continued to
confide her designs to her young lover Briancourt, who was
horrified and tried to dissuade her. When she ignored him,
he even sent a message to Mme Mangot, warning her to
beware of poison. Marie de Brinvilliers was infuriated, and
sent a relative of La Chausée to minister to his needs;
Briancourt gave the man a beating and sent him away. Then
Ste-Croix tried, entering Briancourt's bedroom at night,
only to find him awake and fully dressed. Two days later,
while passing the Church of St. Paul, Briancourt had a

narrow escape when a bullet pierced his coat. In a rage, he went to Ste-Croix's house and denounced him as a scoundrel who would come to a bad end. Soon afterwards, he became a teacher in a religious house in Aubervilliers.

Then, in July 1672, Ste-Croix died. There are two accounts of his death, one of which states that he was bending over a bubbling retort in his laboratory in the rue des Bernadins when he inhaled a deadly poison and collapsed; the other, less dramatic but more plausible, is that he died after an illness lasting five months. He had left instructions that a small box, about 18 inches square and covered with red calfskin, should be handed over to Marie de Brinvilliers. But Ste-Croix's wife, from whom he was separated, insisted that it should be opened in the presence of some officials.

Marie heard the news and rushed from her country home to Paris; she was too late. The box had been opened, and its contents were being discussed all over Paris. There was Ste-Croix's will, demanding that the box should be handed over to Marie de Brinvilliers, and two promissory notes: one from Marie, promising to pay 30,000 francs, and the second, from a wealthy man named Reich de Pennautier, promising to pay 10,000 francs. Pennautier was an old friend of Ste-Croix, and had risen suddenly in the world, owing his present position of Receiver-General to the sudden death of a man called Saint-Laurent. The box also proved to contain various packets of poison, listed as corrosive sublimate, Roman vitriol, powdered vitriol, opium, and antimony, as well as a vial of clear liquid with a white powder at the bottom. Animals and birds to whom this was fed died quickly, but showed no trace of poison on being dissected.

La Chausée was found wandering around Paris and arrested; he was found to be in possession of a packet of "powdered vitriol". Under torture, he finally confessed that he had poisoned the two d'Aubray brothers on the orders of Ste-Croix. La Chausée was sentenced to be broken on the wheel.

Marie fled, first to Germany, then to a convent in Liège, where she took refuge. A police agent named François Desgrais was sent to entrap her. He had a gentlemanly manner, and posed as an abbé, Marie received him without suspicion; by now she was bored and undoubtedly sex-starved after almost three years "on the run." So she had no hesitation in accepting the charming abbé's proposal that they should meet for a drive outside the convent. At a signal from Desgrais, archers rushed out of hiding, and Marie was informed that she was under arrest. In her room in the convent Desgrais found a box containing a confession. This acknowledged that she had commenced her career of "vicious indulgence" at the age of 7, and gave details of poisoning of her father and brothers—mostly with "toad venom"—as well as an indecisive attempt to poison one of her daughters, whom she regarded as a "ninny."

The trial lasted from April 29 to July 16, 1676; one of the chief witnesses against her was her lover Briancourt, whom she taunted with being a weakling. But on the whole, she bore herself with dignity that gained her many sympathizers—even when she was being subjected to the "water torture," which involved being stripped naked and bent backwards over a trestle, which strained her body into an arc, while gallons of water were poured into her mouth through a funnel. When she became unconscious, her confessor was sent for—he seems to have provided her with much spiritual comfort at the end. Finally, dressed only in a shift, she was taken in a cart, with a rope around her neck, to the Place de la Grève, where she was decapitated by a single blow of the headman's sword. The blow was delivered with such precision that her doctor, who was watching, thought for a moment that the executioner had missed; then the head toppled and rolled backwards. The executioner picked up the body under one arm—she was a small woman—and the head in his other hand, and threw them onto a pile of faggots beside the scaffold; an hour later, nothing of them remained.

It is reported that her last words were that it seemed

unfair that she should suffer the penalty of the law when most people of quality were making free use of poison . . .

Pennautier was also tried, charged with having poisoned Saint-Laurent; but he was a great deal richer than Marie, and had no trouble persuading his judges that he was innocent. As to the eminent apothecary Christoph Glaser, he spent some time in the Bastille in 1676, but was soon released; he died two years later, rumor attributing the cause of death to rage and indignation.

———————————— 4 ————————————

The police chief, Nicholas de La Reynie, had good reason to know that Marie's last words were no exaggeration. His predecessor—another Daubray—had been poisoned by his wife. And in the year after Ste-Croix's death, La Reynie began to hear rumors of a large-scale poisoning; two priests informed him that many penitents were asking absolution for murdering their spouses. A young lawyer who was having a meal with a fortune-teller known as La Vigoreux, wife of a tailor, was startled to hear another fortune-teller, Marie Bosse, declare "What a marvelous trade! Duchesses, marquises, princes! Three more poisonings and I'll be able to retire." The lawyer passed on this information to Desgrais, who sent the wife of one of his officers along to ask Marie Bosse's advice about her husband's cruelty. On the second visit, Mme Bosse handed over a vial of a colorless poison, together with precise instructions for using it. And finally, on January 4, 1669, the police descended on Marie Bosse in the early hours of the morning and placed her under arrest. La Reynie was shocked to be told that Marie had been found sharing a huge bed with her two sons and her daughters, for it was believed that magical powers could be passed from one member of a family to another by incest. La Vigoreux was also arrested, and she and Bosse proved more than willing to talk. At first, La Reynie thought he was dealing with a harmless matter of witchcraft—love potions and magic spells—for although belief in magic was still common among the uneducated class, the aristocracy of the Age of Reason was already inclined to dismiss it as pure imagination. But as La Reynie listened to the confessions, he realized with alarm that Marie Bosse had not been exaggerating when she talked about her clients: this affair involved the ''highest in the land.'' Moreover, Bosse and La Vigoreux were associated with an eminent fortune-teller called Catherine Deshayes, known as La Voisin, whose wealthy and aristocratic clients included members of the court. One client, Mme. de Poulaillon, was the wife of the Master of Forests and Waterways in Champagne, while another two, Mme. Leféron and Mme. Dreux, were the wives of Paris magistrates who would probably be called to try these ''witches.'' Finally, with astonishment, La Reynie heard the names of two of the king's mistresses, Louise de la Vallière and Mme. de Montespan, and at that point he knew that the king himself must be informed. And when the king heard the details, he decided immediately that this could not be tried in open court; all this talk of poisons and love potions could only bring the monarchy into discredit. La Vigoreux was tortured—she died under torture—and so were Marie Bosse and La Voisin. They told amazing stories of poison and magic spells. The pretty Mme. Poulaillon, burdened with an aging husband and a demanding lover, had been given shirts treated with arsenic, which would cause her husband to scratch himself, and a ''healing ointment'' that would kill him in 10 weeks. But her husband had come to suspect her designs, and had her confined in a convent. And Mme. de Montespan, for 10 years the king's favorite mistress, had called on the sorceresses whenever the king's affections had seemed to be diminishing, and had been supplied with love potions and aphrodisiacs, including Spanish Fly, mashed blister beetles, cocks' combs and cocks' testicles. And there was worse to come. Montespan had raised the question of whether the queen and Louise de la Vallière might be killed by witchcraft. This was beyond the powers of the fortune-tellers; they sent her instead to the ''high priest of devil worship,'' an evil old man called Abbé

Guibourg. The essence of the black masses performed by Guibourg was the sacrifice of a newborn baby. Mme. de Montespan was made to lie naked on a bed, her feet dangling on the floor, with the sacred chalice on her groin. La Voisin brought in a baby, and Guibourg slit its throat over the chalice, into which he drained its blood, reciting the names of Mme. de Montespan and the king. The child's entrails were removed, and its body burned in a furnace; the entrails were used for distilling a magic potion—which included the Host used in the black mass—and this was given to Mme. de Montespan to administer to the king.

La Voisin's daughter, who described all this, also told how a lady of the court named Mme. des Oeillets had come for a magic potion, accompanied by a man; Guibourg had explained that he would need to mix the sexual discharges of both into the potion. But since Mme. des Oeillets was menstruating, he accepted instead some of her menstrual blood, which he mixed with the sperm which the man had produced by masturbating into the chalice.

The king was horrified. If this became known, he would be the laughing stock of Europe. He therefore gave orders that the case should be tried in private. The trial began in April 1679, and dragged on until July 1683; 104 defendants appeared before a selected panel of 12 judges in a chamber of the old Paris Arsenal; since this was lit by candles and torches it became known as the Chambre Ardente (lighted chamber). Many other priests were found to be involved, and the king was shocked to discover the astonishing extent of black magic in France. Thirty-six death sentences were handed out, and four life sentences to the galleys; another 34 prisoners were sentenced to banishment or heavy fines. No word of the proceedings leaked outside the walls of the "Poison Chamber," but the long and grim series of executions left the public in no doubt of the seriousness of the crimes involved. The name of Mme. de Montespan was never mentioned; she had been replaced by a new favorite, Mme. de Maintenon—who had been her protégée—and retired to a convent. In 1709, the king ordered that all papers relating to the case should be destroyed; but by some error, the minute-book of the clerk of the court was overlooked; it was finally published in the second half of the nineteenth century, revealing for the first time one of the most incredible stories of murder and black magic in the recorded annals of crime.

_____ 5 _____

The first poisoning case in which medical evidence played the decisive role was the trial, in 1751, of Mary Blandy, charged with poisoning her father with arsenic. In 1746, at the age of 26, Mary was still unmarried, although she was an heiress to a fortune of £10,000; her father, a prosperous lawyer of Henley-on-Thames, took exception to most of the young men who showed signs of interest in his plain but good-natured daughter. But in that year, Mary made the acquaintance of a Scottish captain, the Hon. William Henry Cranstoun, who immediately began to pay her attentions. Cranstoun had many disadvantages; he was small, pock-marked, cross-eyed, and already married; none of this prevented him from deciding to win Mary's hand. The first step was to rid himself of his wife, who was being supported by her relatives in Scotland. He wrote to her explaining that his chances of advancement in the army were poor while he was married, and begging her to write him a letter stating that she had merely been his mistress. She was finally persuaded to do this, whereupon Cranstoun circulated copies to his and her relatives, and instituted divorce proceedings. His wife opposed it and proved that their marriage was legal. And Mr. Blandy, who had been prepared to accept Cranstoun as a son-in-law—after all, he was the brother of a Scottish peer—indignantly reproached the ugly little Scot and indicated that the engagement was at an end. Cranstoun nevertheless continued to call, and he and Mary continued to regard themselves as secretly engaged, although she declined his suggestion that they should run away and marry. Mrs. Blandy became the captain's ardent ally after he had given her £40 to pay a debt she had contracted on a visit to London. Soon after this visit, in September 1749, Mrs. Blandy became suddenly ill and died, begging her husband to allow Mary to marry Cranstoun. When Cranstoun wrote to Mary, telling her that he was besieged by the bailiffs, and needed his £40, she borrowed the money and sent it to him.

From this point on, we must accept either the version of those who believe Mary guilty, or those who are convinced she was an innocent dupe. Cranstoun explained to her that he knew a fortune-teller called Mrs. Morgan, whose magic potions could be relied upon to make her father change his mind. And on a visit to the Blandy household in 1750, Cranstoun apparently demonstrated the efficacy of a magic powder by slipping some of it into the old gentleman's tea. He had been in the worst of tempers at breakfast, yet overflowing with benevolence at dinner. Mary allowed herself to be persuaded to continue the doses. And in April 1751, Cranstoun sent Mary some "Scotch pebbles"—a fashionable ornament at the time—together with a white powder for cleaning them. Mary began to administer the powder to her father in small doses. And the fact that Francis Blandy began to suffer acute stomach pains must have made her aware that the potion was less harmless than her lover claimed. And when the servant, Susan Gunnel, tasted some of the gruel that Mr. Blandy was about to eat, she also became ill. After that, Susan poured out the gruel from the pan and noticed a gritty white powder in the bottom; she took this to a neighbor, who sent it to an apothecary. But since no reliable chemical test was known for arsenic, no immediate analysis was attempted. Nevertheless, Susan went to Mr. Blandy and warned him that she thought he was being poisoned by his own daughter. And when Blandy asked Mary if she had put anything into his tea, she became pale, and hurried from the room.

Incredibly, Mr. Blandy took no steps to prevent Mary from meddling with his food. And when he was shown a letter Mary had written to Cranstoun, begging him to take care of what he wrote, he only smiled and said: "Poor lovesick girl! What a woman will do for the man she loves." Then he continued to sink. And when Mary, now in a panic, threw some letters and powder into the kitchen fire, the cook rescued the powder as soon as she left the room. Mr. Blandy asked to see Mary, who fell on her knees and begged him not to curse her; he told her that he blessed her, and hoped God would forgive her. Two days later, he died.

That same afternoon, Mary begged the footman to accompany her to France, and offered him £500, which he refused. The following morning, she ran out of the house and tried to escape, but was soon surrounded by an angry crowd. Her lover was more successful; when he heard news of her arrest, he fled to France.

When Mary was tried, on March 3, 1752, the main witnesses against her were four doctors. They agreed that the condition of Mr. Blandy's inner organs suggested arsenic poisoning, and that the white powder they had analyzed was arsenic. But the only test they had been able to apply involved touching a red-hot iron to the powder, and sniffing the vapor, which they declared to be that of arsenic. In later years such evidence would have been unhesitatingly rejected. On the other hand, servants were able to state, in considerable detail, when and how Mary had administered poison to her father—to such an extent that it now seems astonishing that Mr. Blandy was not warned in time. Mary made a passionate speech in which she flatly denied administering poison although she admitted that she *had* put a powder in her father's food "which had been given me with another intent." She gave her father the powder, she said, to make him fond of Cranstoun. The prosecution rejected this with contempt, pointing out that she had attempted to destroy the powder as soon as she knew she was suspected. And after thirteen hours, the jury took only five minutes to find Mary guilty.

Six weeks later, her hands bound with black ribbon, she mounted the gallows outside Newgate, insisting to the end that she had no intention of killing her father. Her last words were to ask the hangman not to hang her too high "for the sake of decency." Cranstoun survived her by only six months, dying "in considerable agony" at Furnes, in Flanders, in his fortieth year.

Where Cranstoun was concerned, it was the old gentleman who had the last laugh. While Mary was awaiting her trial she was told that her father's estate amounted to less than £4,000. The fortune of £10,000—which had attracted Cranstoun—had either never existed, or been long spent. This was almost certainly the reason that Francis Blandy had set his face against so many aspiring suitors—because he was unable to provide the promised dowry. The irony of the situation must have come home to him on his deathbed; he had wronged his daughter by withholding the truth, and now she had poisoned him to obtain a non-existent fortune. This would seem to explain why he asked the weeping girl: "How canst thou think I could curse thee?"; after all, he had only himself to blame.

---------------------------- 6 ----------------------------

It was at about the time of the Blandy case that Henry Fielding had to interrogate a woman who was accused of causing the death of her husband by poison. No poison was found in her house, and there was no evidence that she had ever purchased poison. And when Fielding applied to doctors to know whether there was any method of detecting poison in the human body, he was told that such a method did not exist. This led Fielding to deplore the absence of some way of "making poison visible." In fact, the only fairly reliable method of testing for poison was one employed in the Brinvilliers case—to feed some of the substance to an animal, and see if it died.

Fielding died in 1754, unaware that a generation of men who would transform the science of chemistry had been born within his lifetime: Joseph Priestley in 1728, Henry Cavendish in 1731, Karl Wilhelm Scheele in 1742, and

Antoine Lavoisier in 1743. These men, and others like them represent the true dividing line between the alchemy of Paracelsus and the chemistry of Dalton and Mendeléeff. They discovered, to begin with, that air was not an "element," as all chemists so far had believed, but a mixture of different gases. Cavendish made hydrogen by dissolving zinc in sulphuric acid. Priestly made oxygen by heating red oxide of mercury. Lavoisier took the all-important step of realizing that oxide of mercury is a combination of oxygen and mercury. And in 1775, Scheele, who had already discovered seven or eight acids, discovered that he could make an acid from arsenic by dissolving the oxide ("white arsenic") in nitric acid or water containing chlorine. And when zinc was dropped into arsenic acid, a dangerous gas that smelt of garlic was given off—arseniuretted hydrogen, or arsine. So clearly, if someone's stomach contents contained oxide, it could be made to reveal its presence as a distinctive gas by a few simple steps.

A decade later, Samuel Hahnemann took this process a significant stage further when he discovered that when sulphuretted hydrogen (the gas that smells like rotten eggs) is bubbled into arsenic acid, the result is a yellow deposit— yellow sulphate of arsenic (which the ancients knew as orpiment, and used as a caustic and depilatory). And this, in turn, when heated produces "white arsenic." So a mixture containing suspected arsenic could again be identified by three simple steps: dissolving in nitric acid, mixing with sulphuretted hydrogen, and heating—alone or with charcoal— to produce white arsenic.

It was only one step from this to the discovery by Johann Metzger that if substances containing arsenic were heated, and a cold plate was held overhead, a white layer of arsenious oxide would form on the plate. And if the arsenic was heated with charcoal to the point of red heat, metallic arsenic would be deposited on a cold plate, or in the cooler part of the test tube—the so-called arsenic mirror.

All this was useful if a chemist was faced with the problem of whether a substance, or the contents of someone's stomach, contained arsenic. But what if the arsenic had already been absorbed into the body? In 1806, Dr. Valentine Rose, of the Berlin Medical Faculty, solved this problem when he cut up the stomach of a possible poison victim and boiled it in water. After many filterings, the liquid was treated with nitric acid, which had the simultaneous effect of getting rid of the remains of the flesh, and of converting any arsenic into arsenic acid, which could then be detected by any of the methods described above. (Rose converted the acid to the carbonate and hydroxide of arsenic with potassium carbonate and calcium hydroxide, then obtained an "arsenic mirror" by heating with charcoal.)

Three years later, all Germany was thrown into a state of shock by the revelations at the trial of a mass murderess, Anna Zwanziger, the most sensational case of its kind since the Marquise de Brinvilliers. But at least Brinvilliers had poisoned for an understandable motive—money. Zwanziger seems to have killed her victims for the sadistic joy of watching them suffer. The German jurist Anselm Ritter von Feuerbach said that she trembled with joy when she looked on the white powder, and quotes her as saying that arsenic was "her truest friend."

The daughter of a Nuremberg innkeeper, Anna Maria Schonleben married a solicitor named Zwanziger who was also an alcoholic, and left her in penury. The constant reading of Geothe's gloomy novel *The Sorrows of Young Werther* led her to attempt suicide on two occasions, and she drifted from place to place, working as a domestic. In Weimar she fled with a diamond ring belonging to her employers, and a public advertisement of the theft came to the attention of her son-in-law, who ordered her out of his home. She found a job as a housekeeper with a judge named Glaser, in Rosendorf, Bavaria. It seems to have struck her that Glaser would make an excellent husband, but there was one impediment: Glaser's wife, from whom he was separated. Anna set about reconciling the two, and was soon able to welcome Frau Glaser back into her home with flowers strewn on the floor. Within a few weeks, Frau Glaser had died in agony. But Judge Glaser showed no sign of wanting to transfer his affection to his housekeeper, who was thin, sallow and 50 years old. Perhaps he was alerted by the stomach ailments suffered by guests after they had eaten meals prepared by Anna; at all events, she decided to move to the house of another judge in Sanspareil, a younger man named Grohmann, who was unmarried but suffered from gout. Regrettably, he had a fiancée, and Anna became increasingly jealous. When the marriage banns were published, Judge Grohmann died suddenly; his doctor attributed the death to natural causes.

Once more Anna found herself a job as a housekeeper to a member of the legal profession, a magistrate named Gebhard. He was also married, and his wife was pregnant; but her health was poor. When she died, accusing the housekeeper of poisoning her, no one took the accusations seriously. But Gebhard, like the others showed no sign of wanting to marry Anna. Moreover, as his servants expressed intense dislike of the skinny widow, and told stories of violent colics suffered by those who incurred her displeasure, he finally decided to dismiss her. Half an hour or so after she had left in a carriage for Bayreuth, most people in the household became ill—including the baby, to whom Anna had given a biscuit soaked in milk. It was recalled that Anna had refilled the salt box before she left, and its contents were submitted for analysis. As we have seen, this was now a simple matter; there were at least three reliable tests for white arsenic. And this is what proved to have been mixed with the salt.

It took the law some time to catch up with her. She lived in Bayreuth a month, then went back to Nuremberg, then tried to persuade her son-in-law in Mainfernheim to take her in. But he was no longer her son-in-law, having divorced the daughter after she had been imprisoned for theft and swindling. Anna went back to Nuremberg, and was arrested on October 18, 1809. In her pockets were found a packet of tartar emetic and a packet of white arsenic.

For six months Anna Zwanziger simply denied everything. But at this point, Frau Glaser's body was exhumed, and the method of Valentine Rose, invented only four years previously, revealed arsenic in the vital organs—arsenic lingers on in the human body (including the hair) for a very long time. When told about this discovery, Zwanziger knew she was trapped; she fell to the floor in convulsions and had to be carried out of court. And a long and detailed confession followed—including the attempted poisoning of fellow servants and guests of her employers, apparently merely for her own entertainment. Sentenced to death, she remarked that it was probably just as well, since it would have been impossible for her to stop poisoning. She was beheaded, by sword, in 1811, more than two years after her arrest.

7

In the year Anna Zwanziger was executed, there finally occurred the major turning point in the history of poisons: at the Paris School of Medicine, a young Spaniard named Orfila obtained his medical degree. It would hardly be an exaggeration to describe Orfila as the Isaac Newton of toxicology; after the publication of his great *Treatise on Poisons* in 1813, the murderer who killed by poison took the same risk as the murderer who killed with a knife or gun.

Mathieu Joseph Bonaventure Orfila was born in Mahon, on the east coast of Minorca, on April 24, 1787. The tiny island was, to put it mildly, a backwater; Mahon did not even have a school. But Mathieu learned to read early, and had soon read all the books in his father's library. In the dazzling sunlight of the Mediterranean, he devoured everything he could find about ancient Greece and Rome. His tutors were a series of priests, and it was probably from one of these—a native of Languedoc who had fled from the Revolution—that he first heard the name of the great chemist Lavoisier, who had been guillotined during the Terror. By the age of 14 he could speak five languages, including Latin and Greek, and had written a Latin thesis on philosophy.

The first ambition of the young prodigy was to become a sailor—understandably, since a youth of his brilliance must have found the island, where life was dominated by the Catholic Church, boring and stifling. But on his first voyage to Alexandria, at the age of 15, he discovered that travel bored him, and preferred to stay in his cabin reading. Sea sickness, terrifying storms, and a close encounter with pirates confirmed his lack of aptitude for the life of a seaman. Back at home a meeting with a German professor named Cook convinced him that his true vocation was medicine; at the age of 16, he enrolled in the chemistry class in Valencia.

Irritated by the old-fashioned doctrines—which regarded air and water as elements—he began to buy more up-to-date works by Lavoisier and Vauquelin, and was soon so excited by them that he slept for only two hours a night. At 18, his exam results were so brilliant that he was chosen for a scholarship to the University of Barcelona. There his successes were also spectacular, and the university decided to send him on to Paris to complete his education: he was then to return to Barcelona, to occupy a chair of chemistry that would be created for him. But fate had other plans.

In Paris, he lived the life of a penniless student; poverty only spurred his ambition. On the day he received his medical degree he had only 6 francs in his pocket. Friends came to his aid; one of them lent him a large room in which he could give lectures on chemistry, and within a few weeks, Orfila had 40 enthusiastic students, each paying 40 francs for the course. Soon he was able to set up his own laboratory, in which he also gave a course in botany.

The revelation that turned him into Europe's greatest toxicologist occurred one day in April 1813, when he had a particularly large audience for his chemistry lecture. He was speaking about arsenious acid, and explaining that when it was mixed with various liquids—wine, coffee, broth—there would always be a white, chalk-like precipitate. Whereupon he took some coffee from a cup on his chair and mixed it with the acid. And instead of a white precipitate, there was a murky grey one. He tried the same experiment with ammoniated copper sulphate, and was again embarrassed to obtain a blackish-green coloring with a bright green precipitate. Blushing with vexation, Orfila told his students that there must be some organic matter in the acid which explained the unexpected result.

Orfila was not the kind of person who liked to be proved wrong in public. Immediately after his lecture, he took samples of broth, wine, tea, milk, and other natural substances, and mixed them with various poisons. Then he performed the standard chemical tests to detect these poisons. And in more than half these tests, he failed to detect them.

That stunned him. For it meant that if a professor of chemistry was called upon to try and detect a poison in soup or wine or coffee—or the organs of the body—he would probably fail. He looked up all the volumes of chemistry he could find in the university library, and various books on forensic medicine. None of them seemed to be aware of this problem. "The central fact that had struck me had never been perceived by anyone else. My first words were these: *toxicology does not yet exist.*" In 19 cases out of 20, the forensic pathologist who was investigating a suspected poisoning would find himself in a state of total confusion.

The challenge was obvious. Could Orfila turn toxicology into a science? His driving ambition told him that here was a chance to become a famous man. And, typically, his first step was to go to a bookseller (in those days most of them were also publishers) and ask if he was willing to bring out a book on poisons in two volumes. An hour later, the contract was signed. Then Orfila went back to his laboratory and settled down to work. And he worked so fast that the first volume of his *Treatise on Poison, or General Toxicology*, was soon published at 6 francs a copy. Its impact was immediate and tremendous. After all, the "Italian school of poisoners" still flourished in many parts of Europe, and old hags prepared solid or liquid poisons according to the formulas attributed to the Borgias—poisoning an animal, rubbing arsenic or strychnine into its flesh, and collecting the liquid that dripped from it as it decayed. And now Orfila had created a science of toxicology that should enable a doctor employed by the police to detect any poison, no matter how it had been prepared. And in an age when poison was one of the most popular means of murder, this was virtually a revolution in criminology. It was also the kind of revolution that appealed to the general public; Orfila was a scientist who was also a detective. To his astonishment, the 26-year-old chemistry teacher suddenly found himself in demand in the salons. In 1815, he made an ''advantageous marriage'' to the daughter of a successful sculptor, and their honeymoon trip to Minorca was a triumphal procession. Back in Paris, Orfila followed up his success with a volume on medical chemistry, and in 1818, at the age of 31, was rewarded with a professorship at the Medical Faculty of Paris—a chair of ''mental maladies'' specially created for him.

The first case of suspected poisoning in which he was consulted took place in 1824. In Montmorency, a woman named Laurent had been married only 10 days when her husband died suddenly; an autopsy was carried out, and the local doctor stated that he had found arsenic. A few years earlier, this might have amounted to a death sentence; but since Paris was now famous for its professors of legal medicine, the contents of the dead man's stomach were sent to the Faculty of Medicine. In August 1824, Orfila was asked to carry out tests: he stated with confidence that he could find no trace of poison. And the widow Laurent was acquitted.

In other cases, Orfila became a kind of court of last appeal. In December 1838, Nicholas Mercier, the idiot son of Louis Mercier, of Villey-sur-Tille, near Dijon, died of severe stomach pains. His father had recently married for the second time, and his new wife had objected strenuously to the presence of the idiot in the house. The father had given way and sent his son to live elsewhere for a while, then allowed the boy to return home. The bitter disputes began again. One day Mercier remarked to his wife: "Don't worry, it will soon be over," and bought an ounce of arsenic. A week later, after severe vomiting, the son died after drinking broth and sugared wine given to him by his father. Two weeks after the funeral, an exhumation was ordered, and three experts performed an autopsy, and testified that Nicholas Mercier had died as a result of poisoning by a metallic substance. But a few days later, two more experts performed another autopsy, and decided that the youth had not been poisoned, by arsenic or any other substance. Finally, Orfila led another group of experts, who examined the remains for the third time; Orfila pronounced that the body undoubtedly contained traces of arsenic. At the trial of the husband and wife at Dijon, another celebrated expert, Raspail, appeared for the defense, and he and Orfila had a spectacular clash in court. But it was Orfila's opinion that prevailed, and Mercier was found guilty and condemned to hard labor for life—he escaped the death sentence because the court found extenuating circumstances. (The wife was acquitted.)

It was this case that led Orfila to investigate another interesting problem. Arsenic, of course, comes from the earth, occurring in an ore called realgar, and in orpiment. And if these happen to occur in the area of cemeteries, then is it not possible that a body that has been buried for several months may absorb arsenic from the soil? With the usual thoroughness, Orfila proceeded to analyze samples of each from various cemeteries, and was able to state that the soil in certain areas contained traces of arsenic, while others were free from it. But the quantities involved would usually be too small to confuse a medical expert.

Three years earlier, in 1836, such delicate tests for arsenic would have been impossible, for there was no known method of detecting the poison in extremely small quantities. But in October 1836, an article in the *Edinburgh Philosophical Journal* described a method that could detect as little as a thousandth of a milligram of arsenic. Its author was a poverty-stricken English chemist named James Marsh.

—————————— 8 ——————————

The man who revolutionized crime detection was no brilliant scientific rebel, but a middle-aged alcoholic who worked in London's Woolwich Arsenal and who stumbled into the business of crime detection by chance. Born in 1794, Marsh at first showed signs of being a scientific prodigy, like the great Michael Faraday, whose assistant he became in 1829. Faraday had started life as a half-starved errand boy, and achieved success with the aid of Sir Humphrey Davy. Marsh had no such luck. All his life he earned a mere 30 shillings a week at the Royal Military Academy, and when he died at the age of 52, he left his wife and children destitute.

Yet he had his minor triumphs. In nearby Plumstead, in 1832, a farmer named George Bodle drank his breakfast coffee, and began to suffer from stomach cramps and vomiting. The old man was much disliked by his family, with whom he played the tyrant, and no one was greatly distressed when he died. A Justice of the Peace called Slace decided to investigate rumors that Bodle's grandson John had expressed the wish that the old man would hurry up and die. For John was a wastrel, and on the day the old man had died, John had taken the kettle out to the well to fill it, an uncharacteristic gesture that had startled the maid of all work. The symptoms sounded very much like poisoning. But who in London was competent to analyze the contents of the coffee pot? Judge Slace heard of the assistant at the Royal Military Academy, and asked him if he knew how to test for poison.

A chemist of Marsh's brilliance found this no challenge. Scheele's test, invented more than half a century before revealed the presence of arsenic when the coffee gave off the typical garlic smell of arseniuretted hydrogen. And when the coffee was subjected to Hahnemann's test, it produced the easily identified yellow precipitate of sulphide of arsenic. Young John's neck seemed destined for the noose. But Marsh had reckoned without a British jury, with its characteristic distaste for abstraction. At the trial in Maidstone that December, John Bodle was found not guilty, and was cheered in court. Ten years later, after being deported for fraud, he confessed to the murder of his grandfather.

Thoroughly irritated—and also, perhaps, fascinated by this glimpse of forensic toxicology, which was certainly more interesting than his work on naval cannons—Marsh decided to continue where Scheele had left off, and try to devise a test that would actually reveal the arsenic to the eyes of the stupidest jury. The most conclusive test would be to show them the arsenic. And Metzger had already shown how to do this: that when arsine gas is heated, it turns into a mixture of hydrogen and metallic arsenic, and the arsenic can be collected by holding a cold dish above the hot charcoal. Marsh saw instantly that the trouble with this test is that most of the gas probably escapes past the dish, and if only a tiny quantity of arsenic is involved, then it has escaped for ever. So he simply devised a sealed apparatus, in which the gas can escape only through a tiny pointed nozzle. First the suspected arsenic compound is dropped into a flask containing zinc and sulphuric acid (which produces hydrogen). The resulting arsine gas, if any, is then heated as it passes along a glass tube; this decomposes it, and the arsenic forms a black "mirror" as soon as it reaches a cold part of the tube. Or, if the gas is burned as it issues from the nozzle, it forms the mirror on a cold dish or plate. It was simple and obvious, and also incredibly sensitive, making it possible to detect as little as a fiftieth of a milligram of arsenic. When he published his result in 1836, the Society of Arts awarded him their gold medal. Poor Marsh would undoubtedly have preferred an appreciation in cash, like the £30 he received from the Board of Ordnance for a percussion grill for naval guns. When he died in 1846, his achievement was promptly forgotten, so that it is nowadays practically impossible to find his name in a work of reference.

It was the sensitivity of his test that enabled Orfila to test the earth in various cemeteries, and to measure precisely how much arsenic it contained. In fact, the sheer sensitivity

of the Marsh test led to a certain alarm when it was found
that substances that contained no arsenic could be made to
deposit that characteristic arsenic mirror. It was then discovered
that the zinc and sulphuric acid used in the tests contained
minute traces of arsenic, and that this possibility had to be
eliminated before the test . . . As to the problem of arsenic in
cemeteries, Orfila demonstrated to his own satisfaction that
arsenic could not enter corpses provided the coffin remained
intact. It was not a completely satisfactory solution, but it
had to serve for the time being.

Meanwhile, Orfila's name continued to be associated
with crimes that excited widespread attention, so that he
achieved the kind of acclaim that Sir Bernard Spilsbury
would receive a century later. In 1839, the year of the
Mercier trial, the French equivalent of the Mary Blandy case,
caused a sensation. A hotelier named Cumon retired in the
village of Montignac. When a gendarme named Dupont
requested the hand of his daughter Victorine in marriage, he
exploded with indignation: the fact that Victorine was eager
to accept failed to dislodge his prejudice against an under-
paid policeman. As Victorine and Dupont continued to
meet, there were violent family quarrels. Victorine confided
her misery to her maid Nini. And then, suddenly, old
Cumon fell ill with an internal complaint; within a month he
was dead. Victorine disdained any hypocritical show of
sorrow; declaring that "What God does must be well done,"
she lost no time in marrying her gendarme.

One day, a condemned man on his way to hard labor—
probably in the hulks—passed through the village, and was
"exhibited," as was the custom, on the village green, as a
salutory warning to other potential miscreants. With tears in
his eyes he begged his audience to conduct themselves
irreproachably, adding with a certain smugness the comment
that no doubt many of them had consciences as bad as his
own. Nini heard all this only at second hand, but it was
enough to release in her a flood of repentance. She now
confessed that she had purchased the arsenic, opium, vitriol,
and other toxic substances which Victorine had administered

to her father. Cumon's body was exhumed, and a panel of experts declared that they suspected poisoning by arsenic. Orfila was called in, and with the aid of the Marsh test, he was able to turn suspicion into certainty. There was a dramatic clash in court in Périgueux between Orfila and the local doctor, who insisted that Cumon's symptoms indicated death by natural causes, but Orfila's expertise prevailed. Victorine was sentenced to life imprisonment with hard labor, and the maid's sensitive conscience was rewarded with 18 years of the same punishment.

But it was in the following year, 1840, that Orfila reached the apex of his fame as a forensic expert. It was in the autumn of that year that he made his sensational intervention in the most notorious poison trial of the period: the case of Marie Lafarge.

_____ 9 _____

On January 16, 1840, a 29-year-old ironmaster, Charles Pouch Lafarge, died of a gastric ailment at his farm at Le Glandier, near Limoges. He had been ill ever since he had eaten a slice of cake sent to him in Paris by his newly wedded wife Marie. Not long before Lafarge's painful death, a maidservant had seen Marie stirring a white powder into a glass of milk she was about to take to her husband. She asked what it was, and Marie replied that it was orange blossom sugar. Later, the servant noticed white flakes on the surface of the half-finished glass of milk, and showed it to a doctor. When the doctor tasted one with the tip of his tongue, he found it bitter. And after seeing Marie surreptitiously stirring white powder into her husband's soup, the maid warned the rest of the family that she suspected Marie of poisoning Lafarge. Even before Lafarge's death, a local doctor had been convinced that he was being poisoned with arsenic. This is why, nine days after her husband's death, Marie Lafarge was arrested and charged with murder. As soon as the arrest was reported in the Paris newspapers,

Marie's case became a *cause célèbre*, for she had aristocratic connections—she was even illegitimately related to the reigning Royal Family.

Marie Lafarge was a romantic dreamer, of the kind that Gustave Flaubert was to portray in *Madame Bovary;* she was also neurotic and hysterical. Born Marie Capelle, daughter of an artillery officer, in 1816, she was an orphan by the time she was 18. She went to live with a wealthy aunt, who regarded her as a burden, and who began to look around for possible suitors who might take Marie off her hands. A respectable subprefect made a proposal, but Marie indignantly turned him down; she was dreaming of handsome aristocrats and of magnificent country estates in which she could play lady of the manor. Her wealthy cousin, Marie de Nicolai, had married a viscount named Léautaud. During a visit to their château, there was an embarrassing incident; a *parure* of diamonds (a necklace with matching earrings) vanished, and Inspector Allard of the Sûreté reached the conclusion that Marie Capelle was probably the thief. Embarrassed at the idea of a scandal involving his bride's best friend, the viscount decided to drop the investigation. Marie was allowed to leave unsearched.

Soon after this, her aunt announced that she had found Marie a husband, a wealthy young ironmaster who lived in an old Carthusian monastery in the Limousin district. What she did not tell her niece was that the suitor had been found through a matrimonial agency, and that he was a widower. Charles Lafarge was fat, coarse, and cunning; he had told the matrimonial agency that he had a property worth 200,000 francs and an income of 30,000 francs a year. In fact, his forge had gone bankrupt, and he was looking around for a rich wife. By Lafarge's standards, Marie was rich—to begin with, she had a dowry of 90,000 francs.

In August 1839, much against her will, Marie Capelle became Marie Lafarge. And when they arrived at Le Glandier, her few remaining day-dreams were shattered. The place was unutterably dreary and provincial, and the monastery was little more than a decaying farmhouse. Her mother-in-law and sister-in-law seemed to her to be peasants. The shock was so great that she locked herself in her room and wrote her husband a long, passionate letter declaring that she was in love with someone else, and that if he would not release her, she would kill herself with arsenic. Charles was deeply upset by the document—Marie was still innocent enough to think that this was because he adored her—and promised not to demand his marital rights until he had refurbished the house and borrowed enough money in Paris to re-finance the ironworks. He had developed a new smelting process which he intended to patent.

For the next few months, Marie lived in a rather gloomy daydream. Her husband had improvements made to the house, took out subscriptions to newspapers, and made his wife a member of a lending library. But she took care not to reveal her misery in her letters to relatives, for the born day-dreamer hates to admit being brought low. There were bitter conflicts with her mother-in-law when she insisted on dismissing old servants, and hiring young girls who were willing to work under the servants Marie had brought from Paris; but eventually, an uneasy peace reigned in the household. On a three-week visit to the town of Tulle, she met a handsome young advocate with whom, under the right circumstances, she would have started a love affair; but she had to return to Glandier. She had a close confidante in the 17-year-old daughter of a local doctor, and when her husband went off to Paris to patent his invention and try to raise money, she actually began to feel happy.

Not long before Christmas 1839, Charles Lafarge received a letter telling him to expect some cakes baked specially for him, at Marie's request, by his mother. What actually arrived was one large cake. He broke off a piece and ate it before he went out to a business appointment; when he returned, he was violently ill.

Back at Glandier, Marie was beginning to suspect the true reason that her husband had married her. Her will vanished from her desk, and when her mother-in-law finally produced it, Marie discovered that it had been changed; legacies to relatives had been cut out, and all her money—and some land she owned—had been left to her husband. The mother-in-law fell on her knees and begged forgiveness, swearing that her son knew nothing of the alterations; finally, Marie agreed to keep silent.

Charles returned home, looking pale and ill; Marie shared some chicken and truffles with him, and he became even sicker. A doctor who was called in diagnosed indigestion. Marie seemed genuinely solicitous, and had him installed in her own bedchamber, which had been decorated according to her Parisian taste. She frequently fed him with her own hand. When someone saw her stirring a white powder into an eggnog, Marie insisted that it was gum arabic, which was good for intestinal complaints. But the family sent some of the eggnog to a local chemist, who declared that the Hahnemann test revealed arsenic. The servant, Anna Brun, had seen her stirring a white powder—taken from a malachite box—into Charles Lafarge's milk. It was she who warned old Mme. Lafarge that she suspected Marie of trying to poison the master. But by now it was too late anyway. Charles Lafarge died, and Marie's 17-year-old confidante, Emma Pontier, exclaimed: "Oh Marie, if you made some fatal mistake . . ." Marie replied indignantly that she was innocent, and went on to demand an inquest on the body.

When the investigating magistrate learned that she had purchased arsenic—"for poisoning rats"—a few days before the cake was sent off to Paris, he had no alternative but to order her arrest. And when the police searched her room, they found the missing diamond *parure* of her best friend. If Marie was not a murderess, it seemed certain that she was a thief.

At least Marie had achieved what she had always wanted: national—even international—celebrity. Her aristocratic relatives all took the view that she was innocent, and their position in society made them a powerful influence on the Parisian press. The middle classes took it for granted that she was guilty. From the day of her arrest, column after column was devoted to the affair, and the interest soon spread to foreign newspapers. But the Vicomte de Léautaud revealed a vindictive spirit when he announced that he would prosecute Marie for the theft of the diamonds even before her trial for murder; this aroused much sympathy on her behalf. He also accused her of being a lifelong kleptomaniac. Charles Lachaud, the handsome young attorney from Tulle, had become Marie's advocate. When he begged her to tell the truth about the diamonds, she declared that Marie de Nicolai, the viscount's wife, had given them to her to sell. Just before her marriage, Marie de Nicolai had become involved with a handsome but penniless young Spaniard named Felix Clavé, who became frantic when he learned she was about to discard him. Terrified that he would divulge the affair to her husband, the countess begged her closest friend to sell her diamonds and give the money to Clavé . . . Approached by Marie's defense lawyer, Mme. de Léautaud indignantly denied Marie's story, declaring that the relationship with Clavé had been no more than a schoolgirl flirtation, encouraged by Marie herself. The Vicomte de Léautaud became even more determined to pursue the case. And Marie Lafarge received thousands of letters of sympathy. But at her trial for theft in Brives, she offered no defense, and was given a two-year sentence, suspended until after her trial for murder.

By British standards, the murder trial, which opened in Tulle on September 3, 1840, was a travesty of justice. From the beginning, the prosecutor branded Marie a monster who had carefully planned her husband's murder, then watched him die in agony; every device of melodrama was used to sway the jury. Many of the witnesses had only hearsay evidence to offer—gossip and rumor. Through all this, Marie bore herself with a grace and dignity that impressed even her enemies. Yet the case against her certainly looked black. It was proved that she had purchased arsenic on two occasions, and that she had been seen stirring powder into her husband's drink and scattering it on his food. The powder in the malachite box had proved to be arsenic, not gum arabic. The local chemist had detected the presence of arsenic in the milk and eggnog, and also in the dead man's vomit and stomach contents.

Now it so happened that Marie's defense lawyer, *maître* Paillet, was an old friend of Orfila. He hurried to Paris to consult the great toxicologist, and showed him the report of the chemists. Orfila was contemptuous. The report demonstrated a lamentable carelessness. They had obtained yellow precipitates that were soluble in ammonia, but there are dozens of yellow precipitates that contain no arsenic. And they had performed the Rose test so carelessly that the apparatus had exploded; therefore there was no proof that the "mirror" was arsenic.

Back in court, Paillet had a field day; with urbane ruthlessness he exposed the incompetence of the local chemists, pointing out that they had not even heard of the Marsh test. But the prosecution called his bluff. They were perfectly willing to allow the contents of the dead man's stomach to be subjected to a Marsh test . . . Paillet protested. Provincial science had already revealed its incompetence; let them send for his friend Orfila. But the prosecution prevailed. The materials were handed over to the chemists, who were instructed to carry out a Marsh test. And, to Paillet's delight, they admitted that the new tests had failed to reveal unmistakable signs of arsenic. Suddenly, the Lafarge supporters began to smile. Marie beamed at her defense attorney, who was unable to restrain tears of joy. The news quickly spread over the town: Marie Lafarge had been proved innocent . . . At this stage, everyone forgot the result of the tests on the milk and eggnog.

But the question was raised again that afternoon. The experts repeated their tests on the eggnog, the malachite box, and other items from Glandier, and this time the tests revealed large quantities of arsenic—enough to kill 10 men. The prosecution lawyer leapt to his feet. Since Paillet had asked for Orfila, let Orfila be brought from Paris; let the great toxicologist himself examine the contents of the dead man's stomach. Paillet was forced to agree.

A telegram was dispatched to Paris, and a week later, on September 13, he arrived in a stagecoach. He demanded that the local chemists should witness his experiments, and for the remainder of that day, and most of the following night, he performed his experiments in a room in the courthouse. The following afternoon, the chemists and doctors followed him into the courtroom. The lean, black-coated man with a hawk-like nose and grey whiskers cleared his throat. "I shall prove that there is arsenic in the body of Lafarge, and that this arsenic cannot have found its way there from the soil . . ."

Paillet was stunned. Marie Lafarge rose to her feet, her hand on her heart. Her supporters sighed with dismay. Orfila seemed oblivious of the effect he was producing. In a dry, detached manner he detailed his tests on the stomach, the liver, the thorax, the heart, the brain, and the intestinal canal; in all these, he said, arsenic had been discovered, though admittedly in small quantities. But, he added, no arsenic had been found in the flesh, so it was just possible that the poison had been placed in the body after death. But as he left the box, Marie Lafarge buried her face in her hands. Outside the courtroom, a storm was raging, but few people noticed it until Orfila had stopped speaking.

Paillet surpassed himself in his final address to the jury, but it was all to no effect. On September 19, 1840, Marie Lafarge was found guilty, and condemned to hard labor for life, and to be exposed at the marketplace at Tulle.

The sentence was, in fact, commuted to one of imprisonment without hard labor. Marie spent 10 years in prison at Montpellier, from 1841 until 1851; a few months after her release, she died of tuberculosis. Her Memoirs, in which she continues to maintain her innocence, reveal considerable literary talent. If Marie had reconciled herself to life at Le Glandier and directed her romantic imagination into the composition of novels, she might well have achieved a success comparable to that of her heroine George Sand.

Was Marie guilty? In retrospect there seems little doubt of it. One of the best books about her, *The Lady and the*

Arsenic by Joseph Shearing (1944), points out that in a modern British or American court she could certainly have been acquitted. Shearing also comes close to convincing the reader that Lafarge deserved to be poisoned; from the beginning, he was determined to lay his hands on Marie's fortune. He obtained bank loans by forging her signature, which she was forced to repay, and he was fairly certainly a party to the swindle involving her will. Yet even Shearing's skillful advocacy leaves the reader in no doubt that Marie poisoned her husband. It is true that he also throws suspicion on Lafarge's assistant manager, Denis Barbier, who hated Marie, and who was a party to the various forgeries. Barbier vanished before the trial, which suggests a guilty conscience. Shearing speculates that he might have known that Marie was introducing small quantities of poison into her husband's food, and decided to strengthen the case against her by planting large quantities of powdered arsenic in her room and in the death chamber. Yet even if this could be proved, it would still fail to acquit Marie of the charge of murdering her husband; Barbier could have had no possible motive to kill his employer.

Why, then, did she do it? Few writers on the case have seized upon the obvious clue: Marie's insistence that the marriage was never consummated. Yet when asked why her relations with her husband had improved in the weeks before he left for Paris, she explained that he had made many attempts to win her affection. "That touched me. I was not able to do otherwise than . . ." (here she hesitated), "than to fulfill my duties, to make life happier for Monsieur Lafarge." She even admitted that at one point she thought she might be pregnant; then she hastened to declare that she considered this some kind of immaculate conception. It sounds as if Marie allowed Lafarge into her bed, perhaps once, perhaps more often. Having yielded, it would seem logical that sexual relations would continue after his return from Paris, and that, in due course, she would find herself pregnant. This may have been the prospect that, in his absence, made Marie determine that she would never again yield her body to the boorish oaf. If this was, in fact, her motive in sending Lafarge the poisoned cake, then it becomes possible to understand why she was so insistent that the marriage had never been consummated; provided this was believed, her motive would remain unsuspected.

10

After the Affair of the Poisons, Louis XIV issued a decree forbidding apothecaries to sell poisons—particularly arsenic—to persons who were unknown to them. He also introduced the law that made it necessary for the purchaser to sign the "poisons book." Other countries soon adopted the same rule. In spite of which, arsenic remained the easiest of poisons to purchase, even in the nineteenth century. In Great Britain, it could easily be obtained in the form of rat poison—although in that case it was mixed with soot or indigo so that it was visible in food—or on fly papers which could be soaked in water. A Breton peasant woman named Hélène Jegado, who shared Anna Zwanziger's sadistic enthusiasm for poison, managed to acquire a fairly large quantity of arsenic at an early stage in her career as a servant, and used it to devastating effect over a 20-year period, enjoying the sense of power that it gave her. In one household where she worked, seven people—including her own sister—died in agony during a three-month period. At least another 16 victims had died by 1851, when she took a job in the house of Professor Théophile Bidard, of the University of Rennes. When a servant named Rosalie Sarrazin, of whom she was jealous, died in agony that July, an investigating magistrate accompanied police officers to the house. "I am innocent!" declared Hélène without preamble. "Of what!" asked the magistrate. "No one has accused you." And an investigation into Jegado's background revealed a toll of deaths even longer than in the Zwanziger case. She was executed in 1852.

In Glasgow in 1855, an attractive but bored 19-year-old

girl named Madeleine Smith, daughter of a well-to-do architect, was introduced in the street to Pierre L'Angelier, a young Frenchman from Jersey, who had gone to considerable trouble to engineer the introduction. Soon afterwards, Madeleine received a letter from L'Angelier declaring his love; she replied encouragingly, using the maid as a go-between. The course of true love was far from smooth; when her parents found out, they ordered her never to communicate with him again. But the lovers continued to snatch brief and frustrating meetings, during which they exchanged hasty kisses and caresses. By December she was addressing him as "My own darling husband." But no real intimacy was possible between them until the following summer, when the Smiths went to their country house at Row; here Madeleine had a chance to take unchaperoned country walks. A letter to L'Angelier in June 1856 begins: "If we did wrong last night, it was in the excitement of our love," and went on to note prosaically: "I did not bleed in the least but I had a good deal of pain during the night."

But later that summer, disillusionment—or perhaps merely satiety—began to set in. This may have had something to do with the attentions of a wealthy bachelor named William Minnoch, a close friend of her father's, who eventually proposed. Madeleine accepted. And at this point, L'Angelier played into her hands with a fit of petulance that led him to return one of her letters; she promptly replied that their engagement was at an end. "My love for you has ceased." L'Angelier's response was to threaten to write to her father revealing all. Madeleine hastily agreed to meet him again; again her letters address him as "dearest pet" and "sweet love"; but no longer as "My darling husband." For the truth was that she loathed the ungentlemanly blackmailer with her whole heart. They had two more meetings, each in the basement of Madeleine's house, and on each occasion he drank a cup of cocoa prepared by Madeleine. After the first meeting, L'Angelier was ill; after the second, in March 1857, he returned home in agony, bent over and clutching his stomach; by 11 o'clock the next morning he was dead.

His doctor insisted on a post-mortem, and 87 grains of arsenic were found in his stomach—the lethal dose being three grains.

Madeleine's letters were found; she immediately became the chief suspect, and was arrested on March 31. But although the case aroused the same excitement as the Lafarge poisoning, Madeleine had no defenders; the notion of a young girl becoming the mistress of a Frenchman horrified Scottish public opinion. Her guilt seemed obvious. Yet although it was proved that she had purchased three lots of arsenic, as rat poison, they had been mixed with soot or indigo. And no signs of soot or indigo were found in the dead man's stomach—but one medical witness commented that the grains of indigo could easily be washed from the arsenic with cold water. Madeleine insisted that her lover was in a habit of taking small quantities of arsenic for health reasons (arsenic is a stimulant and improves the complexion), but the defense offered no proof of this assertion. The jury eventually brought in a verdict of "not proven"—peculiar to Scotland—which implied that they regarded her as guilty, but found the proof insufficient. The crowd in court cheered, evidently feeling that L'Angelier deserved what he got.

Madeleine did not marry William Minnoch. Instead, she went to London, where she married a man named Hora, and became a successful hostess. The artist George du Maurier is said to have attended a Hora soirée and, unaware of the identity of his hostess, remarked "Madeleine Smith's beauty shouldn't have saved her from the scaffold." She later married an artist, George Wardle, who became manager of William Morris's silk weaving firm, and she developed an interest in socialism; Bernard Shaw once ate at her table. She died in America at the age of 92.

--------------------- **11** ---------------------

Although arsenic was the most widely used poison in the nineteenth century, there were dozens of others; antimony, aconitine, prussic acid, belladonna, mercury, lead, strychnine, opium, phosphorus, quinine, chloroform, brucine, codeine, and nicotine. In the early years of the century, new poisons were discovered at such a pace that the chemists were unable to keep up: morphine in 1803, strychnine in 1818, brucine in 1819, quinine in 1820, conium (extracted from hemlock) in 1826, nicotine in 1828, chloroform in 1831, codeine in 1832, and aconite and belladonna (from deadly nightshade) in 1833. Many of these, it will be noticed, are often regarded as medicines or useful drugs: codeine, quinine, nicotine, morphine; yet all, including caffeine, can cause death in sufficient quantities.

Yet although most metallic poisons were easy enough to detect (antimony, for example, could be measured precisely by the Marsh test), the vegetable poisons or alkaloids were a different matter—opium, for example, could vanish and leave no trace within hours. In Edinburgh in 1877, an alcoholic teacher named Eugène Marie Chantrelle poisoned his wife with opium, after insuring her life, and tried to make the death appear accidental by filling the bedroom with coal gas. No opium whatever was found in the body, but Chantrelle was convicted on the evidence of opium found in vomit on the bedclothes. Half a century earlier, the situation was considerably worse in that no chemical tests could reveal the presence of any alkaloid poisons in the body. In 1823, a Paris doctor named Edmé Castaing agreed to help a friend named Auguste Ballet to murder his elder brother Hyppolyte, who was dying of tuberculosis. Hyppolyte was wealthy, and Auguste had learned, to his indignation, that he had been excluded from his brother's will; he asked Castaing's help in destroying the will. When Hyppolyte died suddenly, with Castaing in attendance, the physician suddenly paid off all his debts. But success made Castaing greedy, and he persuaded Auguste to make a will in his favor. He consulted a lawyer to make sure such a will was valid and, having been reassured on this point, invited Auguste to drive with him into the country to inspect some property. That night, Auguste died in a St-Cloud hotel, after drinking mulled wine which had been "sugared" by Castaing. But although Auguste Ballet showed symptoms of morphine poisoning (contraction of the pupils, inflammation of the lungs), it was impossible in 1823 to detect morphine in the body—which is undoubtedly why Castaing chose it. Even the great Orfila had to confess his helplessness at the trial. But the circumstantial evidence against Castaing was strong enough to secure a guilty verdict, and his subsequent execution. As late as 1847, Orfila admitted that it was possible that the vegetable poisons might remain forever undetectable in the body.

Fortunately, it was a mere four years before a young Belgian chemist proved him wrong. The James Marsh of vegetable poisons was Jean Servais Stas, a professor of chemistry at the École Royale Militaire in Brussels.

On November 20, 1850, a man named Gustave Fougnies died on the dining-room floor of Château Bitremont, near the village of Bury, in Belgium. Gustave Fougnies had been a sick man for many years, and the amputation of a leg seemed likely to hasten his death. This prospect was by no means entirely disagreeable to his sister Lydie, who was married to the Count Hyppolyte de Bocarmé. Bocarmé had married Lydie for her money—she was the daughter of a well-to-do apothecary—and then discovered that she had less than he had hoped. The two were deeply in debt. Gustave's death would solve their money problems. Then Gustave had announced that he had decided to marry; he had purchased a château, fallen in love with its previous owner, and been accepted. The Bocarmés were shattered. On November 20, they had invited Gustave to lunch. But the children were sent off to eat in the nursery, and the countess herself served the meal.

In the late afternoon, the servants heard a thud from the dining-room, and the countess calling for help. Gustave was lying on the floor, obviously dead—the countess said she thought it was a stroke. The count ordered a servant to fetch vinegar, then poured a large quantity into the dead man's mouth, apparently in the belief that it would revive him. He then ordered the servant to undress the dead man and wash his body with vinegar. The countess took her brother's clothes and took them to the laundry, where she threw them in boiling water. Then she and the count scrubbed the floor of the dining-room and even scraped it with a knife. When an examining magistrate finally arrived, Gustave Fougnies was lying, naked, on bed in a servant's room; his cheeks were cut and his mouth and throat were scarred with burns.

A post-mortem was carried out; the doctors reported that the death was not due to a stroke, but to drinking some corrosive substance, possibly acid. But vinegar would not, of course, be strong enough to cause burns.

It all looked extremely suspicious. The Bocarmés were placed under arrest, and the contents of the dead man's stomach were sent to the military school in Brussels, to be examined by Stas, a pupil of Orfila.

Stas immediately noted the smell of vinegar in the unpleasant greenish-black mess that had been delivered to him. When told that this had been poured down the dead man's throat, and that the body had also been washed in vinegar, he immediately suspected that this had been intended to mask some other smell.

The stomach contents were preserved in alcohol. Stas's first step was to mix some of them with water, and filter and distill the result. His reasoning was body substances are soluble in alcohol or water, but not in both, so that body substances that passed through the filter with alcohol would be caught by water, and vice versa. The result should be a fairly pure solution of any poison that had been used. When Stas distilled the result repeatedly he thought he could detect a smell like mouse urine—the typical smell of conine, the hemlock derivative. But more washing and filtering produced a stronger smell—that of tobacco.

Nicotine is, in fact, one of the strongest of poisons—Taylor's *Medical Jurisprudence* compares it to prussic acid. Cases had been known of children dying from sucking at old pipes, with their brown deposit, while a rabbit could be killed within minutes from a single drop of nicotine.

The problem now was how to separate the poison from the liquid distillate. Stas had an inspiration. He mixed the liquid with ether—first discovered by the alchemist Raymond Lull, and rediscovered in 1792 by Frobenius—which was lighter than water. After a while, the ether separated out on top of the water, taking with it the brownish coloring. Stas carefully poured off the ether, and left it in an open dish to evaporate. And when it had done so, it left a quantity of a colorless, oily liquid with a strong smell of tobacco. It burned his tongue and filled his mouth with an unpleasant taste. Now Stas only had to prove that it was nicotine by chemical tests with tannic acid, mercuric iodide of potassium, bichromate of potassium, and so on. Each test was positive.

By the time Stas had removed all the nicotine from the stomach's contents, he had enough to fill a small flask—that is, enough to kill several men.

Bocarmé's murder plot had been truly ingenious. The château possessed a laboratory, for Bocarmé was interested in the scientific side of agriculture. Bocarmé had heard of the deadly qualities of pure nicotine, and he also knew that vegetable poisons were undetectable. So he had grown tobacco leaves, and then distilled from them a quantity of the colorless liquid. He had told his feeble-minded gardener that he was making eau-de-Cologne. The police were able to trace a professor of chemistry in Ghent with whom Bocarmé had discussed the problems of extracting nicotine from tobacco leaves (Bocarmé had given the professor a false name).

Gustave had been seized from behind and thrown to the floor; then, as he was held down by Bocarmé, the poison had been poured into his mouth by his sister. When he lost consciousness, more of it was poured down his throat—the inevitable result being that much of it splashed onto the floor. (In fact, in spite of all the scrubbing and scraping, Stas was able to find traces of nicotine on the floorboards.)

Then the count made the mistake that cost him his life and brought Stas immortality. He poured vinegar into the dead man's mouth to mask the smell. But the vinegar combined with the nicotine to produce the burns that had made the police suspicious. (Stas experimented with two dogs, poisoning both with nicotine, and then pouring vinegar into the mouth of one of them. Only this dog developed acid burns.) Moreover, the vinegar then mixed with the alcohol in which the stomach contents were preserved, and this acidified alcohol happened to be exactly the right solution for dissolving certain bodily substances such as sugar and mucus, while other substances dissolved in acidified water.

At the trial, the countess insisted that her husband had used force to make her agree to the murder plot; she was acquitted. But Bocarmé was executed on July 19, 1851, in Mons. And the method of detecting vegetable poisons—on which he had inadvertently collaborated with Stas—is still in use to this day.

_____ 12 _____

By the middle of the nineteenth century, forensic medicine had become a science in its own right. The Scots deserve the credit for recognizing its importance. It was Andrew Duncan, Professor of Physiology at the University of Edinburgh from 1789, who succeeded in persuading the government to create the first chair of forensic medicine at the university in 1807, and his son, another Andrew Duncan, became its first incumbent. The senate of the university intensely disliked this innovation, but in due course, universities all over Europe followed suit—including, of course, Paris, which appointed Orfila.

In 1834, at the age of 28, Alfred Swaine Taylor became Professor of Medical Jurisprudence (as the subject was then called) at Guy's Hospital Medical School, and he went on to become perhaps the most influential forensic scientist, with the exception of Orfila, of the century. The first edition of his classic *Principles and Practice of Medical Jurisprudence* appeared two years later—and in updated editions, is still in use today. Taylor had spent some time studying with Orfila, and he was in Paris during the revolution of 1830, which gave him the opportunity to make a close study of gunshot wounds.

It must nevertheless be admitted that none of the major poisoning cases in which he was involved can be regarded as triumphs of toxicology. The first concerned a Quaker, John Tawell, who was accused of poisoning his mistress with cyanide. Tawell, who began life as a druggist, was transported to Australia for forgery in 1814, but by the time he returned to England, had amassed a fortune of £30,000. His wife fell ill and died, and during her illness, Tawell began a liaison with the attractive girl who nursed her, Sarah Hadler. She later bore him two children, and Tawell moved her to a cottage at Salthill, near Slough. Meanwhile, he married a second time, a Miss Catforth, from whom he took care to conceal the liaison. He paid Sarah Hadler (now known as Hart) £1 a week. After Tawell paid Sarah a visit in September 1844, she fell ill and vomited, but recovered from the attack.

On New Year's Day, 1845, Tawell went down to Salthill from his home in Berkhamsted; a neighbor saw him arrive, and a little later, met Sarah on her way to buy stout, and remarked how happy she looked. Soon after dusk, the neighbor heard Sarah scream, and went to her door with a lighted candle; she met Tawell, hurrying away, and found Sarah writhing on the floor in agony. Before the arrival of the doctor, she was dead.

A telegraph line—one of the first—had recently been constructed from Slough to Paddington, and a message was sent, asking the police to look out for a man in Quaker dress. When Tawell arrived at Paddington, he was followed to the lodging he had taken for the night, and arrested the next morning. He immediately made his first mistake by denying that he had left London the previous day.

Meanwhile, Sarah Hadler's body had been opened, and the bitter smell of prussic acid had been noted. The analyst, Mr. Cooper, mixed the stomach contents with potassium ferrosulfate, and obtained the deep Prussian blue color of potassium ferrocyanide. His conclusion was that Sarah Hadler had been poisoned by prussic acid, probably administered in stout. When it was proved that Tawell had bought the acid at a chemist shop in Bishopsgate, the case against him looked black.

The defending counsel, Fitzroy Kelly, advanced an ingenious defense, probably based on Taylor's suggestion: that apple pips contain prussic acid, and that there had been a barrel of apples in the room in which Sarah Hadler had died. At this, both sets of medical experts proceeded to distill apple pips to see how much cyanide they could obtain. The prosecution said that the amount distilled from 15 apples was not even dangerous; the defense replied that they had succeeded in distilling two-thirds of a grain of pure hydrocyanic acid from 15 apples, and that such a dose could be toxic.

The jury took the view that all this was irrelevant, and sentenced Tawell to death. Shortly before his execution, he confessed to the murder, and to an attempt to poison Sarah Hadler with morphine the previous September. His motive had been financial—his Australian investments had dropped in value, and he wanted to save the £1 a week he paid his mistress. Tawell was hanged in April 1845, and is now remembered mainly as the first murderer to be trapped by the electric telegraph. The defense lawyer became known forever afterwards as "Apple Pip Kelly."

The next major poisoning case in which Taylor was involved became one of the most famous in British criminal history. Dr. William Palmer, of Rugeley, Staffordshire, was accused of poisoning a friend named Cook with strychnine. Palmer, an inveterate gambler on horses, was known to be heavily in debt. On November 13, 1855, Palmer and John Parsons Cook attended the races at Shrewsbury, and Cook's mare, Polestar, won. Back in a hotel in Rugeley, where they were celebrating, Cook took a swallow of his brandy and jumped to his feet crying: "Good God, there's something in that that burns my throat." Palmer retorted "Nonsense," and drained the rest of the brandy. But Cook became increasingly ill. And after taking some pills offered to him by Palmer, his body convulsed so violently that his head touched his heels, and he died a few minutes later. Palmer was not slow to claim that the dead man had negotiated £4,000 for his benefit, and produced a document to prove it.

It was some days before Cook's stepfather became suspicious and demanded an autopsy. Palmer was arrested on a moneylender's writ. Yet, incredibly, he was not only permitted to be present at the autopsy, but to sneak out of the room with the jar containing Cook's stomach—he was caught only just in time.

Now it was recalled that Palmer had been associated with a long series of sudden deaths, and with many dubious financial transactions. As a trainee doctor he had fathered no fewer than 14 illegitimate children, and one of these had died unexpectedly after a visit to Palmer. An acquaintance named Abbey had died in the Staffordshire Infirmary after drinking a glass of brandy with Palmer.

Back in Rugeley with his medical diploma, Palmer had married an heiress, the illegitimate daughter of an Indian army officer; but apparently she was not as rich as he had hoped. Three years later, he invited his mother-in-law to stay with them, and she died suddenly during the visit. Her money passed to her daughter—and in turn to Palmer. In the following year, a bookmaker named Bladon died with equal suddenness when staying with Palmer. A large sum of money disappeared, and so did Bladon's betting book, in which Palmer figured as a heavy loser. His wife was heard to enquire wearily: "Where will it end?"—her own sudden death would occur three years later. But in the meantime, sudden deaths continued to occur with suspicious frequency—a creditor named Bly, an uncle named "Beau" Bentley, and four of Palmer's children, who died in convulsions. Then, in 1853, Palmer insured his wife for £13,000, and she died soon afterwards. The ease with which he had acquired this money—and staved off bankruptcy—evidently decided Palmer to insure the life of his brother Walter for £82,000. But when Walter died suddenly, after a drinking bout, the company was suspicious, and refused to pay. Palmer succeeded in insuring a friend called George Bates for £25,000, who also died unexpectedly; but when a detective employed by the company learned from a boot boy that he had seen Palmer pouring something into Bates's drink, they once again refused to pay. Palmer then had a drinking session with the boot boy, who was severely ill after it.

It was after these setbacks that Palmer attended the Shrewsbury races with Cook, who died in agony a week later.

The bodies of Palmer's wife and brother were now exhumed; and a considerable quantity of antimony was found in Anne Palmer. There was no poison in Walter Palmer, but Taylor pointed out that prussic acid would escape from the body after death in the form of gases.

Cook's stomach had been sent to Professor Taylor for analysis. It had been turned inside out before it had been thrown in the jar, and Palmer had then succeeded in taking the jar out of the room before anyone noticed; when it was returned, there were two slits in its parchment cap. Taylor was able to find a small quantity of antimony in the stomach—not enough to kill a man—but no strychnine. Palmer was still at large when Taylor's letter, containing his results, arrived in Rugeley, and he succeeded in intercepting the letter, and sending the coroner a present of game, pointing out that no strychnine had been found.

If the case had depended solely on Taylor's evidence, there can be no doubt that Palmer would have been acquitted. But the circumstantial evidence was overwhelming. It was proved that he had forged Cook's signature on a cheque for £350 while his friend lay ill, and also forged the document showing that Cook owed him £4,000. So although Taylor's evidence came in for some derision, there was never any doubt about the verdict, and Palmer's guilt. He was hanged at Stafford on June 14, 1856.

Where Taylor was concerned, the case of Dr. Thomas Smethurst was also a fiasco. In 1853, the 48-year-old doctor had retired to a boarding-house in Bayswater with his 68-year-old wife. There he met Miss Isabella Bankes, who was six years his junior, and the acquaintance soon ripened into an intimacy that led the landlady to give him notice. Thereupon, Dr. Smethurst and Miss Bankes moved to Richmond, and he married her bigamously. The following March, 1859, Miss Bankes became ill, with vomiting and stomach pains, and two doctors called in by Smethurst thought the symptoms looked like poisoning. They went to a local magistrate, and when it was learned that Smethurst would gain £1,750 from her will, he was arrested. Miss Bankes died the next day. Some of her excreta was sent to Professor Taylor, who detected arsenic. A bottle of colorless liquid, found in Smethurst's room, was also sent to Taylor, who subjected it to the Reinsch test for arsenic. In this test, the suspected arsenic is mixed with hydrochloric acid, and then a piece of copper gauze is steeped in the acid; if arsenic is present, the gauze becomes black with a deposit of metallic arsenic. In later editions of his famous textbook, Taylor emphasizes that it is important to use copper of a high degree of purity, since ordinary commercial copper contains a small quantity of arsenic. And this, it seems, explains why Taylor believed he had found arsenic in the colorless liquid. In fact, it later proved to be a solution of potassium chlorate. Before the trial began, Taylor was forced to write to the prosecution and defense admitting his mistake. His analysis of the excreta was now obviously suspect.

At the trial, three doctors insisted that the death revealed all the symptoms of irritant poisoning; but Taylor's mistake crippled the prosecution case. The result was that although Smethurst was found guilty, the controversy surrounding the case led the Home Secretary to submit all the evidence to a surgeon, Sir Benjamin Collins-Brodie. Brodie reported that although the case against Smethurst was full of suspicious circumstances, "there was no absolute and convincing proof of his guilt." Accordingly, Smethurst was granted a free pardon.

One interesting piece of evidence was discovered later. Smethurst had written a letter in the *Lancet* in 1844 on the extraction of teeth, and on the opposite page there was a letter from the well-known chemist Frisenius stating that the Reinsch test for arsenic would fail in the presence of potassium chlorate. This has given rise to the speculation that Smethurst may have disguised the poisoning of Miss Bankes by also giving her potassium chlorate. On the other hand, the doctors who attended Miss Bankes were unaware that she was pregnant, or they might have reached the conclusion that her vomiting was due to pregnancy complicated by dysentery. This contradictory evidence helps to explain why the guilt or innocence of Thomas Smethurst has remained a matter of controversy ever since.

The same ambiguity surrounds the case of Dr. Alfred Warder, one of the forensic experts who gave evidence at the trial of William Palmer. In 1866, Dr. Warder and his third wife, Ethel, moved to Brighton. Her health had so far been good, but now she fell ill with symptoms that were curiously similar to those that had preceded the death of Warder's previous wife. A Dr. Taafe, who was called in on the insistence of Warder's brother-in-law, found her to be suffering from bladder pains. Warder said he had prescribed Fleming's Tincture of Aconite. Taafe pointed out that this was supposed to be for external application only, and insisted on substituting a mixture of henbane and opium. He was greatly puzzled that Mrs. Warder failed to improve; Warder told him that his wife had got tired of the medicine and would not take it. Soon after, Mrs. Warder died. Because of the suspicious circumstances, an inquest was held, and her viscera were sent to Professor Taylor for analysis.

He performed a series of tests for metallic poisons— arsenic, antimony, and so on, but all were negative. So were his tests for vegetable poisons, using the Stas method and various color tests. (By then, many reagents had been developed that would reveal the presence of various vegetable poisons—morphine, atrophine, hyoscine, and others—by changing color in the presence of sulfuric acid.) He was not even able to detect aconite, which *had* been administered by Warder. He concluded, nevertheless, that the symptoms observed by the doctors were consistent with slow aconite poisoning. And at the inquest on Mrs. Warder, Dr. Taafe expressed the same opinion.

However, before the jury could return a verdict, Dr. Warder poisoned himself with cyanide. This looked like an admission of guilt, so the jury reached the decision that Mrs. Warder had died of aconite administered by her husband. Yet the unsatisfactory nature of Taylor's conclusions suggests that if Warder had been tried for murder, he would have been acquitted. It is possible that he committed suicide because he realized that he would never escape the suspicion of being a wife-murderer.

It seems clear, on the whole, that as a toxicologist, Taylor was lacking in the brilliance that characterized Orfila and Stas. Yet this in itself is hardly a condemnation; it only underlines the incredible difficulties that face a doctor who has been sent a mass of decaying intestines and half-digested food, and asked to make up his mind whether one of dozens of poisons has been the cause of death. In many of the famous poisoning cases, success has been the result either of luck or of some incredible inspiration on the part of the pathologist. Or, of course, of some fatal oversight on the part of the poisoner . . .

-------------------- **13** --------------------

And what if no chemical test exists to identify a poison— as, for example, in the case of aconite and digitalis? This was the problem that, in 1863, confronted one of France's foremost experts on forensic medicine, Dr. Ambroise Tardieu.

The death that concerned him was that of a young widow

named Mme. de Pauw; the suspect was her ex-lover, a
doctor named Couty de la Pommerais. If the evidence that
was beginning to emerge was correct, he was one of the
most calculating and heartless murderers in medical history.
But if Mme. de Pauw *had* died of poison, then he had used
his medical knowledge to choose a poison for which there
was no known chemical test.

Pommerais had been in Paris since 1859 when, at the age
of 24, he had come from Orléans. His charm and good
looks ensured his success among the aristocracy, and he
himself claimed to be a count (a title to which, in fact, he
had no right). One of his patients was an artist named de
Pauw, and when he died he left behind a pretty widow and
three small children. Pommerais was susceptible, and she
soon became his mistress. Unfortunately, Pommerais was a
gambler, and he needed money. The solution seemed to be
to marry some rich patient. His choice fell upon the daughter of a wealthy widow named Dabizy. The widow was
doubtful about the match, no doubt suspecting the doctor's
motive, so she took the precaution of making sure that her
daughter's money should be placed legally beyond her
husband's reach. But a mere two months after the marriage,
the widow Dabizy died after dining with her daughter and
son-in-law, and Pommerais certified the death as Asiatic
cholera—after all, she was his patient.

Without a husband and without a lover, Mme. de Pauw
was finding it hard to make ends meet, and her children
were suffering from undernourishment. It seems possible it
was she who approached her ex-lover for help; at all events,
in March 1863, they renewed their acquaintance. And eight
months later, on the night of November 17, Mme. de Pauw
died, apparently of cholera. She was buried soon after.

The police had no reason to suspect the personable young
doctor. Then Chief Inspector Claude, of the Sûreté, received
an anonymous letter suggesting that he ought to look into the
question of whether Pommerais would benefit financially
from the death of Mme. de Pauw. When he did so, he
learned that Pommerais had insured Mme. de Pauw's life

for 500,000 francs, and that the insurance company was even now preparing to pay him.

The author of the anonymous letter was almost certainly the dead woman's sister, Mme. Ritter. Five days after Mme. de Pauw's death she called on Claude, and told him an amazing story. Hearing that her sister had had a fall on the stairs, and was confined to her bed, she had gone to call on her. Mme. de Pauw had sworn her to silence, then explained that the fall was all part of an ingenious plot devised by Pommerais, the aim of which was to give her an income for life. The sound of the fall downstairs, which had been heard by neighbors was, in fact, a stuffed sack. The next task, Pommerais had explained, was to convince the insurance company that her life was in danger, so that when she proposed that her life insurance should be exchanged for a small annuity of 5,000 francs a year they would seize the opportunity to save themselves a far larger sum . . .

Mme. Ritter told Claude that she had warned her sister against involving herself in such a plot; but Mme. de Pauw needed the money to support three children. And now she was dead.

Clearly, Pommerais had given Mme. de Pauw some drug that produced symptoms like cholera. And instead of allowing her to live when the insurance company agreed to the annuity, he had increased the dose and killed her.

Claude lost no time in having Mme. de Pauw's body exhumed, and sent to Professor Tardieu. The police called at the doctor's surgery and took away various bottles of poison, as well as some letters from Mme. de Pauw. And Tardieu settled down to trying to determine whether Mme. de Pauw had died of poison. One thing was clear: it had not been from cholera, or any other natural cause. Neither had it been from any metallic poison like arsenic, antimony, or mercury. The alternative was a vegetable poison. But which? Patiently, Tardieu and his assistants applied Stas's method to the contents of the stomach, discouraged by the knowledge that many of the poisons would have disappeared from the system and left no trace. And even if there *were* traces, the poison might be one of those to which no reaction had been found.

On the other hand, the concentrated extract that was now contained in a sealed flask probably contained the poison. And there was at least an obvious way of testing this hypothesis. Tardieu injected it into a dog. And after six and a half hours, the dog's heartbeat slowed to half its normal rate, and it lay gasping on the floor. Then, slowly, it recovered. Tardieu was triumphant. The liquid from Mme. de Pauw's stomach contained a poison; the problem was to identify it.

And now the clue came from the material turned over to Tardieu by the police. One of the letters went out of its way to mention the drug digitalis, with which Pommerais was treating her. Digitalis is an extract of foxglove, and is used to treat heart disease. In large doses, it causes fluctuations in the heartbeat, and a slowing of the heart that can lead to death. Moreover, the bottle containing digitalis, taken from Pommerais's surgery, was almost empty, although the records showed that he had bought three grains of it recently. Injected into a large dog, Pommerais's digitalis caused wild fluctuations of heartbeat; within a few hours, it was dead.

Tardieu now tried his stomach extract on a frog, opening its chest so as to observe the heart. An injection of the stomach extract produced precisely the same effect as an injection of digitalis; the heart beat slower and slower, then stopped.

The body of Pommerais's mother-in-law was also exhumed. It had been buried too long to reveal a vegetable poison, but the symptoms of her short illness were undoubtedly those of digitalis poisoning.

In court, the defense—predictably—challenged Tardieu's medical evidence, arguing that he had failed to demonstrate the presence of digitalis by chemical means. Tardieu's evidence was not the factor that ultimately swayed the jury. They were overwhelmed by the circumstantial evidence, particularly by the method by which Pommerais had almost obtained 500,000 francs from the insurance company. He had not insured Mme. de Pauw's life in his own name—which would obviously arouse suspicion—but had persuaded her to do it, providing her with the premium. But if she died, the insurance money would be paid to her children. To prevent this, Pommerais had visited a lawyer and explained that a close woman friend, now married, owed him 100,000 francs. She lacked the money to pay, but had insured her life for that amount. Would it be legally binding if she signed a document agreeing that she owed him the money? The lawyer assured him that it would be, and drew up the document. Pommerais then changed the amount to 500,000 francs, and persuaded Mme. de Pauw to sign it. It would, he said, be further evidence that she was convinced she was close to death, and that she relied on him to look after her children. But if Pommerais did not intend to kill her, then he could have no possible motive to get her to sign such a document . . .

So Pommerais was found guilty, and executed in June 1864. And Tardieu's method of testing for digitalis—with the aid of a frog—is still to be found in every modern textbook of toxicology.

14

The science of toxicology has undoubtedly made greater advances in the past century than any other branch of forensic medicine. And this has been largely a matter of necessity. If the number of known poisons had remained the same as in the days of ancient Rome, or the court of Louis XIV, the modern toxicologist would have no problems, for arsenic, mercury, conium, belladonna and the rest are relatively easy to detect. But medical science has devoted itself to the discovery of new drugs, and most of these drugs are also poisons. The sheer number of synthetic alkaloids developed since the Second World War—Clarke's standard *Isolation and Identification of Drugs* mentions more than 2,000 of them—means that the modern toxicologist is faced with an apparently impossible task.

It is not, of course, quite impossible, since science has also developed a number of important short cuts. Many alkaloids form distinctive crystals that can easily be recognized under the microscope. Each crystal has its own melting point. In the early days, in the first decade of the century, this test required a fairly large amount of the suspected alkaloid, but by the early 1950s, microscopic amounts could be tested. The discovery of X-rays by Röentgen in 1895 resulted in the new science of X-ray crystallography: when X-rays pass through a crystal, they are diffracted as light is refracted by a prism, and the unique pattern of diffraction can be captured on a photographic plate.

Even more important was the discovery of column chromatography. If a dye solution is poured into an upright glass tube containing fine chalk, the color is filtered out near the top of the tube, and only pure water runs out the bottom. If more water is poured in at the top, the area of color will descend down the tube, meanwhile splitting into different layers representing the different dyes or components. This discovery was made in 1906 by a Russian, Tsvett, and rediscovered in the early 1930s. When filter paper was substituted for the chalk, it could be flattened out, and its various layers examined and tested separately. If one of these contained even a small quantity of an alkaloid poison, it could be revealed by the appropriate reagent.

Another ingenious way of determining the composition of an unknown substance is the spectroscope. When any substance is heated, it atoms vibrate and give off a characteristic light, and if this light is passed through a prism or a narrow slit, the dark background is crossed by a number of bright "emission" lines—they were first carefully studied by Bunsen and Kirchhoff in 1859. Each element has its own characteristic lines, so that it is even possible to tell what elements are present in a star by passing its light through a prism. The intensity of the lines depends upon the quantity of the heated substance in the sample. So if a known poison is sprayed into a flame, the exact amount of poison can be determined by a light meter attached to a spectroscope. Metallic poisons like arsenic could also be measured by electrolysis. When an electric current is passed through a metal salt dissolved in water, the salt is split into its positive and negative constituents (ions), and the positive metal ions move to the negative electric pole (the cathode). So if the cathode is weighed before and after the experiment, it is possible to determine just how much arsenic or antimony or mercury has been deposited.

In the 1950s, an even more ingenious method for detecting arsenic was developed by nuclear physicists. When bombarded with neutrons in a nuclear reactor, arsenic becomes radioactive, and the radioactivity can be measured by a Geiger counter. So a hair that had absorbed arsenic could be made radioactive, and then the exact quantity of arsenic measured. And since the amount of arsenic in a hair is proportional to the amount in the whole body of a poison victim, it could easily be determined whether a fatal dose had been administered.

In spite of these sensitive methods of detecting and measuring poison, there were many setbacks. In the 1870s, an Italian professor of chemistry, Francesco Anselmo, discovered the "cadaveric alkaloids," certain alkaloids that form naturally in corpses, and which can be mistaken for poisons administered with malice. Anselmo had investigated cases in which poisoning by morphine and delphinine were suspected, and in which the "poison" turned out to be alkaloids that had developed naturally in corpses. This discovery caused alarm among experts in forensic medicine, for it complicated the already impossibly complicated problem of detecting vegetable poisons. In 1882, the question of cadaveric alkaloids was raised in a British court of law during the trial of Dr. George Lamson, accused of poisoning his schoolboy brother-in-law with aconite, the poison extracted from monkshood (or wolfbane). For this poison there is—as already noted—no straightforward color reaction test, as there is for morphine, heroin, atropine, hyoscine, and so on.

Lamson undoubtedly knew this, and decided to solve his serious financial problems, which included writing dud checks, with the poison. Another brother-in-law, Herbert, had already died at a convenient moment—later giving rise to the suspicion that Lamson had poisoned him—and the doctor had benefited by £700.

Eighteen-year-old Percy John suffered from curvature of the spine, and was a pupil at a private school in Wimbledon. On December 3, 1881, Lamson called on him there and saw him in the presence of the headmaster. He then went through a pantomime that seems typical of a certain type of murderer, involving an excess of ingenuity. The headmaster offered him sherry, and Lamson said he would like to put some sugar in it; a basin was brought, and Lamson spooned some into his sherry. Then he took out a Dundee cake, cut three slices, and handed one to the headmaster, one to Percy, and ate one himself. The poison had undoubtedly been inserted in Percy's slice of cake before it was baked. After they had eaten, he told the headmaster that he had brought some empty pill capsules from America, which would make it easier for pupils to be persuaded to take medicines. Lamson spooned some sugar into one capsule, and handed it to Percy with the words, "Here, Percy, you are a champion pill-taker." The boy took the "pill," and Lamson left. Within two hours, Percy was dead. Lamson went to Paris, but voluntarily gave himself up on his return, and was arrested.

His excessive ingenuity was his undoing. The pathologist, Dr. Thomas Stevenson (Alfred Swain Taylor's successor at Guy's) applied every possible test to the dead boy's vomit, and from the lack of result, concluded that the poison could only be aconite. And when Lamson was proved to have purchased aconite, the case against him was very strong indeed. Experiments with mice left Stevenson in no doubt that the liquid distilled from the dead youth's organs was a poison.

At the trial, the defense made much of the problem of cadaveric alkaloids, about which Stevenson proved to be ignorant. For a while, it looked as if he had introduced serious doubts into the minds of the jury. But when the verdict came, it meant a sentence of death for Lamson. It emerged later that the verdict had been based on the other evidence—all of which pointed very clearly to a murder plot that was too ingenious and complicated by half. Before his execution on April 28, 1882, Lamson confessed to murdering Percy John, although he continued to deny murdering his other brother-in-law Herbert to the end.

Nevertheless, it was some 40 years before forensic science could assert with confidence that there was no chance of confusing cadaveric alkaloids with vegetable poison.

In a case of the late 1940s, even Orfila's well-established conclusion that arsenic could not enter the body from the surrounding soil came under attack. The accused was a Frenchwoman named Marie Besnard, who came under suspicion after the sudden death of her husband in October 1947. Before he died, he had time to whisper to the local postmistress that he thought his wife was poisoning him. She seemed to have a motive, in that she was suspected of having an affair with the hired man. Her husband was exhumed and found to contain a large quantity of arsenic. Then many other mysterious and sudden deaths were recalled—11 in all—beginning with that of her first husband in 1929. His body was also exhumed and found to contain arsenic. And the same was true of body after body. It looked as if there could not be the slightest doubt of Marie Besnard's guilt. But the defense counsel, Albert Gautrat, thought otherwise. He unearthed recent scientific publications which revealed that certain bacteria in the soil can interact with natural arsenic, causing it to become far more soluble than it is normally. Moreover, when these "anaerobic microbes" extracted hydrogen from sulfur compounds in human hair, they allowed the sulfur to be replaced by arsenic. Tests of these claims took seven years to investigate, and even so, were indecisive. In 1961, 14 years after her arrest, Marie Besnard was acquitted for lack of proof.

Yet, oddly enough, it is these continual doubts and

uncertainties, the apparently endless proliferation of new and more subtle problems, that has made forensic toxicology the most brilliantly successful of all branches of legal medicine.

———— 2 ————
The Sexual Criminal

———— 1 ————

As strange as it sounds, sex crime is a relatively modern phenomenon. Of course, invading armies have always committed rape; so have brigands and burglars. But these might be regarded as crimes of opportunity. A sex criminal like Michael Fairley is an obsessive, for whom sex is the most important thing in life. And as we look back over the history of crime, we find that such people were virtually nonexistent before the nineteenth century.

The reason is obvious. In earlier centuries, most people lived in a state of continuous insecurity. If you are on the verge of starvation, or likely to freeze to death in winter, sexual satisfaction is bound to seem a secondary affair. One of the few true sex murderers of earlier times is the French Marshall Gilles de Rais, executed in 1440 for the sadistic murder of children, who also happened to be at one time the richest man in France; but Gilles began killing children in the course of "magical" operations to make gold, which he believed required human sacrifice. The evidence at the trial makes it clear that, for this spoilt and bored aristocrat, paedophilia and sex murder simply developed into a habit. The case of Gilles makes it plain why "obsessive" sex crime was a rarity in earlier centuries.

The same remains true down to the later eighteenth century, although by now there were a great many spoilt and bored aristocrats. It was the attitude of mind that was absent. The wealthy man who was so inclined could have an endless procession of mistresses and concubines; sex, like good dinners, was easily available. The first comprehensive survey of crime to be published in England, *The Newgate Calendar* (1774), reveals that murder committed in the course of robbery was the commonest offense, and that rape was a rarity. Of its 200 or so cases, only two or three involve "rape," and even in these there is room for doubt. The Revd. Benjamin Russen, executed by Tyburn for the rape of a child named Anne Mayne, was charged with committing the offense several times during a period when his wife was in bed having a baby, and a surgeon who examined the girl could find no sign of violence; it sounds like a case of seduction rather than rape. In 1817, a domestic servant was raped by three boatmen in Rickmansworth, Hertfordshire, and the local justice was so incensed that he financed a private investigation to track down the three men to Derbyshire; but when the victim and one of the rapists published their marriage banns, the charges were dropped.

Another case of 1817 poses an interesting riddle in crime detection; H.T.F. Rhodes devotes a chapter to its consideration in *Clues and Crime*. At 6:30 on the morning of May 27, 1817, a laborer on his way to work noticed a pair of shoes and a bundle of clothes lying close to the edge of a deep pool. He also observed, about 40 paces away, a patch of blood on the grass, and the impression of a human body lying full length; the blood was in the area of the lower part of the impression. There were also imprints of large-toed shoes, and some bloodspots leading towards the pond.

The laborer summoned help; the pond was dragged, and the body of a 20-year-old girl named Mary Ashford discovered in it. Medical examination later established that she had been a virgin, and that she had recently had sexual intercourse; the dress she was wearing was spotted with blood. The men made a careful study of the field, and showed that they had a real flair for detection. They noted several sets of footprints of a man and a woman, and that in one place, there was evidence that the man had run behind the woman to try to catch her up. Other footprints indicated that they had dodged one another. Finally, they had walked together. Then the girl had lost her virginity. No footprints led from this spot to the pond, from which the searchers deduced— rather oddly—that the man had carried her to the pond and thrown her in.

Mary Ashford lived in Erdington, near Birmingham, with her uncle, a small farmer, and was known as the village belle. On the night of the tragedy, Mary had arranged to go to a dance at a small village called Tyburn with a friend named Hannah Cox. She arrived at Hannah Cox's house with her dance frock tied in a parcel, and wearing a pink dress and a straw bonnet. At Hannah's she changed into her dance frock and shoes, and she and Hannah went to Tyburn. There she met the son of a neighboring farmer named Abraham Thornton, and danced with him a great deal. Hannah and a friend left the dance around midnight; so did Mary and Abraham Thornton. At three o'clock, a man who knew Thornton passed him standing at a stile with Mary and said good morning. At 3:30 she was seen walking towards Hannah's house. There, at about 4 a.m., she changed back into her pink dress, and wrapped her dance clothes in a bundle. But, for some reason, she continued to wear her dancing shoes. Hannah watched her change, and said she seemed perfectly normal, and that her clothes were not bloodstained. At 4:15, Mary left Hannah's and began walking back towards her home—three people saw her on the road. (The unusual amount of activity in the area may have been due to the fact that the dance was a major annual event.) Two hours later, the laborer found her clothes in the field near the pond.

The obvious suspect was Abraham Thornton. He had walked back home to Castle Bromwich, arriving about 5:35.

When told the next day of Mary's death, he certainly behaved like a man with nothing to hide: "What! I was with her until four this morning." And he also admitted that he had been responsible for the loss of her virginity—he had told a friend at the dance that he intended to try and seduce her later. He also seemed to have a sound alibi. At roughly the time Mary Ashford must have reached the field where she died, he was seen walking back home by three people, and was at a distance of three miles from the pond. Nevertheless, he was charged with Mary Ashford's murder, and tried at Birmingham. It took the jury only six minutes to find him not guilty.

In retrospect, we can see that the question of his guilt or innocence could have been easily established, even allowing for the condition of forensic science in 1817 (when Orfila was just making a name for himself in Paris). A microscope would have revealed whether the blood on her dress was menstrual blood, or due to her deflowerment. We know that there were spots of blood on her dance frock, which means that she had bled while still wearing it. If it was normal blood, then Mary had voluntarily given herself to Thornton in the field, and gone back to Hannah Cox's to change. In that case, she began to bleed more heavily on her way home, and lay down in the field, near the pond, in an effort to ease it—hence the blood on the grass. (She would naturally raise her dress to prevent it becoming more badly stained.) This scenario suggests that her death was accidental— she walked to the pond to wash off the blood, and slipped in, perhaps weak from loss of blood.

If the blood was menstrual, then Thornton was guilty. He admitted to possessing her, and it is highly unlikely that a girl who is starting to menstruate would feel like surrendering her virginity. In that case, Thornton must have waited for her to return across the field and run after her. She was raped and probably fainted; then Thornton threw her into the pond. But if, in fact, he was seen as early as 4:35 at a farm three miles away, then he cannot have been Mary's killer. Since no other footprints were found in the field—Mary's shoes and Thornton's shoes both fitted the footprints—it seems unlikely that she was attacked by some stranger. In that case, the jury was correct to find him innocent.

Local people were certainly outraged by the "not guilty" verdict; they may have felt that this conceited Casanova— there is some evidence that Thornton regarded himself as a ladies' man—deserved some punishment. A fund was raised to enable Mary's brother William to bring an appeal. And at the appeal, in front of the Lord Chief Justice Lord Ellenborough, Thornton caused considerable surprise by offering to defend his innocence by engaging in single combat—a medieval law that had never been repealed. He threw down a glove on the floor, and William Ashford was on the point of picking it up when he changed his mind—he was apparently a much smaller man than Thornton. So Thornton walked out of the court a free man, and Parliament hastened to pass an act abolishing the "wager of battel."

Rhodes has pointed out that if Mary Ashford had changed into her walking shoes at Hannah Cox's, the case would be solved. If some of the footprints in the field had been those of her walking shoes—particularly those that showed her walking with Thornton—then it would prove that Thornton was present immediately before her death, and was probably guilty of it. Since Mary neglected to change her shoes, her death must remain an unsolved mystery. Yet even so, there is still one more piece of evidence to take into account—the running footprints. The field next to the one that contained the pond had recently been harrowed, and it was in this field that the amateur detectives found signs that the man had pursued the girl across the field and caught up with her; then they had, apparently, walked to the place where blood had been found on the grass. More of the man's footprints— again running—were found going back across the harrowed field in the opposite direction. Now it seems unlikely that this had all occurred earlier in the evening; Thornton was seen talking to Mary at a stile that led to the fields, so why should he then pursue her, unless they had decided to play hide-and-seek at half past three in the morning? It seems more likely that Thornton was unsuccessful in his attempts at seduction, waited for her on her way home, and made an attempt to take her by force. The rape completed, and the unconscious girl assigned to the pond, he then ran back across the field in an attempt to make up for lost time and establish an alibi. Simple logic makes it seem that the acquittal of Abraham Thornton was a miscarriage of justice.

2

1828 saw the trial of Burke and Hare, the Edinburgh "body snatchers." The case might be regarded as a typical example of the type of "economic crime" which is so fully documented in *The Newgate Calendar*; because anatomists would pay a few pounds for corpses (the price between £5 and £10) Burke and Hare decided that it would be a simple matter to manufacture corpses by suffocating vagrants after getting them drunk. After a dozen or so murders they became careless and were caught. Hare turned King's evidence, so only Burke was hanged; Hare later died, a blind old beggar, in London.

But the period that saw the archetypal "economic" murder case also saw the rise of a vigorous new industry: pornography. A kind of pornography had existed in France in the eighteenth century, but it was really a type of anticlerical satire, consisting mainly of tales of monks seducing their penitents and impregnating nuns. In 1740, Samuel Richardson's novel *Pamela, or Virtue Rewarded* caused a sensation, with its tale of a virtuous servant girl who resists all her master's attempts to rape and seduce her; it was the first novel, in our modern sense of the word. Nine years later, a penniless drifter named John Cleland produced the first pornographic novel, *Fanny Hill,* full of minutely detailed descriptions of seduction; but the government awarded him a pension on condition that he wrote no more pornography, and Cleland found few imitators; Henry Fielding's

contemporaries were less interested in reading about sex
than in doing it. After the French Revolution, the works of
the Marquis de Sade caused considerable scandal; but Sade
was so obviously a pathological case—writing about horrible tortures—that people read them to be shocked rather
than sexually titillated.

But by 1820, a new generation was learning from Sade
and Cleland, and England was importing large quantities of
pornography from France. Books like *The Lustful Turk*
(1828) and *The Ladies' Telltale* differed from their earlier
models in one basic respect. Instead of Rabelaisian accounts
of seductions, or nightmarish sadism, they concentrated on
the forbidden—peeping through cracks in doors at women
undressing, drilling holes in lavatory partitions, hiding under beds. Seduction of innocence was a favorite subject:
little girls who see the butler in bed with the chambermaid,
and persuade him to initiate them into the "game," school-
masters who deflower their female pupils after whipping
their bare backsides . . . And as we observe the rise of
pornography, we can see that the blame should be laid
squarely at the door of the virtuous Samuel Richardson, the
printer who claimed that his novels were intended as a
warning against vice. V. S. Pritchett observed accurately:

> Prurient and obsessed by sex, the prim Richardson
> creeps on tiptoe nearer and nearer, inch by inch . . . he
> beckons us on, pausing to make every kind of
> pious protestation, and then nearer and nearer he
> creeps again, delaying, arguing with us in whis-
> pers, working us up until we catch the obsession
> too.

In *Pamela,* the virtuous housemaid holds out for marriage, but in its successor *Clarissa,* the heroine is kidnapped, taken to a brothel, and there drugged and raped.

But Richardson's real importance is that he taught Europe
to daydream. *Don Quixote* and *Robinson Crusoe* had been
mere fairy stories; by comparison, *Pamela* and *Clarissa*

were soap operas about the people who live next door; they had the compulsive quality of gossip. Within a decade, the novel had conquered Europe as the cinema would conquer the world 150 years later. The novel was a kind of magic carpet to a more interesting world.

Under the circumstances, it is surprising that it took so long for unscrupulous hacks to realize that the magic carpet could make highly profitable day-trips to the land of sexual fantasies. But when it happened, pornography ceased to be a vehicle of anticlerical satire, and became an independent literary form, like the historical novel or the Gothic fantasy.

Now the novel in itself might be regarded as a mixed blessing. Human beings learn to cope with life by knocking themselves against its hard corners; personal development is limited by reality. But the world of imagination offers another kind of development, just as authentic in its way, but uncontrolled by harsh realities. Cervantes had already treated this theme satirically—the dreamer who ventures out into the world prepared only by a diet of fantastic daydreams. In the early nineteenth century, thousands of young people served their apprenticeship to life through the pages of romantic fiction, and then found themselves overwhelmed by the physical actuality—one result being an appallingly high rate of suicide.

Pornography offered an alluring alternative to real sex—daydreams of seduction in which the innocent maiden never offered any real objection to the lustful male, and in which all the normal laws of social reality were suspended; daughters yielded to their fathers, mothers to their sons, and no one ever became inconveniently pregnant. In Victorian brothels, clients enacted their fantasies with women dressed as nursemaids or schoolgirls. The male ego was able to blossom like a hothouse plant—for male sexual fulfillment is based upon the assertion of the ego. Sooner or later, all this fantasy was bound to try to come to terms with reality, and the inevitable result would be sex crime.

What prevented an explosion of sex crime in the mid-Victorian era was not religious or social inhibition, but the fact that women were so easily available. The male who walks through a modern city knows that most of the women are unavailable—unless he happens to be a film star or pop idol. In the Victorian age, most of the working-class women *were* available, if he happened to have a few sovereigns in his pocket. The anonymous author of the Victorian autobiography *My Secret Life* describes endless encounters with teenage pick-ups who yielded their virginity for five shillings in some hired room. Only children were "forbidden," and this explains why about three-quarters of Victorian rape cases involved children. But in the second half of the century, an increasing number of women began to earn their own living. We have seen that, in 1841, female shop assistants like Mary Rogers were such a rarity that they became minor celebrities and ensured the success of the business; by the 1890, every large store employed hundreds of them, and although a few of them might be available to the predatory male, most were intent on marriage. And since Victorian morality preached the importance of virtue, the female sex was suddenly divided sharply into two classes: respectable women and whores. Now that most women were "forbidden," children ceased to constitute the majority of the rape statistics. Yet social taboos were still so powerful that the rape of a shop assistant or typist was still a relatively rare crime.

This explosive situation was complicated by Victorian prudery. The Victorian heroine, particularly as portrayed by female novelists, was a high-minded creature who would have regarded sex out of wedlock as horribly sinful. These same novelists made sure that the "fallen" woman always ended in ruin and despair. As far as the normal Victorian male was concerned, this only made them ten times as desirable, so that the very idea of femininity became sexually stimulating. In 1886, the Victorian medical establishment was deeply shocked by Dr. Richard von Krafft-Ebing's *Psychopathia Sexualis,* a book that revealed the extraordinary extent of sexual deviations on the Continent. Many of these deviations were variants of sadism and masochism; but the majority were forms of fetishism, in which sexual excitement is derived from some object connected with woman—hair, shoes, nightcaps, underwear, even crutches. "Woman" had become so forbidden and so desirable that her magic could operate just as potently even, so to speak, at second hand.

Yet at the time of the publication of *Psychopathia Sexualis,* sex crime was still rare. In 1867, a clerk named Frederick Baker had lured an 8-year-old girl named Fanny Adams away from her companions and then dismembered her. The main piece of evidence was an entry in his diary reading, "Killed a young girl today. It was fine and hot." Baker tried to persuade a jury that it merely meant: "Killed today—a young girl. The weather was fine and hot," but they disbelieved him and he was executed. But Baker came from a family with a history of mental illness, and the murder was regarded as an expression of "moral insanity" rather than as an explosion of obsessive sexuality. Four years later, in 1871, a Frenchman named Eusebius Pieydagnelle became obsessed by the smell of blood in the butcher's shop where he worked, and committed six murders with a knife, mostly of young women; he admitted that the murders were always accompanied by orgasm. In Italy in the same year, a youth named Vincent Verzeni was charged with a number of sex crimes, including two murders—he experienced a compulsion to strangle women until he experienced orgasm. And in Boston, Massachusetts, in 1874, a 14-year-old boy named Jesse Pomeroy was charged with two sex murders of children, and sentenced to life imprisonment. In 1880, 20-year-old Louis Menesclou lured a 5-year-old girl into his room in Paris and killed her; he concealed the body under his mattress overnight. When neighbors complained about choking black smoke issuing from the chimney, police found a child's head and entrails burning in his stove. Menesclou denied raping the child, but became embarrassed when asked why the genitals were missing; a poem in his notebook began: "I saw her, I took her." But what all these cases had in common was that the murderer was mentally subnormal, so the sexual motivation could be subsumed under the heading "hereditary degeneracy" and dismissed.

———————————— 3 ————————————

The Jack the Ripper murders, which occurred in 1888, created a world-wide sensation because they refused to be dismissed—they were, in fact, the first "sex murders" in our modern sense of the term. All occurred in the Whitechapel area of east London and the known victims total five, although it is possible that a prostitute named Martha Turner, stabbed 39 times on the landing of a slum tenement on August 7, brings the total to six.

Most of the murders displayed the same gruesome trademark; the disemboweling of the victim and the removal of certain inner organs, such as liver or kidneys. In the early hours of the morning of August 31, 1888, a prostitute named Mary Ann Nicholls was found lying on the pavement in Bucks Row, Whitechapel; when removed to the mortuary, it was discovered that her stomach had been cut open. Death was due to the severing of the windpipe. Eight days later, on September 8, a prostitute named Annie Chapman was killed in an almost identical manner in a backyard in Hanbury Street; the head was almost severed from the body, and her kidneys and ovaries had been removed and taken away. On September 28, the Central News Agency received a letter signed "Jack the Ripper," threatening more murders; two days later, the "Whitechapel maniac" killed two women in a single night. Interrupted soon after he had cut the throat of a prostitute named Elizabeth Stride in the backyard of a working men's club, the Ripper immediately went in search of another victim. In Mitre Square, half a mile away, he met a prostitute named Catherine Eddows, who had just been released from police cells, and killed and disemboweled her in less than a quarter of an hour—a policeman passed the spot at half past one and a quarter to two, and found the body on his return.

The final murder was the only one that took place indoors. On the morning of November 9, 1888, a rent collector peered through the broken window of a room in Miller's Court, and saw a mutilated body lying on the bed. The victim was a 24-year-old prostitute named Mary Kelly, and the murderer had obviously spent several hours in the room, opening the body and removing most of the inner organs, and stripping the skin from the legs; he had apparently worked by the light of rags burning in the grate.

This was almost certainly the last of the crimes of "Jack the Ripper," although three other murders with similar features occurred during the next three years. The general public was horrified at the sheer savagery of the mutilations, and the fact that the women were prostitutes touched some deep spring of morbidity in the Victorian mentality. Prostitution was unmentionable in decent society; the kind of men who made use of such women were supposed to be unspeakably degenerate, while the women themselves were— in modern phraseology—"non-persons." Yet the thought that such "creatures" existed aroused mixed feelings in the Victorian middle classes, a mixture of revulsion and envy. (They were known euphemistically as "daughters of joy," apparently in the belief that they did it for pleasure.) By drawing attention to these women in such a horrifying manner, Jack the Ripper had aroused, in an amplified form, these same morbid emotions of revulsion and envy. And, for the first time, the Victorians became aware of the immense reservoir of sexual frustration that lay just below the surface of their prim and orderly society.

The police were horrified for a more practical reason. For more than half a century—since the foundation of Scotland Yard in 1829—crime detection had been improving steadily. And crime detection meant discovering a link between the crime and the criminal, and tracing the thread back to the criminal. Yet these casual sex murders by a maniac with a knife seemed virtually unsolvable. In theory, they should have offered no more difficulty than a series of burglaries—for, after all, the burglar also selects his target more or less at random. But the burglar may be identified by his *modus operandi,* by clues he leaves behind, and by his method of disposing of the stolen goods. By comparison, Jack the Ripper might have been the Invisible Man.

A mere nine years after the Ripper murders, finger-printing solved its first murder in India, and within another four years, was in use at Scotland Yard. But would fingerprinting have enabled the police to catch the Ripper? On the available evidence, the answer is no. Mary Kelly's murderer undoubtedly left behind fingerprints in her room in Miller's Court, but unless they were the prints of a known criminal, or of someone the police arrested as a suspect, they would have been unhelpful. In fact, Jack the Ripper might have gone on killing for years, if he had chosen to do so, and remained uncaught—as Peter Sutcliffe, the "Yorkshire Ripper" (whom we shall discuss later) demonstrated in the 1970s. After half a century of scientific crime fighting, the police found themselves virtually back to square one—to the sense of helplessness that had led the police of earlier centuries to rely on torture.

Why *did* the murders cease? The police were inclined to assume that it was because the Ripper committed suicide, or was confined in a mental home. This is why their favorite suspect was an unsuccessful barrister named Montague John Druitt, who committed suicide by throwing himself into the Thames on December 3, 1888. Druitt was named in the papers of Sir Melville Macnaghten as his chief suspect—together with two other men named Kosminki and Ostrog. But then Macnaghten came to the Yard in the year after the murders, and so had no direct experience of the case. And the information he gives about his suspect—in his private papers, and in his autobiography *Days of My Years*—is so inaccurate that it throws doubt on the whole theory. Macnaghten describes him as a doctor who lived with his family, and who committed suicide immediately after his last murder, when his mind collapsed as a result of "his awful glut." Druitt was a barrister (although he never practiced) who lived alone in the Temple; he committed suicide four weeks after the murder of Mary Kelly, not "immediately" after. And we know precisely why he committed suicide, since he left a suicide note: because his mother had become insane, and he was afraid that the same thing was happening to him. He was also undoubtedly depressed because he had been dismissed from the school in Blackheath where he worked as an usher—possibly for homosexual offenses. And only six hours after the murder of Annie Chapman, Druitt was playing cricket at Rectory Field in Blackheath—he was an enthusiastic cricketer. On the whole, it seems likely that Macnaghten was merely repeating garbled rumors when he named Druitt as his chief suspect.

Other suspects* have included the Duke of Clarence (Queen Victoria's grandson), Clarence's tutor, J. K. Stephen (the cousin of Virginia Woolf) and the Queen's physician, Sir William Gull. The Duke of Clarence must be excluded, since he was celebrating his father's birthday at Sandringham at the time of the last murder. His tutor and close friend J. K. Stephen was a homosexual aesthete who seems an even less likely candidate than Clarence. The Sir William Gull theory, advanced by Stephen Knight in a book called *Jack the Ripper: the Final Solution*, was based on a story told by Joseph Sickert, the son of the printer Walter Sickert, according to which the Duke of Clarence had outraged his grandmother by marrying a Catholic artists' model named Annie Crook, who bore him a child. Mary Kelly, the final victim, was the nurse of this child. Annie Crook was kidnapped on the orders of the Royal Family, and Sir William Gull induced to perform a sinister brain operation to destroy her memory. Then, since Mary Kelly and some of her Whitechapel friends were trying to blackmail the Royal Family, Gull was given the

---

*For a comprehensive discussion of the murders and suspects, see *Jack the Ripper: Summing Up and Verdict*, by Colin Wilson and Robin Odel (1987).

task of hunting them down and murdering them one by one.

Soon after Knight's book appeared, Joseph Sickert admitted that his whole story had been a hoax. But since Gull had suffered a severe stroke in the year before the Ripper murders, he could have been excluded as a suspect even without this admission.

If the Ripper murders produced dismay at Scotland Yard, the police must have been encouraged by their success in arresting two more mentally disturbed killers, both of whom have been suspected of being Jack the Ripper. Dr. Thomas Neill Cream, who obtained his medical degree in Canada, was a bald-headed, cross-eyed man, who arrived in London in 1891. He picked up young prostitutes in the Waterloo Road area, and persuaded them to take pills containing strychnine, apparently from motives of pure sadism; four of them died in agony. But Cream was undoubtedly insane: he wrote confused letters accusing well-known public men of the murders, and went to Scotland Yard to complain of being followed by the police. A young constable who had followed him from the house where two prostitutes had been poisoned explained why he suspected the cross-eyed doctor, and Cream's arrest followed swiftly. After his arrest, he wrote to a prostitute to tell her that his name would be cleared by a Member of Parliament, who had over 200 witnesses to prove his innocence. Cream should undoubtedly have been found guilty but insane; he told one prostitute that he lived only for sex, and was probably suffering from tertiary syphilis, with softening of the brain. After his execution in 1892, it was frequently suggested that Cream was Jack the Ripper. This seems unlikely for two reasons. No sex murderer has been known to change his *modus operandi* from stabbing to poisoning, and at the time of the Ripper murders, Cream was serving a term in Joliet penitentiary in Chicago for the murder by poison of his mistress's husband. So although Cream's last words on the scaffold were, "I am Jack the . . . ," there can be no doubt that he is the least likely suspect.

George Chapman, a Pole whose real name was Severin

Klossowki, *was* in Whitechapel at the time of the Ripper murders, and was suspected at the time by Detective Inspector Frederick Abberline, one of the officers in charge of the investigation. A doctor named Thomas Dutton suggested to Abberline that he should be looking for a Russian or Pole with a smattering of surgical knowledge—it was often asserted, inaccurately, that the mutilations showed medical skill. Chapman, who was 23 in 1888, practiced the trade of "barber-surgeon"—one writer asserts that he rented a shop in the basement of George Yard Buildings, the slum tenement where Martha Turner was stabbed 39 times. But in 1888, Klossowski had no known criminal record. In 1890, he married (bigamously) and went to America. In 1892 he returned to England, met Annie Chapman, a woman with a private income, and allowed her to set him up in a barber's shop in Hastings. But in 1897, she died after a great deal of vomiting; her death was attributed to consumption. In the following year, Klossowski—who was now a publican—married his barmaid Bessie Taylor; she died in 1901 after a long period of vomiting and diarrhea. He married another barmaid, Maud Marsh, but his mother-in-law became suspicious when her daughter fell ill, and even more suspicious when she herself almost died after drinking a glass of brandy prepared by Chapman (as he now called himself) for his wife. When Maud Marsh died, an autopsy revealed arsenic poisoning, and Chapman was arrested. A second inquest revealed that the poison was antimony, not arsenic; and when the bodies of the previous two women were exhumed, it was discovered that they had also died from antimony poisoning. Although there was no obvious motive for the murders, the evidence against Chapman was overwhelming, and he was sentenced to death.

Abberline had continued to regard Chapman as a prime suspect in the Ripper murders; he had questioned the woman who was his mistress at the time—Lucy Baderski—and she said that Chapman was often out until four in the morning. When Chapman was arrested by Detective Inspector George Godley, Abberline remarked to Godley, "You've got Jack the Ripper at last." But although Chapman certainly had the opportunity to commit the Whitechapel murders, the same objection applies to him as to Neill Cream: a sadistic killer who has used a knife is not likely to switch to poison.

So although the police had reason to congratulate themselves on the arrest of two multiple murderers, they must also have recognized that detecting a poisoner is far easier than tracking down a sadistic "slasher." It was obvious that the Ripper-type killer was by far the most serious challenge so far to the science of crime detection.

This view was confirmed by a series of murders which began in France in 1894. In May of that year, a 21-year-old mill-girl named Eugénie Delhomme was found behind a hedge near Beaurepaire, south of Lyon; she had been strangled, raped, and disembowelled. And during the next three years, the "French Ripper" went on to commit another 10 sex murders of the same type. The next two victims were teenage girls; then a 58-year-old widow was murdered and raped in her home. In September 1895, the killer began killing and sodomizing boys, also castrating them: the first victim was a 16-year-old shepherd, Victor Portalier. Later that month, back near the scene of his first crime, he killed a 16-year-old girl, Aline Alise, and a 14-year-old shepherd boy. Soon after this, he was almost caught when he tried to attack an 11-year-old servant girl, Alphonsine-Marie Derouet, and was driven off by a gamekeeper, who was walking not far behind her. A man was stopped by the police, but allowed to go after producing his papers. He was, in fact, the killer—a 26-year-old ex-soldier (and inmate of an asylum) named Joseph Vacher, whose face was paralyzed from a suicide attempt with a revolver.

Imprisonment as a vagrant stopped the murders for six months, but almost as soon as he was released he raped and disemboweled Marie Moussier, the 19-year-old wife of a shepherd; three weeks later, he murdered a shepherdess, Rosine Rodier. In May 1897 he killed a 14-year-old tramp,

Claudius Beaupied, in an empty house, and the body was not found for more than six months. The final victim was Pierre Laurent, another 14-year-old shepherd boy, who was sodomized and castrated. On August 4, 1897, he came upon an Amazonian peasant woman named Marie-Eugénie Plantier, who was gathering pine cones in a forest near Tournon, and threw himself on her from behind, clamping a hand over her mouth. She freed herself and screamed; her husband and children, who were nearby, came running, and her husband threw a stone at Vacher, who in turn attacked him with a pair of scissors. Another peasant appeared, Vacher was overcome and dragged off to a nearby inn. There he entertained his captors by playing the accordion while awaiting the police. The "disemboweler of the southeast" (*l'éventreur du sud-est*) was finally trapped.

There had been a massive manhunt for the disemboweler, and dozens of vagabonds had been arrested on suspicion. An extremely accurate description of Vacher had been circulated, which mentioned his twisted upper lip, the scar across the corner of his mouth, the bloodshot right eye, the black beard and unkempt hair. Yet he committed 11 murders over three years, and if he had not been caught by chance, might well have gone on for another three.

The great Alexandre Lacassagne, Locard's mentor, spent five months studying Vacher, and concluded that he was only pretending to be insane. Vacher insisted that he had been abnormal since being bitten by a mad dog as a child. Tried for the murder of Victor Portalier, he was sentenced to death in October 1898 and guillotined on December 31. But there seems to be little doubt that Lacassagne was mistaken; Vacher was undoubtedly insane, and his random mode of operation had enabled him to play hide-and-seek with the combined police forces of southeastern France.

It was a disturbing lesson for the police and the crime scientists; in the 1890s, the random sex killer constituted a virtually insoluble problem.

Fortunately, rippers and disembowelers remained a rarity. In 1901, Paul Uhlenhuth was able to use his newly discovered precipitin test to help convict the sadistic child-killer Ludwig Tessnow. But it must be admitted that his contribution was not crucial; the jury hardly needed to be convinced that the man who had been questioned about the murder of two schoolgirls in 1898 was the same man who had murdered two schoolboys in 1901. All the same, it was plain that Uhlenhuth's method would one day spell the difference between a guilty and not guilty verdict for some-one who had shed human blood.

------------------------ 4 ------------------------

On the morning of June 11, 1904, a boatman on the River Spree in Berlin hooked a floating parcel; it proved to contain the torso of a young girl, whose developing breasts indicat-ed that she had not yet reached adolescence. Two days earlier, a workman named Friedrich Berlin had reported the disappearance of his 9-year-old daughter Lucie; now, from the underwear on the body, the torso was identified as that of the missing child. The police surgeon established that Lucie Berlin had been raped.

She had last been seen shortly after lunch on June 9, when she had asked for the key to the toilet on the next landing—the family lived in an overcrowded apartment building. A few doors away from the Berlins lived a prostitute named Johanna Liebtruth; but since she had been in jail on the day of Lucie's disappearance, the police decided she could tell them nothing. They also ignored her pimp, a man named Theodor Berger. They were seeking someone who had a penchant for young children. In due course, such a man was arrested, but proved to have a cast-iron alibi. And by this time the police had learned that the prostitute's male guest, Theodor Berger, was not a casual visitor, but actually lived with Johanna Liebtruth. And the occupants of the room above theirs reported that they had heard a child cry "No!" at about 1:30 on the day of the murder.

Lucie Berlin's head was found floating in the ship canal, with two arms attached to it with string. The police took Berger to view the remains, hoping to shock him into confessing. Berger strenuously protested his innocence, claiming that his sister was in the room cooking his lunch at the time Lucie Berlin had disappeared. But a lengthy interrogation of Johanna revealed a new piece of information. She had quarrelled violently with Berger when she came out of prison because she discovered that a wicker suitcase was missing; Berger had finally confessed that he had had another woman up to the apartment—he was a highly sexed man who needed regular satisfaction—and that, having no money to pay her, he had given her the suitcase. And then, to Johanna's astonishment, he had taken her in his arms and declared that he had decided to marry her immediately, a promise that had the effect of dissolving all her resentment—they had been living together for 18 years and he had so far resisted all her attempts to drag him to the altar.

To the police, this was a highly significant admission. Why indeed should Berger decide to marry the woman who supported him, simply because she was angry about a missing suitcase? It argued that the suitcase was of considerable importance. The police let it be known through the newspapers that they were seeking a wicker suitcase in connection with the murder of Lucie Berlin. Berger and Johanna were taken into police custody. Meanwhile, a brilliant forensic investigator named Dr. Paul Jeserich studied the Berger apartment at 130 Ackerstrasse through a magnifying glass, and left with a number of items that appeared to be bloodstained. By using Uhlenhuth's method, he could now tell whether it was human blood, animal blood, or only some fruit or wine stain. His results were disappointing. Most of the stains were not human blood. Some clothing contained a few light stains that could have been blood, but they had been carefully washed, making them too faint for forensic identification.

Two weeks after the discovery of the body, the break

came: a bargeman reported finding a wicker suitcase soon after Lucie had vanished. He had simply not heard that the police were looking for one.

Johanna immediately identified the case as her own. And the police were delighted to notice a few brown spots on the inside of the case. It had been found floating close to the spot where Lucie's torso had been discovered.

Jeserich now repeated his Uhlenhuth test, and this time it gave a positive result: the spots were human blood. This forged the last link in the case, enabling the police to build up a picture of how Lucie Berlin became a murder victim. Johanna Liebtruth had known her well, and Lucie had often been in the apartment; she called Berger "uncle." In fact, on the day before Johanna had been taken to jail (for insulting a customer) Lucie had been playing with Berger's dog on the floor of the room, kicking her shapely legs in the air—she was exceptionally well-developed for her age. Berger was the kind of man who needed a woman every day; when drunk he became—in Johanna's words—"like a bull." When Lucie had gone up to the lavatory, on the day of her disappearance, neighbors had seen Berger standing in the doorway of his room. What had happened, almost certainly, was that Berger had invited her into the room to play with the dog, then made advances to her. Lucie had shouted "No," and Berger, too sexually excited to stop, had throttled her, then raped her. Then, terrified of being found with the body, he had dismembered it, removed the limbs so it would fit into the suitcase—wrapping the limbs in newspaper to absorb blood— then taken them down to the river after dark.

The jury declined to believe Berger's insistence that he was "as innocent as Christ," and he was sentenced to 15 years in prison.

5

On the other side of the Atlantic, the transition from the age of Victorian morality to the age of sex crime was less brutally obvious than in Europe; there were no American Jack the Rippers or Joseph Vachers. (The nearest American equivalent, H. H. Holmes, will be considered in the next chapter.) America's first recorded sex murder took place in 1852—15 years before England's Frederick Baker case; a man named Charles Steingraver raped and murdered a 10-year-old girl who was blind, deaf, and dumb in Jackson, Ohio. Hundreds of spectators cheered as he fell through the trapdoor of the scaffold, and then seized his body and tore it to pieces.

The crimes of a Boston bell-ringer, Thomas W. Piper, challenge Jack the Ripper's claim to be the first sex killer in the modern sense of the term. Piper, a black-moustached young man in his mid-20s, was held in high esteem as the sexton of the Warren Avenue Baptist church in the early 1870s. In 1873, a curious change came over his character, and he began to cause scandal by leering at young ladies and whispering indecent suggestions in their ears. In December 1873, in nearby Dorchester, a servant girl named Bridget Landregan was attacked and battered to death with a club; then her killer stripped her, and was in the process of raping her when a passing stranger came to investigate the sounds issuing from the thicket. The killer ran away, leaving his club behind, and escaped over a railway embankment. Hours later, a girl named Sullivan was knocked unconscious and raped; she died later in hospital. The next victim was a prostitute named Mary Tynam, who was battered unconscious as she slept; she died later in hospital.

After church on May 23, 1875, Thomas Piper invited a 5-year-old girl named Mabel Young to come and see the pigeons in the belfry. Once there, he battered her unconscious with a cricket bat; but at that point, he heard the sounds of a search party ascending the stairs. He descended to a lower floor before they caught sight of him, and scrambled out of a window, dropping to the ground. Then he strolled back into the church. Meanwhile, his victim had recovered consciousness enough to scream in reply to the

shouts of the search party. The door of the belfry was
forced, and the child taken to hospital. But she died before
being able to describe what had happened to her. However,
the bloodstained bat was identified as Piper's, and he had
been seen leaping from the window. Charged with the
child's murder, he protested his innocence. But the evidence
against him was overwhelming, and he was sentenced to
death. A few days before his hanging, he sent for his
lawyers, and confessed to killing Mabel Young, and to four
earlier murders, as well as to several rapes of children. He
was executed in May 1876. Piper seems to have been a
heavy drinker—he admitted to being drunk when he attacked
Mabel Young—who experienced the urge to rape under the
influence of whisky. (He was also a drug addict who took
laudanum.)

Twenty years later, a strangely similar case was to take
place in San Francisco, and was duly recorded by Thomas
S. Duke, a captain of that city's police force, in his
Celebrated Criminal Cases of America (1910). Theodore
Durrant was a medical student and a Sunday school teacher
at the Emanuel Baptist church, a good-looking and highly
regarded young man, who was much attracted by a pretty
girl named Blanche Lamont. But Blanche was not entirely
happy about her admirer. Some time before, he had taken
her for a walk in the park, and made some bold advance
that had outraged the virtuous young lady, who refused to
speak to him for several weeks afterwards. Another girl
named Anne Whelming had even more reason to avoid
Durrant; he had invited her into the church library, made
some excuse to leave her, then suddenly reappeared
completely naked. The girl had screamed and fled, but
decided to tell no one.

On April 3, 1895, Blanche Lamont left her cookery class
in the early afternoon and met Theodore Durrant; they took
a ride on a streetcar and he was seen toying with her glove.
At 4:15, they were seen entering the Baptist church on
Bartlett Street, to which Durrant had a key. What happened
there is a matter of conjecture, but it seems likely that

Durrant left her in the library, and reappeared naked. When she screamed, he strangled her, carried her up to the belfry, and stripped off her clothes. Three-quarters of an hour later, the church organist arrived, and found Durrant looking pale and shaken; Durrant explained that he had accidentally inhaled some gas . . .

Blanche vanished, and no one knew where to find her. A week after her disappearance, Durrant persuaded her friend Minnie Williams to accompany him into the church library. When he reappeared naked, Minnie screamed. Durrant pulled her skirt over her head and rammed it into her mouth to choke her screams. After this he raped her and stabbed her to death so violently that the walls were covered with blood; he then raped her a second time. Durrant then went off to attend a meeting of young church members. Towards midnight, he returned to the library, and probably raped her again.

The body was found the next morning by women who had come to decorate the church for Easter. They found the partially clothed body in the library, with the blade of a broken knife still in her breast. The police soon established that Theodore Durrant was the last person to be seen with Minnie Williams; he was arrested near Walnut Creek, where he was training with the state militia. Meanwhile, Blanche Lamont's body had been found in the belfry, looking "white as marble," although it quickly began to decay and turn black when removed downstairs, so that the doctor who performed the post-mortem was unable to say whether she had been raped.

Durrant protested his innocence, but more than 50 witnesses had seen him with either Blanche or Minnie. (This seems to establish that neither crime was planned.) The jury found him guilty. For the next two years, Durrant made a series of appeals, and the case was widely publicized in European as well as American newspapers—an indication that sex murder was still a rarity. He was hanged on January 7, 1898, but feeling against him was so strong that it took his parents six days to find a funeral parlor willing to cremate him.

In retrospect it seems clear that both Thomas Piper and Theodore Durrant were mentally abnormal, and that both were subject to violent urges that temporarily robbed them of all self-control. That is to say, both cases may be seen as a violent and irrational revolt against the rigid morality of the Victorians.

It is interesting to note that Duke's *Celebrated Criminal Cases of America* contains only two sex crimes—in more than 100 cases—and that the second of these would hardly rate a mention in a modern work on American crime.

On January 8, 1902, an advertisement appeared in the *San Francisco Chronicle and Examiner* asking for a nanny to take care of a young baby. A 15-year-old girl named Nora Fuller answered it, and was asked to go to a restaurant in Geary Street by a man who called himself John Bennett. She never returned home. A month later, an estate agent who had let a house to a man who called himself Hawkins sent someone to collect the rent. The house proved to be empty, but the naked body of Nora Fuller was found upstairs in bed. She had been raped and strangled, and the body mutilated. A letter addressed to "Hawkins," and found in the dead girl's jacket, was postmarked 10 days after her disappearance, indicating that her killer had returned to the house.

The room was probably full of the man's fingerprints—for example, on an empty whisky bottle on the shelf—but 1902 was too early for fingerprint identification in San Francisco. But a handwriting expert called Theodore Kytka decided to try and track down the killer by the old-fashioned "needle-in-the-haystack" method. His examination verified that "John Bennett" of the advertisement and "C. B. Hawkins" of the house contract were the same person. Then he went through the only extensive collection of signatures in San Francisco—the Post Office's "change of address" file. He had studied 32,000 signatures before he found what he thought he was looking for. A detective rushed off to Kansas City to question an ex-resident of San Francisco about the murder of Nora Fuller—only to find that the man had a watertight alibi.

At this point, a local newspaper told the police that a clerk named Charles B. Hadley had disappeared, taking some of the firm's cash with him. The mistress with whom he had lived produced a photograph of Hadley with his signature on the back. The initials were obviously the same as those of "C. B. Hawkins," and the handwriting expert verified that they were written by the same hand. The mistress admitted that Hadley had shown an obsessive interest in the Nora Fuller case, reading every report about it. "C. B. Hawkins" had a moustache, while Hadley was clean shaven; then it was discovered that Hadley had purchased a false moustache just before the crime.

Now the hunt was on for Hadley. His photograph—plus an added moustache—was published in all the newspapers. So was his signature. It should have been merely a matter of time before he was caught; the whole country was on the lookout for him. But Hadley was never found; Thomas Duke suggests that he committed suicide.

Eight years later, in 1910, handwriting analysis again played the central part in identifying a sex murderer. A 16-year-old stenographer named Ruth Wheeler received a postcard, forwarded from the Bankers' and Merchants' Business College of New York, asking her to call at an address in 71st Street, on the Manhattan waterfront, for a secretarial job. When the girl failed to return home, her sister found the postcard in her room, mentioning the address; the card was signed "C. Walker." The apartment proved to belong to a young German immigrant named Albert Wolter, who lived there with his common law wife. Wolter was obviously nervous, and he admitted that Ruth Wheeler had been to see him; but he insisted that she had left. And he denied knowing anything about the postcard signed "C. Walker."

The following day, neighbors noticed a sack on the fire escape outside Wolter's room. It proved to contain a charred body, so badly burned as to be unrecognizable, but a gold chain around the neck identified her as Ruth Wheeler. Still Wolter insisted that he knew nothing about her death. But the police noticed that the fireplace in Wolter's room had been repainted—obviously because a very large fire had caused its paint to peel. Wolter was asked to provide a sample of his handwriting; he did, but it looked different from the writing on the card. A handwriting expert suggested that Wolter had disguised his writing in the "C. Walker" postcard, and suggested that he should be made to write page after page. And when Wolter did this, certain German characteristics—due to the fact that he had learned to write German script before English—began to emerge. The expert was able to point to the same characteristics in the handwriting on the postcard. Faced with this evidence, Wolter confessed. He had lured the girl to his apartment knowing that his "wife" would be out all day, and had strangled and raped her. Then he proceeded to burn the body in the grate. But it was still unburnt when his wife returned; Wolter was forced to thrust the remains hastily into a sack and push it out onto the fire escape. It was a singularly inept crime, and Wolter died in the electric chair in Sing Sing.

These early sex crimes all have the same curious characteristics: an attitude of obsession on the part of the murderer that meant that his chances of escaping detection were minimal. Charles Hadley went to the length of renting a house and placing an advertisement in a newspaper; Wolter of writing to a business college; both left an obvious trail behind. A century earlier, such crimes would have been incomprehensible; no criminal would have felt it worthwhile to go to such lengths merely for sexual satisfaction. Such crimes spring out of a preoccupation with sex that was largely the result of Victorian prudery. And that preoccupation was shared by the rest of society. William Randolph Hearst was one of the first newspaper magnates to realize that sex will sell out edition after edition. That he understood his readers is demonstrated by the most widely publicized murder case of 1913.

On Saturday, April 26, 1913, a 14-year-old named Mary

Phagan went to the paper factory in Atlanta where she worked to collect her wages, then went to the toilet in the basement. She failed to return home, and the next day her body was found in the basement, her dress around her waist and a cord knotted tightly around her throat. An autopsy later revealed that she had not been raped, but the motivation was obviously sexual.

Two notes were found near the body, both written in an illiterate hand. The writer obviously hoped that police would assume Mary Phagan had written them; one of them stated that she had been attacked by a "tall, sleam negro." The night-watchman, who was tall, and slim, and black, was arrested, but soon released. In his place, the factory manager, Leo Frank, was arrested; he was Jewish, and there was a great deal of anti-Semitism in Atlanta.

Another Negro named Jim Conley—who was short and fat—admitted that he had been sleeping off a hangover in the basement that Saturday; he also insisted that he could not write, and was believed. When it was later discovered that he could write, he stated that he had written the notes on the orders of Leo Frank. It should now have been obvious to everyone that Conley, not Frank, had killed Mary Phagan; but the citizens of Atlanta preferred a Jewish scapegoat.

One obvious clue was ignored: there were teeth-marks on Mary Phagan's shoulder. A few years later, they would have led to the conviction of the murderer; yet even when it was shown that they did not correspond to Frank's teeth, this evidence was dismissed. The newspapers sold endless editions by headlining the Frank case, and they were largely responsible for his final conviction in August 1913. His attorneys published a letter of protest that contained the sentence, "The temper of the public mind was such that it invaded the courtroom and invaded the streets and made itself manifest at every turn the jury made." Appeals were rejected. But in June 1915, Frank's sentence was commuted to life imprisonment. On August 16, a mob that called itself "the Knights of Mary Phagan" broke into the Milledgeville prison, overpowered the guards, and dragged out Leo Frank; hours later, weak from beating and loss of blood, he was lynched in Marietta, 125 miles away. Although the identity of the "executioners" was well known, no one was ever charged.

In 1982, Alonzo Mann, who had been a 14-year-old boy at the time of the Phagan murder, testified that he had seen Jim Conley dragging the body of Mary Phagan along the ground, and that Conley had threatened to kill him if he told anyone. Mann's evidence was validated by lie detector. In 1986, Leo Frank was granted a posthumous pardon by the State of Georgia.

----------- 6 -----------

Even after Frank's death, the case continued to exercise a morbid fascination; there were several books about it, and no fewer than three films. The newspaper accounts of the time make it obvious that, while everyone expressed horror, the underlying emotion aroused by the case was a kind of prurient interest. A journalist only had to invent some new absurdity—such as that the walls of Frank's office were covered with nude photographs—to sell out an edition of his newspaper.

What had happened was simply that half a century of Victorian morality and Victorian prudery—when even table legs were covered up in case they reminded people of the real thing—had generated a feverish sexual obsession. Now in a sense, there was nothing very new in this—we can observe the same thing in the novels of Samuel Richardson. But for all his gloating interest in seduction and rape, Richardson never for a moment presents Pamela and Clarissa as mere sex objects; they always remained individuals. It was not until the pornography of the 1820s that the "heroine" ceased to be an individual, and became a completely unbelievable combination of modesty and nymphomania. It was the phenomenon that Karl Marx would call "alienation," the breakdown of human relationships that causes human beings to treat one another as mere objects. But at this early stage, the social pruderies had not yet dammed up the sex urge until it was ready to explode into violence; this happened only in the second half of the century. And even so, it remained a frightening rarity until the First World War. Nineteen-thirteen, the year of the Mary Phagan murder, may be regarded as a kind of watershed: it was the beginning of the modern age of sex crime.

It seems to have been the anarchic violence of the First World War that released the age of sex crime in Europe. The dubious distinction of being its inaugurator probably goes to the Hungarian Bela Kiss, whose crimes presented an apparently insoluble problem to the Central Police Medical Laboratory in Budapest.

In 1916, the Hungarian tax authorities noted that it had been a long time since rates had been paid on a house at 17 Rákóczi Street in the village of Cinkota, 10 miles northwest of Budapest. It had been empty for two years, and since it seemed impossible to reach the owner, or the man who rented it, the district court of Pest-Pilis decided to sell it. A blacksmith named Istvan Molnar purchased it for a modest sum, and moved in with his wife and family. When tidying up the workshop, Molnar came upon a number of sealed oildrums behind a mess of rusty pipes and corrugated iron. They had been solidly welded, and for a few days the blacksmith left them alone. Then his wife asked him what was in the drums—it might, for example, be petrol—and he settled down to removing the top of one of them with various tools. And when Molnar finally raised the lid, he clutched his stomach and rushed to the garden privy. His wife came in to see what had upset him; when she peered into the drum she screamed and fainted. It contained the naked body of a woman, in the crouching position; the practically airless drum had preserved it like canned meat.

Six more drums also proved to contain female corpses. Most of the women were middle-aged; none had ever been beautiful. And the police soon realized they had no way of identifying them. They did not even know the name of the man who had placed them there. The previous tenant had gone off to the war in 1914; he had spent little time in the house, and had kept himself to himself, so nobody knew who he was. The police found it difficult even to get a description. They merely had seven unknown victims of an unknown murderer.

Professor Balazs Kenyeres, of the Police Medical Laboratory, was of the opinion that the women had been dead for more than two years. But at least he was able to take fingerprints; by 1916, fingerprinting had percolated even to the highly conservative Austro-Hungarian Empire. However, at this stage, fingerprinting was unhelpful, since it only told them that the women had no criminal records.

Some three weeks after the discovery, Detective Geza Bialokurszky was placed in charge of the investigation; he was one of the foremost investigators of the Budapest police. He was, in fact, Sir Geza (lovag), for he was a nobleman whose family had lost their estates. Now he settled down to the task of identifying the female corpses. If Professor Kenyeres was correct about time of death—and he might easily have been wrong, since few pathologists are asked to determine the age of a canned corpse—the women must have vanished in 1913 or thereabouts. The Missing Persons' Bureau provided him with a list of about 400 women who had vanished between 1912 and 1914. Eventually, Bialokurszky narrowed these down to 15. But these women seemed to have no traceable relatives. Eventually, Bialokurszky found the last employer of a 36-year-old cook named Anna Novak, who had left her job abruptly in 1911. Her employer was the widow of a Hussar colonel, and she still had Anna's "servant's book," a kind of identity card that contained a photograph, personal details, and a list of previous employers, as well as their personal comments. The widow assumed that she had simply found a better job or had got married. She still had the woman's trunk in the attic.

This offered Bialokurszky the clue he needed so urgently:

a sheet from a newspaper, *Pesti Hirlap*, with an advertisement marked in red pencil:

> Widower urgently seeks acquaintance of mature, warm-hearted spinster or widow to help assuage loneliness mutually. Send photo and details, Poste Restante Central P.O. Box 717. Marriage possible and even desirable.

Now, at last, fingerprinting came into its own. Back at headquarters, the trunk was examined, and a number of prints were found; these matched those of one of the victims. The post office was able to tell Bialokurszky that Box 717 had been rented by a man who had signed for his key in the name of Elemer Nagy, of 14 Kossuth Street, Pestszenterzsebet, a suburb of Budapest. This proved to be an empty plot. Next, the detective and his team studied the agony column of *Pesti Hirlap* for 1912 and 1913. They found more than 20 requests for "warm-hearted spinsters" which gave the address of Box 717. This was obviously how the unknown killer of Cinkota had contacted his victims. On one occasion he had paid for the advertisement by postal order, and the post office was able to trace it. (The Austro-Hungarian Empire at least had a super-efficient bureaucracy.) Elemer Nagy had given an address in Cinkota, where the bodies had been found, but it was not of the house in Rákóczi Street; in fact, it proved to be the address of the undertaker. The killer had a sense of humor.

Bialokurszky gave a press conference, and asked the newspapers to publish the signature of "Elemer Nagy." This quickly brought a letter from a domestic servant named Rosa Diosi, who was 27, and admitted that she had been the mistress of the man in question. His real name was Bela Kiss, and she had last heard from him in 1914, when he had written to her from a Serbian prisoner of war camp. Bialokurszky had not divulged that he was looking for the Cinkota mass murderer, and Rosa Diosi was shocked and incredulous when he told her. She had met Kiss in 1914; he had beautiful brown eyes, a silky moustache, and a deep, manly voice. Sexually, he had apparently been insatiable . . .

Other women contacted the police, and they had identical stories to tell: answering the advertisement, meeting the handsome Kiss, and being quickly invited to become his mistress, with promises of marriage. They were also expected to hand over their life savings, and all had been invited to Cinkota. Some had not gone, some had declined to offer their savings—or had none to offer—and a few had disliked being rushed into sex. Kiss had wasted no further time on them, and simply vanished from their lives.

In July 1914, two years before the discovery of the bodies, Kiss had been conscripted into the Second Regiment of the Third Hungarian Infantry Battalion, and had taken part in the long offensive that led to the fall of Valjevo; but before that city had fallen in November, Kiss had been captured by the Serbs. No one was certain what had become of him after that. But the regiment was able to provide a photograph that showed the soldiers being inspected by the Archduke Joseph; Kiss's face was enlarged, and the detectives at last knew what their quarry looked like. They had also heard that his sexual appetite was awe-inspiring, and this led them to show the photograph in the red-light district around Conti and Magyar Street. Many prostitutes recognized him as a regular customer; all spoke warmly of his generosity and mentioned his sexual prowess. But a waiter who had often served Kiss noticed that the lady with whom he was dining usually paid the bill . . .

Now, at last, Bialokurszky was beginning to piece the story together. Pawn tickets found in the Cinkota house revealed that the motive behind the murders was the cash of the victims. But the ultimate motive had been sex, for Kiss promptly spent the cash in the brothels of Budapest and Vienna. The evidence showed that he was, quite literally, a satyr—a man with a raging and boundless appetite for sex. His profession—of plumber and tinsmith—did not enable him to indulge this appetite, so he took to murder. He had received two legacies when he was

23 (about 1903) but soon spent them. After this, he had taken to seducing middle-aged women and "borrowing" their savings. One of these, a cook named Maria Toth, had become a nuisance, and he killed her. After this—like his French contemporary Landru—he had decided that killing women was the easiest way to make a living as well as indulge his sexual appetites. His favorite reading was true-crime books about con-men and adventurers.

Bialokurszky's investigations suggested that there had been more than seven victims, and just before Christmas 1916, the garden in the house at Cinkota was dug up; it revealed five more bodies, all of middle-aged women, all naked.

But where was Kiss? The War Office thought that he had died of fever in Serbia. He had been in a field hospital, but when Bialokurszky tracked down one of its nurses, she remembered the deceased as a "nice boy" with fair hair and blue eyes, which seemed to suggest that Kiss had changed identity with another soldier, possibly someone called Mackavee; but the new "Mackavee" proved untraceable. And although sightings of Kiss were reported from Budapest in 1919—and even New York as late as 1932—he was never found.

7

In the year 1913 another notorious sex killer committed his first murder. On a summer morning, a 10-year-old girl named Christine Klein was found murdered in her bed in a tavern in Köln-Mülheim, on the Rhine. The tavern was kept by her father, Peter Klein, and suspicion immediately fell on his brother Otto. On the previous evening, Otto Klein had asked his brother for a loan and been refused; in a violent rage, he had threatened to do something his brother "would remember all his life." In the room in which the child had been killed, the police found a handkerchief with the initials

"P. K.," and it seemed conceivable that Otto Klein had borrowed it from his brother Peter. Suspicion of Otto was deepened by the fact that the murder seemed otherwise motiveless; the child had been throttled unconscious, then her throat had been cut with a sharp knife. There were signs of some sexual molestation, but not of rape, and again, it seemed possible that Otto Klein had penetrated the child's genitals with his fingers in order to provide an apparent motive. He was charged with Christine Klein's murder, but the jury, although partly convinced of his guilt, felt that the evidence was not sufficiently strong, and he was acquitted.

Sixteen years later, in Düsseldorf, a series of murders and sexual atrocities made the police aware that an extremely dangerous sexual pervert was roaming the streets. These began on February 9, 1929, when the body of an 8-year-old girl, Rosa Ohliger, was found under a hedge. She had been stabbed 13 times, and an attempt had been made to burn the body with petrol. The murderer had also stabbed her in the vagina—the weapon was later identified as a pair of scissors—and seminal stains on the knickers indicated that he had experienced emission.

Six days earlier, a woman named Kuhn had been overtaken by a man who grabbed her by the lapels and stabbed her repeatedly and rapidly. She fell down and screamed, and the man ran away. Frau Kuhn survived the attack with 24 stab wounds, but was in hospital for many months.

Five days after the murder of Rose Ohliger, a 45-year-old mechanic named Scheer was found stabbed to death on a road in Flingern; he had 20 stab wounds, including several in the head.

Soon after this, two women were attacked by a man with a noose, and described the man as an idiot with a hare lip. An idiot named Stausberg was arrested, and confessed not only to the attacks but to the murders. He was confined in a mental home, and for the next six months, there were no more attacks. But in August, they began again. Two women and a man were stabbed as they walked home at night, none of them fatally. But on August 24, two children were found dead on an allotment in Düsseldorf; both had been strangled, then had their throats cut. Gertrude Hamacher was 5, Louise Lenzen 14. That same afternoon, a servant girl named Gertrude Schulte was accosted by a man who tried to persuade her to have sexual intercourse; when she said "I'd rather die," he answered, "Die then," and stabbed her. But she survived, and was able to give a good description of her assailant, who proved to be a pleasant-looking, nondescript man of about 40.

The murders and attacks went on, throwing the whole area into a panic comparable to that caused by Jack the Ripper. A servant girl named Ida Reuter was battered to death with a hammer and raped in September; in October, another servant, Elizabeth Dorrier, was battered to death. A woman out for a walk was asked by a man whether she was not afraid to be out alone, and knocked unconscious with a hammer; later the same evening, a prostitute was attacked with a hammer. On November 7, 5-year-old Gertrude Albermann disappeared; two days later, the Communist newspaper *Freedom* received a letter stating that the child's body would be found near a factory wall, and enclosing a map. It also described the whereabouts of another body in the Pappendelle meadows. Gertrude Albermann's body was found where the letter had described, amidst bricks and rubble; she had been strangled and stabbed 35 times. A large party of men digging on the Rhine meadows eventually discovered the naked body of a servant girl, Maria Hahn, who had disappeared in the previous August; she had also been stabbed.

By the end of 1929, the "Düsseldorf murderer" was known all over the world, and the manhunt had reached enormous proportions. But the attacks had ceased.

The capture of the killer happened almost by chance. On May 19, 1930, a certain Frau Brugmann opened a letter that had been delivered to her accidentally; it was actually addressed to a Frau Bruckner, whose name had been misspelled. It was from a 20-year-old domestic servant named Maria Budlick (or Butlies), and she described an alarming adventure she had met with two days earlier. Maria had travelled from Cologne to Düsseldorf in search of work, and on the train had fallen into conversation with Frau Bruckner, who had given the girl her address and offered to help her find accommodation. That same evening, Maria Budlick had been waiting at the Düsseldorf railway station, hoping to meet Frau Bruckner, when she was accosted by a man who offered to help her find a bed for the night. He led her through the crowded streets and into a park. The girl was becoming alarmed, and was relieved when a kindly-looking man intervened and asked her companion where he was taking her. Within a few moments, her former companion had slunk off, and the kindly man offered to take the girl back to his room in the Mettmänner Strasse. There she decided his intentions were also dishonorable, and asked to be taken to a hostel. The man agreed; but when they reached a lonely spot, he kissed her roughly and asked for sex. The frightened girl agreed; the man tugged down her knickers, and they had sex standing up. After this, the man led her back to the tram stop, and left her. She eventually found a lodging for the night with some nuns, and the next day, wrote about her encounter to Frau Bruckner.

Frau Brugmann, who opened the letter, decided to take it to the police. And Chief Inspector Gennat, who was in charge of the murder case, sought out Maria Budlick, and asked her if she thought she could lead him to the address where the man had taken her. It seemed a remote chance that the man was the Düsseldorf murderer, but Gennat was desperate. Maria remembered that the street was called Mettmänner Strasse, but had no idea of the address. It took her a long time and considerable hesitation before she led Gennat into the hallway of No. 71, and said she thought this was the place. The landlady let her into the room, which was empty, and she recognized it as the one she had been in a week earlier. As they were going downstairs, she met the man who had raped her. He went pale when he saw her, and walked out of the house. But the landlady was able to tell her his name. It was Peter Kürten.

Kürten, it seemed, lived with his wife in a top room in the house. He was known to be frequently unfaithful to her. But neighbors seemed to feel that he was a pleasant, likeable man. Children took to him instinctively.

On May 24, 1930, a raw-boned middle-aged woman went to the police station and told them that her husband was the Düsseldorf murderer. Frau Kürten had been fetched home from work by detectives on the day Maria Budlick had been to the room in Mettmänner Strasse, but her husband was nowhere to be found. Frau Kürten knew that he had been in jail on many occasions, usually for burglary, sometimes for sexual offenses. Now, she felt, he was likely to be imprisoned for a long time. The thought of a lonely and penniless old age made her desperate, and when her husband finally reappeared, she asked him frantically what he had been doing. When he told her that he was the Düsseldorf killer, she thought he was joking. But finally he convinced her. Her reaction was to suggest a suicide pact. But Kürten had a better idea. There was a large reward offered for the capture of the sadist; if his wife could claim that, she could have a comfortable old age. They argued for many hours; she still wanted to kill herself. But eventually, she was persuaded. And on the afternoon of the 24th, Kürten met his wife outside the St. Rochus church, and four policemen rushed at him waving revolvers. Kürten smiled reassuringly and told them not to be afraid. Then he was taken into police custody.

In prison, Kürten spoke frankly about his career of murder with the police psychiatrist, Professor Karl Berg. He had been born in Köln-Mülheim in 1883, son of a drunkard who often forced his wife to have sexual intercourse in the same bedroom as the children; after an attempt to rape one of his daughters, the father was imprisoned, and Frau Kürten obtained a separation and married again. Even as a child Kürten was oversexed, and tried to have intercourse with the sister his father had attacked. At the age of 8 he became friendly with a local dog-catcher, who taught him how to masturbate the dogs; the dog-catcher also ill-treated them in the child's presence. At the age of 9, Kürten pushed a schoolfellow off a raft, and when another boy dived in, managed to push his head under, so that both were drowned. At the age of 13 he began to practice bestiality with sheep, pigs, and goats, but discovered that he had his most powerful sensation when he stabbed a sheep as he had intercourse, and began to do it with increasing frequency. At 16 he stole money and ran away from home; soon after, he received the first of 17 prison sentences that occupied 24 years of his life. And during long periods of solitary confinement for insubordination, he indulged in endless sadistic day-dreams, which "fixed" his tendency to associate sexual excitement with blood. In 1913, he had entered the tavern in Köln-Mülheim and murdered the 10-year-old girl as she lay in bed; he had experienced orgasm as he cut her throat. The handkerchief with initials P. K. belonged, of course, to Peter Kürten.

And so Kürten's career continued—periods in jail, and brief periods of freedom during which he committed sexual attacks on women, sometimes stabbing them, sometimes strangling them. If he experienced orgasm as he squeezed a girl's throat, he immediately became courteous and apologetic, explaining "That's what love's about." The psychiatrist Karl Berg was impressed by his intelligence and frankness, and later wrote a classic book on the case. Kürten told him candidly that he looked with longing at the white throat of the stenographer who took down his confession, and longed to strangle it. He also confided to Berg that his greatest wish was to hear his own blood gushing into the basket as his head was cut off. He ate an enormous last meal before he was guillotined on July 2, 1931.

Kürten was only one of many sex killers who gained notoriety after the First World War. Fritz Haarmann, a Hanover butcher who was also homosexual, picked up vagrant youths at the railway station—in the post-war period Germany was full of young unemployed workmen—and took them back to his lodging. There he murdered them, dismembered the bodies, and sold them for meat. He was also a police informer, so escaped suspicion of being the murderer who tossed bones and skulls into the river. It was only after his arrest for indecency in 1924 that his room was searched and various male garments discovered. Haarmann then confessed to a whole series of murders, all sexually motivated. He insisted to the end that he had killed his victims by biting them through the windpipe. He was guillotined in 1925.

Karl Denke, a church organist and landlord of a house in Munsterberg, Silesia, also made a habit of murdering strangers who were looking for lodgings. In December 1924, a coachman who lived above Denke heard cries and rushed down to investigate; he found Denke in the process of battering a young journeyman with an axe. When the police searched the house, they found the remains of 30 bodies pickled in tubs of brine, both men and women. Denke had been living off human flesh for at least three years, since 1921, and kept a ledger of his victims. Denke hanged himself with his own braces before he could be tried. In Germany in the mid-1920s, schoolchildren had a joke that went, "Who is the world's worst murderer?" and the child being questioned was encouraged to answer, "Haarmann, ich denke"—which may either be translated, "Haarmann, I think" or, "Haarmann, I, Denke."

Georg Grossmann was a Berlin pedlar who had lived in a flat near the Silesian railway terminal since the beginning of the First World War; when he took it, he specified a separate entrance. In 1921, the tenant of the flat above heard sounds of a struggle and called the police; they found the trussed-up carcass of a girl lying on the bed, tied as if for butchering. For many years, Grossmann had been picking up girls in need of a bed and killing them, then selling the bodies for meat. The number of victims is unknown, but it was established that he had killed three women in the three weeks before his arrest. Like Denke, Grossmann committed suicide in jail before he could be brought to trial.

But the most extraordinary sexual criminal of the post-war years was undoubtedly the Hungarian sadist Sylvestre Matuska, the "man who played with trains."

On August 8, 1931, a bomb had exploded on the Basel-to-Berlin express near Jüterbog (not far from Potsdam) injuring 100 passengers, some of them seriously. On January 30 of that year, there had been an unsuccessful attempt to derail a train near Anspach, in Lower Austria, and it seemed likely that both crimes had been committed by the same man—perhaps for political motives. On a telegraph pole there was a notice with swastikas and "Attack! Victory!"

Only a month after the Jüterbog attack, on September 12, 1931, a tremendous explosion shook the Budapest-Vienna express as it crossed a viaduct near the station of Torbagy, hurling five coaches into the depths below. Twenty-two people were killed, and many more injured. A 20-year-old reporter on the *Vienna Morning Post* named Hans Habe was asked to rush to the scene of the disaster. He found dozens of ambulances, stretchers taking away the injured, and wooden coffins beside the track. Some victims had been blown into pieces, and he saw two heads in one coffin and three legs in another. While Habe was talking to Superintendent Schweinitzer, who was in charge of the investigation, a short, well-built man with a military haircut came up to them. He introduced himself as Sylvestre Matuska, a Hungarian businessman who had been in one of the coaches. He seemed a lively, friendly man, and had apparently had a miraculous escape from one of the wrecked carriages that lay below the viaduct. Habe agreed to give him a lift back to Vienna. The next day, Habe met him by appointment in a café and found him describing the accident—complete with sketches—to a crowd of fascinated onlookers. "I saw one woman with her arm torn off..." Habe quoted him at length in his story, which brought the young journalist much favorable notice from colleagues.

But Superintendent Schweinitzer was suspicious. Matuska looked healthy and unshaken—quite unlike a man who had just survived a train wreck. He questioned all the surviving passengers on the train; none could recall seeing Matuska.

Forensic examination had established that the train had been
blown up by an "infernal machine" in a brown fibre
suitcase—virtually a mine which had exploded by the weight
of the train. A great deal of explosive must have been used,
and explosive was not easy to come by. A few days after the
explosion, a taxi-driver came to the Vienna police and told
them that he had been hired by a short-haired man to take
him on a long journey to two munitions factories, where he
had bought sticks of dynamite. This raised the question of
how the man had managed to obtain an explosives permit.
The answer came a week later when a society woman named
Anna Forgo-Hung went to the police with another piece of
the jigsaw puzzle. Sylvestre Matuska had approached her
about leasing some of her property, but had finally rented
only a quarry, explaining that he wanted to do some blasting.
This is how he had obtained his permit to buy explosives.

Matuska was arrested and charged with blowing up the
Torbagy express. When Habe heard the news, he hastened
to see Matuska's wife, a pretty blonde with an obviously
gentle nature. Frau Matuska told him that her husband was
undoubtedly innocent; he was travelling on the train himself, and she had seen his ticket. Yet her attitude convinced
Habe that she herself had her suspicions; a wife who
believes her husband incapable of a crime says so plainly,
and does not talk about tickets and other "proofs" of his
innocence.

In fact, Matuska soon confessed. He *had* been on the
train from Budapest; but he had got off at the next station,
hired a car, and drove to Torbagy in time for the explosion.
Forensic examination of the trousers he was wearing at the
time showed semen stains, and psychiatrists who examined
Matuska verified that he was a sadist. He was also, like Bela
Kiss, a man of insatiable sexual appetite, who slept with a
different prostitute each night when he was away from home
on business trips. Yet his gestures in courts—his trial began
in Vienna on June 15, 1932—were oddly effeminate. From
the beginning, Matuska set out to give the impression that
he was insane, declaring that he had been persuaded to

wreck the train by a right-wing guru called Bergmann, who
had tried to persuade Matuska to have intercourse with his
incredibly beautiful wife—Matuska rolled the word "intercourse" round his tongue—and then persuaded him to help
him found the religious sect. Matuska spoke of spiritualist
seances, and claimed that he had been under the telepathic
influence of an occultist called Leo since he was 14. But
perhaps the most interesting piece of evidence was that he
had bought his son an electric train set, then spent all his
time playing with it.

The jury was unconvinced by all this talk of mysticism
and occultism, and sentenced Matuska to life imprisonment—
there was no capital punishment in Austria. He was retried
in Budapest, and this time sentenced to death; but since the
Viennese court had sentenced him to life imprisonment, the
sentence was not carried out.

At the end of the Second World War, a reporter asked the
Hungarian authorities what had become of Matuska, and
learned—after many evasions—that the train-wrecker had
been released.

In 1953, towards the end of the Korean War, an American
patrol near Hong-Song captured some North Korean com-
mandos who were about to blow up a bridge; they were led
by a white man who seemed to be about 60. After long
interrogation, during which he apparently failed to answer
the questions, the man announced, "I am Sylvestre Matuska."
His interrogator was obviously unimpressed, at which point
the man explained with pride, "I am Matuska, the train-
wrecker of Bia-Torbagy. You have made the most valuable
capture of the war."

An American report of the incident stated that Matuska
had been freed from his Hungarian prison by the Russians,
and told them that he had wrecked the Jüterbog train on the
orders of a Communist cell of which he was a member; this
is how he came to be accepted as a volunteer on the side of
the North Koreans. As a saboteur trained to blow up
bridges, he must have felt as contented as a necrophile
placed in charge of a morgue. Habe is of the opinion that

Matuska betrayed Communist military secrets to the Americans, and was then released. What became of him after the Korean War is unknown.

—————————————— 8 ——————————————

In America, as in Europe, sex crime became increasingly frequent after the end of the First World War. And the American police, like their colleagues in Europe, found it equally difficult to deal with. Sex crime often appears to be strangely motiveless—as in the case of Matuska—and since most crimes are solved by tracing the motive back to the criminal, such crimes present the most baffling problem to the investigator.

On the morning of May 22, 1924, a Polish immigrant crossing a marshy area near Wolf Lake, not far from Chicago, saw two bare feet protruding from a culvert pipe above a pond. He summoned help, and the naked body of a boy was removed from the culvert. One of the workmen picked up a pair of glasses from the ground close to the body. Later that day, the dead boy was identified as Bobby Franks, the 14-year-old son of wealthy Jewish parents. He had vanished after school on the previous day, and his parents had received a letter demanding a $10,000 ransom, assuring them that their son was safe and well. The boy had been killed by violent blows on the head, and the face had been disfigured with hydrochloric acid.

Clues seemed to be minimal. The spectacles might or might not have been connected with the case—it seemed unlikely, since they were small, and probably belonged to a woman. The kidnap note had been written on a typewriter that had a worn "t" and "d"; but unless this could be located, this clue was useless. Three of the dead boy's schoolteachers were "grilled" by the police for hours, but seemed to have no connection with the murder. One theory was that the boy had been killed by a sexual pervert, who

had then lost his nerve and failed to complete the assault—
there was no sign of sexual interference.

The area where the body had been found was a nature
reserve. The game warden was asked for the names of
frequent visitors, and mentioned that of a 19-year-old ornithologist named Nathan Leopold, the child of wealthy parents who lived in south Chicago. Three days after the
finding of the body, Nathan Leopold was asked to go to the
local police station; there he signed a statement declaring
that he and another ornithologist had been bird-watching in
the Wolf Lake area the Sunday before the murder. A few
days earlier, Leopold had passed his exams in criminal
law.

A week after the murder, a reporter named Alvin Goldstein,
who was working on the case, attended a fraternity lunch
for students of the University of Chicago, and discussed the
case with Richard Loeb, another son of a wealthy Jewish
family, and a close friend of Nathan Leopold. Loeb suggested
that Goldstein should check with drug stores to ask about
anyone making suspicious telephone calls soon after the
murder; Goldstein, who respected Loeb's "hunches," left
early to pursue this line of inquiry.

Meanwhile, the police were following their only promising lead: the glasses. The lenses had been made by a huge
optical firm called Almer Coe and Company, who were able
to identify them as theirs. But both lenses and the frames
were of a common prescription. However, the hinges were
more distinctive, having been made by the Bobrow Optical
Company in Brooklyn. The Almer Coe Company kept
excellent records, and were able to state that, out of 54,000
pairs of spectacles sold by them in Chicago, only three pairs
had the Bobrow hinges. And one of the three purchasers—
who had each paid $11.50 for their glasses—was the young
ornithologist Nathan Leopold.

This, of course, meant little; Leopold had already described his bird-watching trip of the Sunday before the
murder. They had probably fallen out of his pocket. Nevertheless, he was brought in for questioning. He declared at

first that his spectacles were at home. But when a long search failed to unearth them, he admitted that he had probably lost them on the bird-watching trip. How had he lost them?, asked the interrogators. Leopold said that he had stumbled at one point, close to the culvert where Bobby Franks was later found. They asked him to demonstrate; Leopold obligingly put the glasses in his top pocket, and then fell down flat on the floor. The glasses remained where they were. He tried again; the glasses still stayed in the pocket.

Now the questioners asked Leopold about his whereabouts on the day of the murder. His replies were irritatingly vague. But he insisted that, at about the time Bobby Franks must have been kidnapped, he and his friend Richard Loeb had picked up two young women. When the girls had failed to ''come across,'' they had dropped them off, then gone home . . .

Loeb was taken to another police station and questioned separately. At first he said nothing about the two women; then he described how he and Leopold had got drunk and picked up two ''cheap girls'' in Leopold's roadster. The police became increasingly convinced that they were questioning two innocent men.

The reporter Goldstein was meanwhile doing a little sleuthing of his own. He had seen the ransom notes, and now decided to try and check against notes typed by Leopold. He learned that Leopold was a member of a group of law students who prepared information sheets for one another. He called on another member of the group, and succeeded in examining some of these sheets. He immediately noticed that two of those typed by Leopold were on different machines. And the law student remembered: in fact, Leopold had a second typewriter, a portable. Goldstein was excited; typewriter experts had declared that the ransom notes were written on a portable Underwood or Corona. Goldstein borrowed the information sheets, and took them back to his newspaper, the *Daily News*. The editor contacted an expert from the Royal Typewriter Company. And the expert pointed out similarities between the information sheets and the ransom notes: the "t" printed light, the "i" was twisted, the "m" was slanted . . .

Confronted with this new evidence Leopold admitted that he had used a portable typewriter, but insisted it did not belong to him, but to a friend who was now on holiday in Italy. However, it should still be in his house . . . A lengthy search failed to reveal the portable typewriter. But perhaps the friend had taken it away. Once again, the police decided that they were on the wrong track. Both boys had rich parents, and it would be impossible to hold them much longer.

The interrogator, Detective Bert Cronson, decided to try just one more possibility. The one person in the Leopold household he had not yet questioned was the chauffeur, Sven Englund; he asked a policeman to bring him in.

Englund remembered the day of the murder clearly because Nathan Leopold had asked him to repair the brakes on his sports car, a red Willys-Knight; they had been squeaking.

"Then they took the car and left?"

"No," said Englund; "the car stayed in the garage all day."

Now Cronson was excited. "Are you quite sure of the date?"

Englund said that his daughter had been to the doctor that day, and they had picked up a prescription from the doctor. The police hurried to see Mrs. Englund, and she was able to find the prescription. It was dated May 21, the day of the murder.

When Richard Loeb was asked about the car, he went pale and asked for a cigarette. Then he confessed. They had hired a car from the Rent-A-Car Company for the murder, because Nathan's red sports car would be too conspicuous. Nathan had given his name as Morton D. Ballard, and his address as the Morrison Hotel. They had waited for Bobby Franks to come out of school, and offered him a ride. Then, according to Loeb, Nathan Leopold had struck the boy on the head with a heavy chisel. They had stripped the body, poured hydrochloric acid on it to render identification more difficult, and pushed it into the culvert near Wolf Lake. They had posted the kidnap letter, written by Leopold on a stolen portable typewriter, then gone to Richard Loeb's home, where they had burned Bobby Frank's clothes in the furnace. They had already thrown the chisel out of the car window—it was found by a night-watchman . . .

When Leopold was told Loeb had confessed, he laughed and said, "Do you think I'm stupid?" But the details of the confession convinced him; he immediately decided to make his own confession, implicating Loeb as the killer.

Why had they chosen Bobby Franks as the victim? It had been pure chance. Leopold and Loeb had decided to commit a murder "for kicks." They had driven around that afternoon looking for a child to lure into the car—male or female. (At one stage they had planned on kidnapping a girl and raping her.) The child had to be wealthy, so they could also demand a ransom; when Leopold wrote the ransom note, he had no idea to whom it would be addressed. They hid in an alleyway, watching a group of boys playing baseball through a pair of binoculars. But after two hours of looking for victims, they saw Bobby Franks walking towards them—he was a friend of Loeb's younger brother. And Bobby agreed to accept a lift home.

Leopold and Loeb, it emerged at their trial, had been lovers since Leopold was 13 and Loeb was 14. Loeb was daring, charismatic and handsome; Leopold was studious and shy. Leopold fell in love with Loeb, and Loeb agreed to submit to his desires if Leopold signed a contract agreeing to become a partner in crime. For years they committed petty crimes—such as breaking into the fraternity house where they stole the typewriter. It was all part of a fantasy game in which they were master criminals, Nietzschean supermen. Loeb was undoubtedly the leading spirit of the two; Leopold took a masochistic delight in describing himself as Loeb's slave. Eventually, master and slave decided to confront the ultimate challenge, murder. "The plan was broached by Nathan Leopold," according to Loeb, "who suggested it as a means of having a great deal of excitement, together with getting quite a sum of money."

The state demanded the death penalty, but a brilliant defense by the lawyer Clarence Darrow led to life sentences. Nathan Leopold became the librarian in the Stateville penitentiary. Eleven years after his conviction, Richard Loeb was slashed to death with a razor by a fellow prisoner, who alleged that he had made homosexual advances.

After his release on parole in 1958, Leopold decided to sue the novelist Meyer Levin, whose novel *Compulsion* had fictionalized the murder; he demanded almost three million dollars for alleged invasion of privacy. The case was eventually dismissed, the judge pointing out that, since Leopold had "encouraged public attention" by committing the murder, he could not complain at someone writing about it. Leopold's biographer Hal Higdon* speculates that what really upset Leopold was an episode towards the end of the novel in which a psychiatrist analyzes the murder of Bobby Franks as a sex crime, with the chisel as a symbolic penis and the culvert into which the naked body had been thrust a symbolic vagina. The Freudian interpretation may lack subtlety; but there can be little doubt that the underlying compulsion of the murder was sexual.

———————————— 9 ————————————

The case illustrates the baffling and paradoxical nature of sex crime. Henry Fielding would have found it totally incomprehensible that two brilliant university students from wealthy backgrounds should have wanted to commit crimes as a kind of game. In Fielding's day, crime was motivated by quite straightforward "deprivation needs," such as starvation. And even if someone had explained to him that

* *The Crime of the Century,* by Hal Higdon (1975).

Leopold and Loeb were *too* comfortable, and wanted to seek out challenges, like a mountain climber or explorer, he would still have found it quite absurd. Fielding would also have been baffled by the crime of Charles Hadley: to rent a house under a false name and lure a girl there, purely for the purpose of rape . . . He *would* have understood the compulsion that makes Lovelace, the villain of Richardson's *Clarissa*, lure the heroine to a brothel to drug and rape her. But to go to so much trouble for *any* girl—a girl Hadley had not even seen until she came to answer his advertisement: that would have struck him as a kind of insanity.

What Fielding would have found impossible to understand is that, in the course of two centuries, civilized man had learned to use his imagination, so that *he lives with only one foot in the real world*. We have become so accustomed to this condition, with books, films, and television, that we accept it as normal; but in the evolutionary sense, it is thoroughly abnormal. Living in this strange, airless world inside our own heads, we experience a compulsion to "get back to reality." The sexual urge has this power to restore contact with reality; this is why the twentieth century has become "the age of sex crime." In that sense, Hal Higdon was right to describe the murder of Bobby Franks as "the crime of the century."

It is the fact that sex crime is the outcome of fantasy that makes the random sex criminal so difficult to detect. Two years after the murder of Bobby Franks, the American police found themselves confronting the same problem that had perplexed the London police force during the Ripper's "autumn of terror." On February 24, 1926, a man named Richard Newman went to call on his aunt, who advertised rooms to let in San Francisco; he found the naked body of the 60-year-old woman in an upstairs toilet. She had been strangled with her pearl necklace, then repeatedly raped. Clara Newman was the first of 22 victims of a man who became known as "the Gorilla Murderer." The killer made a habit of calling at houses with a "Room to Let" notice in the window; if the landlady was alone, he strangled and

raped her. His victims included a 14-year-old girl and a
8-month-old baby. And as he travelled around from San
Francisco to San Jose, from Portland, Oregon to Council
Bluffs, Iowa, from Philadelphia to Buffalo, from Detroit to
Chicago, the police found him as elusive as the French
police had found Joseph Vacher 30 years earlier. Their
problem was simply that the women who could identify
"the Dark Strangler" (as the newspapers had christened
him) were dead, and they had no idea of what he looked
like. But when the Portland police had the idea of asking
newspapers to publish descriptions of jewelry that had been
stolen from some of the strangler's victims, three old ladies
in a South Portland lodging-house recalled that they had
bought a few items of jewelry from a pleasant young man
who had stayed with them for a few days. They decided—
purely as a precaution—to take it to the police. It proved to
belong to a Seattle landlady, Mrs. Florence Monks, who had
been strangled and raped on November 24, 1926. And the
old ladies were able to tell the police that the Dark Strangler
was a short, blue-eyed young man with a round face and
slightly simian mouth and jaw. He was quietly spoken, and
claimed to be deeply religious.

On June 8, 1927, the strangler crossed the Canadian
border, and rented a room in Winnipeg from a Mrs. Catherine
Hill. He stayed for three nights. But on June 9, a couple
named Cowan, who lived in the house, reported that their
14-year-old daughter Lola had vanished. That same evening, a man named William Patterson returned home to find
his wife absent. After making supper and putting the children to bed, he rang the police. Then he dropped on his
knees beside the bed to pray; as he did so, he saw his wife's
hand sticking out. Her naked body lay under the bed.

The Winnipeg police recognized the *modus operandi* of
the Gorilla Murderer. A check on boarding-house landladies
brought them to Mrs. Hill's establishment. She assured
them that she had taken in no suspicious characters recently—
her last lodger had been a Roger Wilson, who had been
carrying a Bible and been highly religious. When she told

them that Roger Wilson was short, with piercing blue eyes and a dark complexion, they asked to see the room he had stayed in. They were greeted by the stench of decay. The body of Lola Cowan lay under the bed, mutilated as if by Jack the Ripper. The murderer had slept with it in his room for three days.

From the Patterson household, the strangler had taken some of the husband's clothes, leaving his own behind. But he changed these at a second-hand shop, leaving behind a fountain pen belonging to Patterson, and paying in $10 bills stolen from his house. So the police now not only had a good description of the killer, but of the clothes he was wearing, including corduroy trousers and a plaid shirt.

The next sighting came from Regina, 200 miles west; a landlady heard the screams of a pretty girl who worked for the telephone company, and interrupted the man who had been trying to throttle her; he ran away. The police guessed that he might be heading back towards the American border, which would take him across prairie country with few towns; there was a good chance that a lone hitchhiker would be noticed. Descriptions of the wanted man were sent out to all police stations and post offices. Five days later, two constables saw a man wearing corduroys and a plaid shirt walking down a road near Killarney, 12 miles from the border. He gave his name as Virgil Wilson and said he was a farm-worker; he seemed quite unperturbed when the police told him they were looking for a mass murderer, and would have to take him in on suspicion. His behavior was so unalarmed they were convinced he was innocent. But when they telephoned the Winnipeg chief of police, and described Virgil Wilson, he told them that the man was undoubtedly "Roger Wilson," the Dark Strangler. They hurried back to the jail—to find that their prisoner had picked the lock of his handcuffs and escaped.

Detectives were rushed to the town by aeroplane, and posses spread out over the area. "Wilson" had slept in a barn close to the jail, and the next morning broke into a house and stole a change of clothing. The first man he

spoke to that morning noticed his dishevelled appearance
and asked if he had spent the night in the open; the man
admitted that he had. When told that police were on their
way to Killarney by train to look for the strangler, he ran
away towards the railway. At that moment, a police car
appeared; after a short chase, the fugitive was captured.

He was identified as Earle Leonard Nelson, born in
Philadelphia in 1897; his mother had died of venereal
disease contracted from his father. At the age of 10, Nelson
was knocked down by a streetcar and was unconscious with
concussion for six days. From then on, he experienced
violent periodic headaches. He began to make a habit of
peering through the keyhole of his cousin Rachel's bedroom
when she was getting undressed. At 21, he was arrested
after trying to rape a girl in a basement. Sent to a penal
farm, he soon escaped, and was recaptured peering in through
the window of his cousin as she undressed for bed. A marriage
was unsuccessful; when his wife had a nervous breakdown,
Nelson visited her in hospital and tried to rape her in bed.
Nothing is known of Nelson's whereabouts for the next three
years, until the evening in February 1926, when he knocked on
the door of Mrs. Clara Newman in San Francisco, and asked if
he could see the room she had to let . . .

What disturbed the police about the Nelson case was that
even after they had obtained a reliable description of the
strangler from the three old ladies, it was still more than
seven months before he was caught; it demonstrated that,
where the unbalanced sex killer was concerned, crime
detection had made no marked advance since the days of
Jack the Ripper. The point was underlined by a widely
publicized kidnapping that took place in the year of Nelson's execution.

10

On May 28, 1928, a mild-looking old man knocked on the
door of a basement at 406 West 15th Street, in the Chelsea

district of Manhattan; he introduced himself as Frank Howard, and said he was looking for the young man who had advertised for a job in the *New York World Telegram,* Edward Budd. The old man explained that he owned a farm at Farmingdale, Long Island, and would be willing to pay $15 a week for a good worker. The Budd family was delighted; Albert Budd, a doorman, found it hard to support his wife and four children. The old-man agreed to return the following week for their decision. He failed to keep the appointment, but sent an explanatory telegram. The next day he arrived, full of apologies, and had lunch with the Budds, who were impressed by his expensive clothes and good manners. They were even more impressed when he took out a huge roll of dollar bills, and presented the eldest children with two of them to go to the cinema. And when the kindly old man offered to take their 10-year-old daughter Grace to a birthday party at the home of his married sister, they had no hesitation in giving permission. It was to be held in a house at 137th Street and Columbus. Grace went off in her white confirmation dress, holding the old man's hand.

When she had failed to return by the next morning, Albert Budd went to the police; they were able to tell him immediately that there was no such address as 137th and Columbus; Columbus only went as far as 109th.

There was also, of course, no Frank Howard in Farmingdale, Long Island. Nor was there any other clue to his identity. He had taken back the telegram he had sent, claiming that he intended to complain to the post office for getting Albert Budd's name wrong. The first thing that Detective Will King of the Missing Persons Bureau did when he was placed in charge of the investigation was to launch a search for the original telegraph form. It took three clerks 13 hours of sifting through tens of thousands of telegrams before they found it. It had been sent from the East Harlem office of Western Union. But the task of making a search of every house in East Harlem for the missing child would be immense. Instead, King set out to trace a pail of pot cheese

that "Frank Howard" had brought Mrs. Budd as a present.
The police had tried every hardware store in East Harlem
before they found the street pedlar who had sold the pail.
His description of Frank Howard was accurate, but he could
give the police no further information.

Newspapers and radio stations publicized the kidnap; the
police received hundreds of letters and tips from the public.
All led nowhere. After several months, the police abandoned the case as hopeless. Only Detective Will King
refused to give up. When he heard of a forger named
Corthell, who had attempted to abduct a little girl from an
adoption agency, he travelled 40,000 miles trying to track
him down. Finally run to earth, Corthell proved to have a
perfect alibi; he had been in jail in Seattle at the time of the
kidnapping.

On November 11, 1934, six years after the disappearance
of Grace Budd, her mother received an unsigned letter. It
began by claiming that a friend of the writer named Captain
John Davis had acquired a taste for human flesh in China,
when children were eaten during a famine. On returning to
New York, Davis had kidnapped two small boys, beaten
them "to make their meat good and tender," then killed and
eaten them. When Davis told the letter-writer "how good
human flesh was," he decided to try it. As he was eating
lunch with the Budds, and Grace was sitting on his knee, he
had made up his mind to eat her. He had taken her to an
empty house in Westchester, then left her picking flowers
while he went in and stripped himself naked. Then he called
her in. She began to cry and tried to run away. He stripped
her, then choked her to death. After this, he cut her into
small pieces, and took her back home, where he proceeded
to eat her. "How sweet her tender little ass was, roasted in
the oven. It took me nine days to eat her entire body. I did
not fuck her though I could of had I wished. She died a
virgin."

Edward Budd brought the letter to Detective Will King
almost as soon as it arrived. King had declined retirement
two years before so he could fulfill a vow to track down the

kidnapper of Grace Budd. Now, at last, he had his second clue—the first had been the telegram written by "Howard." When he compared letter and telegram, it was immediately obvious that they had been written by the same man.

The flap of the envelope contained a design that had been partly blacked out with ink. Under a spectroscope, this proved to be the letters of N.Y.P.C.B.A. From his Manhattan telephone directory, King deduced that this stood for the New York Private Chauffeurs Benevolent Association. Its address was at 627 Lexington Avenue. Later that day, King spent hours at the Association, comparing the handwriting of every employee—400 of them—with the Grace Budd letter. In the early hours of the following morning he realized he had again reached a dead end; none of the signatures bore the least resemblance to the handwriting of "Howard."

Next, King addressed the assembled employees. Had any of them taken the Association's stationery for his personal use? If so, he need not be afraid to say so; no action would be taken. Then King sat alone in the president's office and waited. There was a knock on the door. A nondescript little man in chauffeur's uniform identified himself as Lee Siscoski, and admitted that he had used the Association's envelopes. King asked if he had given any of them away, or left them anywhere. Siscoski said that he had left some behind in a room at 622 Lexington. King rushed to the address, and borrowed a pass key to the room. There were no envelopes there. He telephoned Siscoski to ask him to think again. This time, the chauffeur recalled that he had also had a room at 200 East 52nd Street.

This proved to be a cheap boarding-house—what the Americans call a flophouse. When he described "Frank Howard" to the landlady, she immediately nodded. "That sounds like the man in number seven—Albert Fish."

In the register, there was a signature "A. H. Fish." King saw at a glance that it had been written by the same man who had written the letter and telegram.

Where was Fish? He had moved away, said the landlady.

But he would undoubtedly be back to collect his check—the monthly check sent to him by one of his sons. She expected him in a couple of days . . . King rented a room at the top of the stairs—where he could see down to the hallway—and settled down to wait.

He waited for more than three weeks. Then, on December 12, 1934, he found the landlady waiting for him. Mr. Fish, she said, had been back half an hour; she was afraid he was going to leave. King checked his .38, then went and knocked on the door; a voice called ''Come in.'' A little old man with a grey moustache and watery blue eyes smiled at him as he opened the door. He agreed unhesitatingly to go to headquarters for questioning. But as they neared the street door, the old man turned suddenly and lunged at King, an open razor in each hand. King grabbed his wrists, and pounded them against the banister until he dropped them. Then he handcuffed the old man, and searched his pockets. They were full of knives and razor blades.

Fish confessed to the murder of Grace Budd without any attempt at evasion. His original motive, he said, was to kill Edward Budd, the 18-year-old youth who had advertised for a job. Instead, he decided that he preferred Grace. They had caught the underground to Sedgwick Avenue, and Fish had left his bundle behind on the train. But Grace noticed it, and ran to fetch it before the train started. The bundle contained a saw, a cleaver, and a butcher's knife.

They had walked out to a place in Worthington Woods, a cottage where Fish used to live. There—as he described in his letter—Fish had stripped naked, called Grace, then killed her. After this, he cut off her head, and drank some of her blood. It made him vomit, so he dissected the body at the waist with a knife . . .

The detectives took Fish back to the empty house, Wisteria Cottage. There they unearthed the bones of Grace Budd.

Back at headquarters, Fish at first denied that he had committed other murders. Then, under intensive questioning, he began to tell the story of his life. Fish ended by confessing to 400 child murders, committed between 1910, when he was 40 years old, and 1934. This figure was never verified, and is undoubtedly exaggerated, but there can be no doubt that Fish murdered dozens of children in 24 years.

The psychiatrist Frederick Wertham was asked to examine Fish in jail. Fish came to like and trust him, and the relationship between the two men was not unlike that between Peter Kürten and Professor Karl Berg; Wertham was later to include a chapter on Fish in his book *The Show of Violence*. In this he states that Fish looked "a meek and innocuous little old man, gentle and benevolent, friendly and polite. If you wanted someone to entrust your children to, he would be the one you would choose." He also described Fish as the most complex example of a "polymorphous pervert" that he had ever encountered; Fish apparently practiced every known form of sexual deviation, from sodomy and sadism to eating human excrement and driving needles into his scrotum. (X-rays revealed the remains of rusted needles still in his body.) He even enjoyed inserting cotton wool soaked in alcohol into his anus and setting it alight. Wertham's study convinced him that Fish was insane, and had been suffering from delusions and "voices" for years. The jury disagreed, and Fish was sentenced to death. He told reporters: "Going to the electric chair will be the supreme thrill of my life." But his last words in the execution chamber were: "I don't know why I'm here."

_____ **11** _____

By comparison with America and the rest of Europe, England remained relatively free of sex crime, and the few that occurred were usually solved by skillful detection.

Nellie Trew was the daughter of an employee of the Woolwich Arsenal in southeast London and, at the age of 16, she was also given employment there as a clerk.

On Saturday, February 9, 1918, she went off to the

Plumstead Public Library to change her book; when she had not returned home by 10 o'clock that evening, her parents began to worry. At eight o'clock the next morning, her body was found on a corner of Eltham Common, not far from her home. She was lying on her back with her dress around her waist, and although her knickers seemed undisturbed, Spilsbury's medical examination established that she had been raped. Cause of death was strangulation.

It had been raining most of the night, and the grass close to the body was muddy and trampled. On this muddy patch a policeman found a military badge and a black overcoat button; the badge was of the Leicestershire regiment "the Tigers." The button had apparently been attached by a piece of wire, which was still on it.

Pictures of the badge and button were published in the newspapers. On the following Thursday morning, these were seen by a youth named Edward Farrell, who worked at the Hewson Manufacturing Company, off Oxford Street—a factory engaged in producing parts for airplanes. The man who worked on the lathe next to Farrell was a recently discharged soldier named David Greenwood, who was 21; on a previous Saturday, he had been wearing a military badge displaying a tiger. Farrell asked him what he had done with it, and Greenwood explained that he had sold it to a man on a tram for two shillings. "In that case," said Farrell, "you ought to go to the police and tell them about it." Greenwood agreed, and Farrell accompanied him to the Tottenham Court Road police station. There Greenwood made a statement to the sergeant in charge, describing how he had sold his badge to a man wearing a black overcoat and bowler hat, and speaking with a Belfast accent. He signed it and was allowed to go.

The detective in charge of the case, Chief Inspector Carlin of Scotland Yard, hurried to the factory and interviewed Greenwood in the office of the works manager. When he learned that David Greenwood lived close to Eltham Common, he must have been fairly certain that he was speaking to the murderer of Nellie Trew. But proving it was a different matter, even when Greenwood acknowledged that the tiger badge had belonged to him. A jury might not believe the story about the man with the Belfast accent, but might still feel obliged to give the young ex-soldier the benefit of the doubt. He asked Greenwood to accompany him to Scotland Yard. And when Greenwood returned wearing an overcoat without any buttons, Carlin asked what had happened to them. "Oh, they've been off for a long time."

Closer examination of the overcoat revealed that most of the buttons had been sewed on with thread, and that this was still sticking out of the overcoat. Only the bottom position but one had a ragged hole where the button should have been. Carlin picked up the overcoat button found near the body and placed it against the hole. It seemed an exact fit.

Greenwood was placed in custody, and Carlin once again interviewed the factory manager, whose name was Hewson. On his way through the factory, he picked up several pieces of wire from the floor—the factory manufactured its own wire. In Hewson's office he asked: "Could you unfailingly identify your own wire?" Hewson said he could. "In that case, would you mind going out of the room?" Carlin then placed several pieces of wire on the desk, including the length from the button. Hewson was called back in. Before he allowed him to see the wire, Carlin warned him of the gravity of what he was about to do. Hewson went pale; he understood that a man's life depended on what he said next. Carlin allowed him to see the pieces of wire.

"Which of these is yours?"

Hewson studied them for a moment and said, "All of them."

"Are you sure?"

"Quite sure."

The experiment was repeated with the foreman, and the result was the same.

At the trial, Spilsbury gave evidence that the girl had been unconscious but alive when she was raped. (This would be indicated by the flow of blood; if the heart had stopped, it would be minimal.) The implication was that she had been killed during the course of the rape, or afterwards. Greenwood's alibi was that he was in the YMCA at the time the girl was attacked; but since this was close to the scene of the rape, it was hardly an effective alibi. Greenwood was sentenced to death. But there was a great deal of public sympathy for a soldier who had been discharged with shell-shock, and the sentence was commuted to 15 years.

Greenwood's crime was obviously committed on the spur of the moment. The curious case of Thomas Allaway belongs in the same premeditated category as those of Charles Hadley and Albert Wolter.

On December 22, 1922, the *Morning Post* carried an advertisement: "Lady Cook (31) requires post in school." The salary she demanded was a modest £65 a year. On the same day, Irene Wilkins received a misspelled telegram from Bournemouth, "Come immediatly [*sic*] 4:30 train," and was signed "Wood, Beech House."

On the train she was noticed by an engineer called Frank Humphris, who later saw her in a green-grey touring car driven by a chauffeur in uniform. Since Humphris was waiting for a car to pick him up, he paid particular attention to this one, observing a luggage carrier of unusual design.

At half past seven the next morning, a farm-laborer on his way to work saw a woman's body lying in a field near Boscombe. He called the police, who discovered that the woman was lying on her back, with her dress pulled up. The face was covered with blood, and there was a trail of blood on the ground. Medical examination revealed that the woman—Irene Wilkins—had been struck in the face several times by a man's fist, then battered to death with a hammer. But her attacker had either been interrupted, or sickened by the injuries he had caused; the rape had not been completed.

On the other side of the hedge from the place where the body was found, the police discovered tire tracks on the muddy road—it had been raining much of the night. The tracks had sunk more deeply into the mud at one point, indicating that the car had been parked there for some time.

The road itself was so muddy that the police were able to follow the tracks for some distance in either direction. An expert identified them as those of a steel-studded Dunlop Magnum tire. It had been on the nearside rear wheel.

Frank Humphris saw the newspaper account of the murder, and told the police about the grey-green touring car and the man in chauffeur's uniform. Every chauffeur in Bournemouth was interviewed. Among these was a man called Thomas Allaway, who worked for a Mr. and Mrs. Sutton. He drove a grey-green touring car, but the nearside rear wheel had a Michelin tire; the other three were Dunlop Magnums. Asked if he had changed the tire recently, Allaway said no. He gave as his alibi a visit to the local pub. And since his employer said that the car had not been out of the garage after six that evening, the alibi was not even checked.

It seemed that Irene Wilkins was only one of several women that the unknown chauffeur had tried to lure to Bournemouth; in the week before the murder, two other telegrams had been sent from the local post office, requesting women to catch the next train to Bournemouth. The clerk recalled that these had been sent by a man in chauffeur's uniform; she had spoken to him, and thought she would recognize his voice.

Two weeks after the murder, Frank Humphris was on his way to Bournemouth station when he recognized the grey-green touring car with the distinctive luggage holder. He told his son to take down its number and later passed it on to the police. This should have been the turning point in the case. In fact, with incredible incompetence, the police failed to follow up the lead. They later explained that they were overworked.

The investigation was very obviously bogged down when, a month later, the female clerk who had spoken to the chauffeur was transferred to the Boscombe post office, and one day heard a voice which she recognized. She told a fellow clerk, but by the time she had reached the door, the chauffeur had gone. However, a few weeks later, the fellow clerk saw the same man standing by a grey-green car. She took its number and passed it on to the police. But the police had obviously given up interest in the case, and again failed to follow it up. A few days later, the clerk again saw the chauffeur, and told a fellow worker, who grabbed his hat and followed the man to an address in Portman Mews, the home of Mr. Sutton. And, incredibly, still the police did nothing.

In April, Thomas Allaway left Sutton's employment and took Sutton's checkbook with him. As a result of several forged checks, the chauffeur was arrested in Reading. And now, at last, the police began to review the evidence, and realized to their surprise that it all pointed towards Allaway as the murderer of Irene Wilkins. Betting slips were found in Allaway's pockets; they checked against the telegrams, and found the handwriting to be identical.

Allaway was an ex-soldier, 36 years of age and married; he also had a mistress. A week after the murder, he had driven his mistress to tea with her sister, and waited for her. Irene Wilkins's attaché case had later been found outside this house.

The police also looked more closely at the tires on the car, and now observed that the Michelin tire was badly worn, although the spare tire—a Dunlop Magnum, was new. A witness was found who had seen Allaway changing the tire—the Michelin had been the spare—on the day after the murder, when local newspapers had mentioned the Dunlop Magnum tire tracks. The final piece of evidence was a garage key which Allaway's successor had found in Allaway's old room. Only Mr. Sutton was supposed to have a garage key; Allaway had obviously had a spare key cut. This explained how he had been able to use the car without his employer's knowledge.

At the trial, Allaway insisted on his innocence; his defense rested on an alibi which, so many months after the murder, could not be positively disproved. His handwriting and the handwriting on the telegrams were not quite identical, but a handwriting expert testified that it had been disguised. And various misspellings in the telegrams convinced the jury that they had been sent by Allaway: asked to write "immediately," "Bournemouth," and "advertisement," he spelled them all without the middle "e." Allaway was sentenced to death, and shortly before his execution, confessed to the murder of Irene Wilkins.

Yet here, even more than in the case of Hadley or Wolter, the most baffling question remains that of motive. If Allaway had been a single man, his attempts to lure women to Bournemouth might be just comprehensible—although he would certainly have found no lack of willing partners on the Bournemouth seafront. But he was a married man with a mistress. To describe him as a "sex maniac" only begs the question. We are simply forced to recognize that, in the twentieth century, social tensions have produced a type of crime that would have been incomprehensible in the eighteenth, and accept that, under these conditions, the roots of crime are to be sought in the imagination as much as in social reality.

The Allaway case demonstrates that the Bournemouth police were rather less competent than their colleagues in America or on the Continent. The tire tracks, which should have led to Allaway's arrest within 24 hours, were ignored, while the sightings of thc car, which should have clinched the case, were simply overlooked. Altogether, the police displayed a vagueness that would have been endearing if it had not been so very nearly disastrous.

Fortunately, their colleagues at Scotland Yard had a more thorough training in scientific crime detection, as well as the support of an up-to-date laboratory. Both these advantages were brought to bear in the investigation of one of the most brutal sex crimes of the 1930s.

On the morning of December 15, 1931, a milkman entering a garden in Addison Road, Holland Park, saw the body of a child lying on the lawn. She was identified as 10-year-old Vera Page, who had been missing from her home at 22 Blenheim Crescent, in the Notting Hill area of London, since the previous evening. She had been raped and then manually strangled. When the body was moved, a finger-stall fell out from the crook of the arm.

A number of clues enabled the police to reconstruct roughly what had happened. Vera Page had last been seen alive at a quarter to seven on the previous evening; she had been on her way back from the house of an aunt, and had been seen looking in the windows of shops decorated for Christmas. Spilsbury's examination indicated that she had been raped and strangled not long after she was last seen, close to her home. Since she was a shy child, it seemed clear that she had been murdered by someone she knew and trusted. This man had probably taken her to a warm room—decomposition had already set in—and raped and killed her there. Then he had hidden the body in a coal cellar—this was indicated by coal dust on her clothes. The cellar had no electric light; this was suggested by spots of candle grease on the child's clothes. Some time around dawn, the murderer had retrieved the body and taken it to the garden in Addison Road, probably using a barrow. It had rained for much of the night, but the child's clothes were dry. As he removed his hands from under her arms, the bandage had slipped off his finger.

The murder caused intense public indignation, and the police mounted an enormous operation to track down the killer. Door-to-door inquiries were made over the whole area, and they quickly located a suspect. He was a 41-year-old laborer named Percy Orlando Rush, and he lived in a flat in Talbot Road, close to Vera Page. Moreover, his parents lived in the same house as Vera Page, so he often saw her. On the evening of the murder, his wife had been visiting her mother, and had not arrived home until later. So Rush could have murdered Vera Page, then taken her down to the coal cellar in the basement before his wife arrived home. Moreover, Rush had a wound on his left little finger, and had been wearing a finger-stall until recently.

The finger-stall was examined by Dr. Roche Lynch, the Home Office analyst. He found that it had covered a suppurating wound, and that the bandage had been soaked in ammonia. Percy Orlando Rush worked in Whiteley's Laundry, near Earls Court, and his job involved placing his hands in ammonia.

There was another damning piece of evidence against Rush. At dawn on December 15, a man of his description had been seen pushing a wheelbarrow covered with a red cloth near the garden where the body had been found. When the police searched Rush's home, they found a red tablecloth.

From the point of view of forensic science, the most interesting clue was provided by the candle grease. In the previous year, an Austrian engineer had invented a new method of testing candle wax. It was melted, with careful temperature control, on a microscope slide, and allowed to cool. Examined through a microscope under polarized light, the wax would reveal its "fingerprinting," a characteristic crystalline structure. The wax on Vera Page's clothing was examined in this way, and compared with candles in her own home. They proved to be quite different. But it was identical with the wax of a candle found in Rush's home. So were certain spots of candle grease on Rush's overcoat.

But the crucial piece of evidence was the bandage. And here Superintendent George Cornish recognized that he may have made a mistake. He had let his suspect know about the finger-stall. And when he asked Rush for samples of bandage from his own house, Rush had handed them over with a faint smile that Cornish found disturbing. In fact, Roche Lynch's microscopic examination of the bandage established that it was not the same as that of the finger-stall.

Cornish's men scoured every chemist's shop in west London to try to find if anyone could recall selling bandages to Rush or his wife. If he could establish that Rush had bought some other type of bandage, and it proved identical with the finger-stall, then his case was complete.

Unfortunately, this attempt was a failure. The circumstantial evidence against Rush was overwhelming. But unless the bandage could be traced to him, the case had a fatal flaw. This became clear at the coroner's inquest, conducted by Dr. Ingleby Oddie, on February 10, 1932. Rush proved to be a short, thick-set man who wore horn-rimmed glasses and a black moustache. His evidence was punctuated by angry cries of "Liar!" from the spectators. But Rush stuck to his story that he had ceased to wear his finger-stall some days before the disappearance of Vera Page; he explained that he wanted to "harden" the wound. All the coroner's questions—and those of jurymen—make it clear that they were convinced of Rush's guilt. But no one had actually seen Rush with Vera Page, and after only five minutes, the jury decided there was insufficient evidence to charge him with her murder.

_____ 12 _____

Sex crimes invariably increase during wartime. This is partly because the anarchic social atmosphere produces a loss of inhibition, partly because so many soldiers have been deprived of their usual sexual outlet. Nevertheless, the rate of sex crime in England during the Second World War remained low, while the murder rate actually fell. One of the few cases to excite widespread attention occurred during the "blackouts" of 1942. Between February 9 and 15, four women were murdered in London. Evelyn Hamilton, a 40-year-old schoolteacher, was found strangled in an air raid shelter; Evelyn Oatley, an ex-revue actress, was found naked on her bed, her throat cut and her belly mutilated with a tin-opener; Margaret Lower was strangled with a silk stocking and mutilated with a razor blade, and Doris Jouannet was killed in an identical manner. The killer's bloody fingerprints were found on the tin-opener and on a mirror in Evelyn Oatley's flat. A few days later, a young airman dragged a woman into a doorway near Piccadilly and throttled her into unconsciousness, but a passer-by overheard the scuffle and went to investigate. The airman ran away, dropping his gas-mask case with his service number stenciled on it. Immediately afterwards, he accompanied a prostitute to her flat in Paddington and began to throttle her; her screams and struggles again frightened him away. From the gas-mask case the man was identified as 28-year-old Gordon Cummins, from north London, and he was arrested as soon as he returned to his billet. The fingerprint evidence identified him as the "blackout ripper," and he was hanged in June 1942. Sir Bernard Spilsbury, who had performed the post-mortem on Evelyn Oatley, also performed one on Cummins.

Of more interest, from the forensic point of view, is a murder that took place near an RAF camp in 1944. On the evening of November 8, two WAAFs, Corporal Margaret Johns and Radio Operator Winifred Evans, attended a dance at an American army camp near Beccles in Suffolk, and returned to their own camp around midnight. Winifred Evans was due to go on duty, so the two women said good-night. At this point, Corporal Johns walked into the ablution hut, and discovered a man in RAF uniform leaning against a wall. He claimed that he had lost his way in the dark and asked how to get back to his own section of the camp. Corporal Johns did not believe his story, but she told him that he had better leave before he got into trouble. The man—a Leading Aircraftman—went off in the same direction that Winifred Evans had taken a few minutes earlier.

The following morning, a policeman cycling past the camp saw the body of a woman lying in a ditch. Medical evidence revealed that she had been raped after a violent struggle, and it was as a result of this struggle that she had died of asphyxia.

This had taken place very soon after Corporal Johns had sent the man on his way, so the search focused upon Leading Aircraftmen. An LAC named Arthur Heys had returned to his billet in the early hours of the morning, and had undressed in the dark, although some of his friends were awake and spoke to him. The next morning, he was seen cleaning mud from his shoes and trousers. And later that day, Corporal Margaret Johns picked him out of a line of men who were sitting waiting for their pay. Detective Chief Inspector Ted Greeno, who had been sent from

Scotland Yard, was certain that Heys was the rapist; but he was also aware that the corporal's identification would not prove it to a jury. Heys's clothes were sent for examination to the Scotland Yard laboratory.

Microscopic examination revealed the remains of mud and brick dust on his trousers, in spite of a brushing that had apparently left them spotless. There were also some rabbit hairs. Examination of the dead girl's clothing also revealed the same brick dust, mud, and rabbit hairs.

Meanwhile, the pathologist, Dr. Eric Biddle, had found bloodspots on Heys's tunic. A blood test revealed that they were of the same group as the dead girl, but not of Heys himself. Heys was placed under arrest and charged with the murder of Winifred Mary Evans.

On the day before the hearing, January 9, 1945, the Commanding Officer of Heys's squadron received an anonymous letter, written in block capitals with a blue pencil. It read:

> Will you please give this letter to the solicitors for the airman who is so wrongfully accused of murdering Winifred Evans. I want to state I am responsible for the above-mentioned girl's death. I had arranged to meet her at the bottom of the road where the body was found, at midnight. When I arrived she was not there. I waited some time, and decided to walk towards the WAAF quarters. Just before I reached this I heard a voice and stood close to the hedge. I heard footsteps. It proved to be an airman. I don't think he saw me. I then saw someone I recognized as Winnie. She said I should not have come down to meet her. A WAAF friend had offered to go along with her as the airman ahead was drunk and had lost his way. She had a bicycle with her. No one will ever find this.

The envelope bore a Norwich postmark, and Greeno's immediate suspicion was that Heys was the author. He discovered that prisoners in Norwich jail could borrow a blue pencil to write letters, and that its color was identical with that of the anonymous letter. The next task was to find samples of Heys's block writing. In a watch taken from him at the time of his arrest, there was a slip of paper with the words "Hair spring straightening," evidently intended for the watch repairer. But this was not long enough for proper comparison; Greeno also went through all the leave application forms Heys had completed in the orderly-room files. These, together with the watch message, were all sent to the Yard's fingerprint expert Fred Cherrill, who explains in his autobiography: "Fingerprints and handwriting have something in common. A fingerprint possesses a host of intricate and minute details. So does handwriting, if one has the ability to detect them."

Cherrill was struck by the "p" in "watchspring," which was written in a distinctive manner—exactly like those in the anonymous letter. Other letters were also unusual, and Cherrill found many exact counterparts in the application forms.

When Cherrill appeared at Heys's trial at Bury St. Edmunds, he found that the airman seemed confident and relaxed; when asked if he murdered Winifred Evans, he replied in a firm voice "I did not."

But Cherrill had noted something else about the anonymous letter: the phrase, "as the airman ahead was drunk and had lost his way." But if the letter-writer was *not* Heys, how did he know that the airman had lost his way? Heys had said this to Corporal Johns, and unless the "stranger" had been lurking close enough to overhear this comment, then he could not possibly have known. When the prosecuting counsel, John Flowers, began to question Heys, the airman looked calm and self-confident; he denied writing the anonymous letter with an assurance that might have sprung from a clear conscience. But as Flowers read out the sentence about the airman being drunk, his gaze wavered. Flowers pointed out that Winifred Evans had parted from Corporal Johns before he—Heys—followed her into the darkness. So it was impossible that the "WAAF friend" (Corporal Johns) had offered to accompany her because Heys was "drunk and had lost his way."

"But *you* were the airman who had lost his way," said Flowers. "How could anyone else in the world have the knowledge to put it in this letter but you?"

Heys was pale as he replied in a low voice, "I did not write this letter." At that moment, he must have realized that the letter was virtually a confession that he was the murderer.

Heys was sentenced to death, and his appeal was rejected. But, as the judge who rejected the appeal made clear, it was the anonymous letter rather than the handwriting or forensic evidence that established Heys's guilt beyond all doubt. Heys was hanged in Bury St. Edmunds.

———————————— 13 ————————————

By 1950, it was obvious that sex crime had ceased to be a rarity, or an exceptional abnormality, as it had been in the days of Jack the Ripper, or even of Peter Kürten. Although crime figures in general began to fall in the early 1950s, sex crime continued to rise. A series of experiments performed by the American psychologist John B. Calhoun on rats suggested a possible reason for this.* Calhoun discovered that when rats are grossly overcrowded, a small proportion of them—5 per cent to be precise—develop "criminal" behavior, such as cannibalism and rape. It had been known since early in the century that 5 per cent of any animal group possesses "dominance"—certain leadership qualities. Calhoun's experiment suggested that, under conditions of stress, this 5 per cent expresses its aggression in crime, including rape. In the early 1950s it was observed that the homicide

* In 1954 at Palo Alto, and later at the National Institute of Mental Health in Bethesda, Maryland. See *Mysterious Senses,* by Vitus B. Dröscher, Hodder & Stoughton, London, 1962, Chapter 9: "Degeneration of Community Life."

rate in large American cities was three times higher than in small towns, and that the rate of sex crime was four times higher.

Calhoun's conclusions might seem to suggest that the criminal—particularly the rapist—is some kind of heroic rebel. But modern studies of the criminal personality make it clear that this is not so. In a study called *The Authoritarian Personality* (1940), sociologist Donald Clemmer presented the result of a survey of 110 inmates of San Quentin prison, and concludes that criminals are not genuine rebels with a feeling of sympathy for the underdog; on the contrary, they are inclined to be childishly self-centered and oblivious to the feelings—and the basic reality—of other people.

Similar conclusions were reached by two other sociologists, Samuel Yochelson and Stanton E. Samenow, in a remarkable study, *The Criminal Personality* (1976). Their studies of criminals in St. Elizabeth's Hospital, New York—studies that will be further discussed in a later chapter—led them to conclude that the chief characteristic of the criminal is a self-centeredness that often makes him almost oblivious of the existence of other people. But they also noted the close relation between sexuality and crime—a connection that had been noted as far back as 1864 by the "father of criminology" Cesare Lombroso when he served in the army. Lombroso commented, "From the very beginning I was struck by a characteristic that distinguished the honest soldier from his vicious comrade: the extent to which the latter was tattooed, and the indecency of the designs that covered his body." And Yochelson and Samenow noted that a large percentage of the criminals they observed had started sexual activity very early—such as peeking through keyholes at sisters undressing or going to the lavatory—and had always indulged in a great deal of sexual fantasy. Sex was exciting because it was "forbidden," and crime itself was an exercise in the forbidden, and therefore carried some of the excitement of a sexual act. This curious confusion between sex and criminality can be seen in the case of the teenage sex murderer William Heirens, a student at the University of Chicago, who began his career of crime as an underwear fetishist, breaking into apartments to steal women's panties; Heirens soon began to achieve orgasm as he entered the window—the window having become a kind of symbolic vagina. Like so many sex killers, Heirens was caught by accident, when someone heard him prowling around an empty apartment and contacted the police; fingerprints left at scenes of crime identified him as the murderer of ex-Wave Frances Brown—over whose body he had scrawled in lipstick "For God's sake catch me before I kill more"—and of 6-year-old Suzanne Degnan, whose body he had dismembered and thrown down manholes and sewers. In 1946 Heirens was sentenced to life imprisonment.

In November 1944, Los Angeles police had been confronted with a case that bore alarming resemblances to the Jack the Ripper murders. On November 15, in a hotel at Fourth and Main Street, a chambermaid discovered the mutilated body of a woman lying on the floor. An enormous cut from the throat to the vagina had opened the body, and the intestines had been pulled out. One arm and one leg had been partly severed at the joint, and the breasts had been removed. These injuries had been inflicted by a carving knife that lay beside the body. The man who had accompanied the woman in the hotel on the previous day had been tall and slender, with a face resembling the film star Robert Taylor, and he had spoken to hotel staff quite openly—indicating that the crime had not been premeditated. The woman was identified as a prostitute named Virginia Lee Griffin, who had often been arrested for drunkenness.

Later the same day, a second "mutilation murder" was reported from a hotel only three blocks away. This time the mutilations were less savage, but the woman's body had been opened from the throat to the left knee, and the face had been gashed. She was soon identified as a prostitute named Lillian Johnson, 38, and the man who had accompanied her to the room was evidently the same man who had killed Virginia Griffin.

It was obvious that the sex killer was choosing victims at random and would continue to do so until he was caught. The police decided to conduct a blanket search of the 20 blocks around the murder area, reasoning that since the killer had already chosen two victims there, he might now be looking for a third. One of the officers walked into a bar on Fourth Street and glanced around; in one of the booths he noticed a man answering the suspect's description, drinking wine and talking to a brunette in a tight red dress. The officer arrested the man on suspicion. The suspect identified himself as Otto Stephen Wilson—he preferred to be called Steve—and when he lit a cigarette, the policeman noticed that the matchbook bore the address of the hotel where Virginia Griffin had died. Like Heirens, he was identified by fingerprints left at the scenes of crime, and confessed to both murders. He was examined by the psychiatrist Paul de River, who concluded that Wilson had strong sadistic tendencies that emerged when he was drunk. His first wife had left him because he liked to creep up on her when she was naked, and cut her buttocks with a razor; later he would apologize and kiss the wounds. He had experienced the compulsion to murder Virginia Griffin after they had gone to the room, and had gone out again to buy a large carving knife. Then he had strangled and mutilated her. After the murder he went to see a horror film, then picked up the second prostitute, took her to another hotel, and murdered her in the same way. Then he went out to a bar and picked up a third prostitute, who would undoubtedly have died later in the day.

From the point of view of crime detection, the most noteworthy feature of the case is that Wilson was so easy to catch. He knew the police had a good description of the killer; he knew he must have left fingerprints in the rooms. Yet he was sitting quietly in a bar close to the scene of both crimes, as if waiting to be arrested. Before his execution in the San Quentin gas chamber in September 1946, he declined any final requests. "I've caused enough trouble for people already . . . I'll be better off out of the way."

Compare this case with the "phantom bank robbers" who went to such immense trouble to cover their tracks, and we become aware that, in some basic sense, sex crime differs from most other types of crime. It seems to contain a powerful "suicidal" element. The same element can be observed in the case of Neville Heath, who murdered Margery Gardner in a sadistic frenzy in June 1946, then killed a second girl in Bournemouth shortly after; he had then telephoned the police saying that he wanted to assist in their inquiries, virtually giving himself up. After the first murder, the second was a kind of gesture of abandonment, like throwing himself off a cliff. He had accepted that he had entered on a course of self-destruction. The same observation tends to support the view that Jack the Ripper committed suicide in 1888.

Another interesting psychological feature of sex crime lies in the number of false confessions received by the police. One of the most gruesome cases of post-war years was the murder of a 22-year-old waitress called Elizabeth Short, known as the Black Dahlia because of her preference for black underwear. In January 1947, her body was found on a vacant lot in Los Angeles, severed in half at the waist. Medical examination revealed that she had been suspended upside down and tortured to death. The horror of the case made it headline material for many months, and in a short time the police had received 28 confessions, all of which proved to be false. And as the years went by (the murder was never solved) they received many more. It was clear that the crime aroused a kind of *envy* in people suffering from psychological imbalance. Yet the morbid interest aroused by the Mary Phagan case three decades earlier makes it clear that this feeling is not restricted to the psychologically sick; we are speaking of an element of sexual obsession that permeates modern society.

Inevitably, then, such murders will give rise to imitative crimes; in the case of the Black Dahlia there were six in the Los Angeles area within a year—one victim had "B.D." scrawled in lipstick on her breast. This raises the frightening notion of a society in which sex crime continues to propagate itself like a nuclear reaction—a notion which, fortunately, disagrees with our observation of reality. The "suicide factor," as illustrated in the case of Steve Wilson or Neville Heath, seems to operate in the same way as the heavy water that acts as the moderator in nuclear fission.

—————————— **14** ——————————

A case in point is the series of murders committed in the 1940s and 1950s by John Reginald Halliday Christie in London's Notting Hill area. Christie, a bald-headed, bespectacled hypochondriac, suffered from problems of sexual impotence that led him to prefer his victims to be unconscious or dead. He achieved this by an ingenious arrangement which enabled him to bubble coal gas through a mixture of Friar's Balsam, designed to clear the sinuses and cure catarrh. Women were lured to his shabby flat in Rillington Place, and persuaded to sit in a chair with their heads covered with a cloth, breathing in the steam of Friar's Balsam mixed with coal gas; when they were unconscious, they were raped and strangled. The first victim, an Austrian girl named Ruth Fuerst, was lured back to the flat in September 1943, when his wife was away visiting relatives; she was buried in the back garden. So was a woman from his place of work, Muriel Eady, three months later. For the next nine years there were no more victims; then, in December 1952, Christie strangled his wife Ethel and placed her body under the floorboards in the front room. After this, he seemed to lose all control, and murdered three more women in the course of a few weeks, placing their half-naked bodies in a large kitchen cupboard. Then he wallpapered the cupboard, abandoned the flat, and became a vagrant. The bodies were discovered almost immediately by the landlord; there was widespread public alarm, and Christie was frantically sought by all the police forces of Great Britain. The panic was unnecessary; Christie was wandering around harmlessly, sleeping in Salvation Army hostels and dozing over cups of tea in cheap cafés. Like Steve Wilson, he had simply given up; all the instinct of self-preservation had evaporated. When recognized by a policeman near Putney Bridge, he made no attempt to resist arrest or deny his identity.

The three corpses in the cupboard were all of women in their mid-20s: two prostitutes named Rita Nelson and Kathleen Maloney, and a woman named Hectorina MacLennan, who had stayed in Christie's flat with her boyfriend, then been murdered as soon as he left. The pathologist, Dr. Francis Camps, found traces of sperm in the vaginas of all three. The bones of the two earlier victims were dug up from the back garden; one of them had been used to prop up a fence.

In the abandoned flat, police found a tobacco tin containing four lots of pubic hair, "artistically arranged." Three were taken from the three women in the cupboard; but whose was the fourth? It was not from Mrs. Christie, whose body had been found under the floorboards, and it seemed unlikely that it dated back to the murders of 10 years earlier. The likeliest assumption was that it came from another woman who had died in the house in 1949, Mrs. Beryl Evans, for whose murder her husband Timothy had been executed. The Evanses, who lived above the Christies, had a 1-year-old daughter named Geraldine, and in the summer of 1949, Beryl had become pregnant again. She and her husband— who was illiterate and mentally retarded—quarreled a great deal. On November 20, 1949, Evans had walked into the police station at Merthyr Vale, in South Wales, and announced that he wanted to confess to "disposing" of his wife, who had died in the course of an abortion operation— he later said it had been performed by Christie. He had pushed his wife's body down a drain, arranged to have the baby taken care of, and sold all the furniture.

The police had found no body down the drain, but they *did* find the bodies of Beryl and Geraldine Evans in the wash-house; both had been strangled. Soon after, Evans made a statement in which he described how he had struck his wife in the face during the course of a quarrel, then strangled her with a piece of rope. He had later strangled the baby with his tie. (The tie was still around the baby's throat when the body was found.) Thirteen days later, Evans retracted his confession. But it was too late. At his trial in January 1950, Evans accused Christie of strangling his wife and child, but no one believed him, and he was sentenced to death.

And now that Christie stood accused of six murders, it suddenly began to look as if there had been a terrible miscarriage of justice. And in fact, Christie soon added his confession of the murder of Beryl Evans to the others; his story was that she had wanted to commit suicide, and offered to let him have sexual intercourse if he would help her. He had rendered her unconscious by turning on the gas tap, then strangled her . . . That seemed to settle it. Evans was obviously innocent, and the apparently incredible coincidence of two stranglers living under the same roof shown to be an absurdity.

Christie was tried only for the murder of his wife. The defense was insanity, but it stood little chance of succeeding— Christie was so obviously a sane and thoroughly cunning individual. He had killed, quite simply, for the immense pleasure of sexual possession. (Francis Camps even found sperm on Christie's shoes, indicating that he had stood over the corpses and masturbated.) The jury took an hour and twenty minutes to decide that he was guilty, and he was sentenced to death. He was hanged on July 15, 1953.

Now only one question remained: was Timothy Evans innocent of the two murders for which he was hanged? In view of Christie's confession, the answer may seem self-evident. But we have to bear in mind that it was Christie's defense who suggested to him that he should confess to the murder of Beryl Evans, on the grounds that a man who had killed seven women might be regarded as slightly more insane than a man who had killed six. Christie replied cheerfully "The more the merrier," and accordingly confessed.

But clearly, this proves nothing, except that Christie wanted to be found insane.

In 1961, Ludovic Kennedy published a book called *Ten Rillington Place*, in which he argues strongly that Evans was innocent. Kennedy's belief is that Christie offered to perform an abortion, but that when Beryl Evans had undressed, he became so overwhelmed with excitement that he hit her in the face until he had subdued her, then strangled her with a rope. After this he raped her. When Evans came home, Christie told him that Beryl had died during the course of the abortion, and pointed out that they would both face criminal charges if her death was discovered. That night, he persuaded Evans to help him carry the body down to the wash-house. Later, Christie told Evans that he would arrange to have the baby looked after by some friends. That day, Christie also strangled Geraldine, and placed her body in the wash-house. After this, he persuaded Evans to sell his furniture and flee to his aunt's house in Merthyr Vale . . .

There is an obvious objection to this scenario. If Evans was Christie's dupe from start to finish, why did he not denounce Christie as soon as he learned that Geraldine had been found dead in the wash-house? Why, in fact, did he then go on to confess—not once but three times—to murdering his wife and baby? Kennedy gets around this supreme difficulty by suggesting that Evans was in such a state of shock that he was virtually "brainwashed," and would have confessed to anything. And he points out that Evans *did* later withdraw his confession and blame Christie, by which time no one believed him. But the difficulty remains. Surely no sane man is going to confess in detail to strangling his wife and baby when he knows he has been "framed" by the real murderer? It is like asking us to believe that black is white.

In fact, after Christie's conviction—but before he was hanged—the question of whether Evans was innocent had become such a public issue that the body of Beryl Evans was once again exhumed. It took place at dawn on May 18,

1953, and the bodies of Beryl and Geraldine Evans were taken to Kensington mortuary, where they were examined by a team of London's three foremost pathologists—sometimes known to the Press as the Three Musketeers—Francis Camps, Keith Simpson, and Donald Teare. Teare had, in fact, performed the original post-mortem on Beryl Evans in 1949. Christie's later confession alleged that he had gassed Beryl, then strangled her, but Teare had certainly noticed no sign of death from carbon monoxide poisoning—a distinctive pink coloration—at the first autopsy. What he *had* noticed was a black eye, bruising on the upper lip, and also on her thigh and lower leg. He had also noticed a bruise on the wall of the vagina, which could have been caused by an attempt at forced intercourse, or by a syringe she had used to try and abort herself.

How would it have been possible to decide whether Beryl Evans had been murdered by Christie or by her husband? Teare could, admittedly, have taken a vaginal swab at the first post-mortem—he was told by a policeman not to bother, since Evans had already confessed—and according to Kennedy, this would infallibly have revealed signs of Christie's sperm. Kennedy is probably correct; where he is incorrect is in believing that this would prove that Christie murdered Beryl Evans. According to Evans, he strangled Beryl before going to work, and left the corpse in the house all day. Christie was a necrophile. The conclusion is obvious: there would have been sperm present in the vagina whether Christie killed her or not.

But the pubic hairs could have been altogether more significant. Christie later took "souvenirs" from his three final victims. If the fourth lot of hair in the tobacco tin was from Beryl Evans, then it would certainly be a strong additional piece of evidence that Christie killed Beryl too. Christie himself claimed that the fourth lot of hair was taken from his wife, but microscopic examination showed this was impossible. So *was* the fourth lot of hair from Beryl Evans? The answer was apparently no. Under the microscope, it was seen to be of the same type as Mrs. Evans's hair. But the hair on Beryl Evans's pubis was uncut. If Christie had taken it from her, then it must have been months before her death, to allow it to regrow. Then whose hair was it? The answer may well lie in the comment in Kennedy's book (p. 216): "[Christie] had met Kathleen Maloney before. About three weeks before Christmas he, Maloney and a prostitute called Maureen had all gone to a room off Marylebone Lane where Christie had taken photographs of Maureen in the nude while Maloney looked on." The fourth lot of hairs could have been taken from some prostitute in circumstances like these, if not on this actual occasion. This would also account for Christie's unwillingness to reveal their source; he always maintained a pose of being a highly moral man, who would never have confessed to taking "dirty photographs" and persuading the woman to allow him to take snippings from her pubis.

The inquiry into whether Christie had murdered Beryl Evans was placed in the hands of Scott Henderson, QC. He interviewed Christie in prison, and concluded that his confession to the murder of Beryl Evans was false; his report, published on the day of Christie's execution, stated that Evans had undoubtedly murdered both his wife and child.

This was not the end of the matter. Books about Christie continued to insist on Evans's innocence, with the result that, in 1968, the case was reheard at the Royal Courts of Justice before Mr. Justice Brabin. The hearing lasted for several months, and the case for Evans's innocence was powerfully presented by the psychiatrist Dr. Jack Hobson. The final result was surprising. Brabin concluded that Christie's confession to the murder of Beryl Evans was false, and that it was probable that Beryl was murdered by her husband. But he added the startling rider that Christie probably killed Geraldine.

What evidence led him to this view? We have seen, to begin with, that Christie had good reason to confess to Beryl's murder; his defense was insanity, and "The more the merrier." In his book *Forty Years of Murder*, Keith

Simpson points out the sheer unlikelihood of Christie's confession. Would Beryl Evans lie down passively and allow Christie to gas her? And if he had done so, there would certainly have been signs of carbon monoxide poisoning when Teare examined the body. Aware of this problem, Christie explained that "the gas wasn't on very long, not much over a minute I think." But, as Simpson points out, if it had been on long enough to cause Beryl Evans to lose consciousness, then it would have left the unmistakable pink coloration in the tissues. This pink coloration would certainly have vanished by the time of the second autopsy, four years later, as all the pathologists agreed. In fact, tests showed no carbon monoxide in the tissues. But Camps—who, unlike Simpson, was representing the prosecution—noted that the teeth showed pink coloration, and tested them for carbon monoxide. He found none, but in his book *Medical and Scientific Investigations in the Christie Case* (1953) nevertheless argues that the pink teeth *could* indicate carbon monoxide poisoning. That still fails to explain why a pathologist as experienced as Teare should have failed to notice it at the first autopsy. We may therefore take it as fairly certain that Beryl Evans was not gassed.

In that case, what of Ludovic Kennedy's suggestion that Christie was engaged in a pretended abortion when he became sexually excited and strangled her? It *is* possible—it would account for the black eye and the bruises. But, as Simpson points out, Christie hated violence—partly because he was convinced that he was a sick man. Moreover, if he battered Beryl Evans unconscious, surely she would have screamed and fought? And since there were workmen carrying out repairs in the yard below, she would certainly have been heard. On the other hand, we know that Beryl and Timothy Evans often had violent quarrels. According to Evans's confession, he and Beryl had been quarreling about debts—particularly about some furniture, on which she had failed to keep up the payments. They had quarreled several times on the Sunday before her death. The following morn-

ing she told him she intended to leave him and go home to
her father; but she was still there when he came home from
work. They quarreled yet again. "I told her that if she
didn't pack it up I'd slap her face. With that she picked up a
milk bottle to throw at me. I grabbed the bottle out of her
hand . . ." The following day they were squabbling again.
"I came home at night about 6:30 p.m., my wife started to
argue again, so I hit her across the face with my flat hand.
She then hit me back with her hand. In a fit of temper I
grabbed a piece of rope from a chair which I had brought
home off my van and strangled her with it." The following
day, according to Evans, he fed the baby, left her in the cot,
and strangled her when he came home from work that
evening. This, as Ludovic Kennedy points out, is impossible. A 1-year-old baby cannot be left alone all day without
crying, and in a house the size of 10 Rillington Place, the
Christies would have heard her. (Ethel Christie, of course,
was still alive at this time.)

But at least the account of Beryl's murder has the ring of
truth—the dreary squabbling that went on day after day,
ending in a quarrel during which he strangled her. After
signing this statement, Evans repeated it the following
day—not once but twice, to a police inspector and to the
prison medical officer. Yet two weeks later, he withdrew it
and accused Christie of murdering his wife and child. Why?

The answer is suggested by Rupert Furneaux, in a book
called *The Two Stranglers of Rillington Place* (1961). Furneaux
reveals that while Evans was in Brixton prison, he met an
accused murderer named Donald Hume, who had been
charged with the killing of a dealer in stolen cars called
Stanley Setty, and scattering parts of his body out of an
airplane over the Essex marshes. Hume stuck to his story
that he was merely an accomplice, and was sentenced to 12
years. In 1958, when Hume came out of prison, he confessed
to the murder of Setty, and also admitted to the *Daily
Express* that it was he who had caused Evans to change his
plea. He had advised him: "Don't put your head in a noose.
Make up a new story and stick to it." When Evans asked his

advice on the "new story," Hume asked him whether he murdered his wife, and Evans denied it. Hume then went on to make the following strange statement:

> He told me that when he and his wife went to live at Rillington Place, Christie came to an arrangement with his wife and that Christie had murdered her. Then he told me about the child. He said, "It was because the kid was crying." I said, "So you did it?" He said, "No, but I was there while it was done." He told me that he and Christie had gone into the bedroom together, that Christie had strangled the kid with a bit of rag while he stood and watched.

Here, at last, we can begin to glimpse a plausible outline of what really happened. There seems to be no reason why Evans should tell Hume that Christie murdered the baby—with Evans looking on—unless it really happened. Evans, then, was an accomplice in the murder, which would explain the sense of guilt that led him to confess. The confession to the murder of his own child is incomprehensible if Christie had committed the murder alone.

But if Evans stood by and consented to the murder of his own baby, the rest of the story immediately becomes suspect: that Christie killed Beryl, and later told Evans that she had died in the course of an abortion. Even if Christie had assured Evans that they would both go to jail if the truth should become known, this would still not explain why Evans was terrified enough to allow Christie to kill the baby. The very idea is an absurdity.

There is only one other explanation. Evans killed his wife, exactly as he confessed. *That* could be the only possible reason that he would allow Christie to kill the baby. His neck was already at risk because he had killed his wife. With a baby on his hands, he stood no chance of remaining undetected. But if both bodies could be concealed, he might escape. He went off to Merthyr Vale believing that Christie would put both bodies down the drain. In Merthyr, he was overcome by guilt and fear. The more he thought about it, the more obvious it became that the bodies must be found, and that he had admitted his own guilt by fleeing. His only chance lay in going to the police and telling a story in which he was only an accomplice. Such a story would, of course, put the blame squarely on Christie...But when he was taken back to London, and charged with the murder of his wife and child, he could no longer maintain the deception; he broke down and confessed. This time he admitted to killing the baby, for what point would there be in accusing Christie if he was already admitting to strangling his wife?

One other odd puzzle remains. What did Hume mean when he stated, ''[Evans] told me that when he and his wife went to live in Rillington Place, Christie came to an arrangement with his wife...''? He appears to be saying that some kind of intimacy developed between Christie and Beryl Evans. This, admittedly, sounds unlikely. When Timothy and Beryl Evans moved into 10 Rillington Place, during the Easter of 1948, they were still a happily married couple. But they had been forced to move because Beryl was pregnant with Geraldine, and the single room in which they had been living would obviously be inadequate for a family. After the birth of the baby, tensions began to develop, and they often quarreled. Both Beryl and her husband were immature; Christie became their friend and adviser. His only motive can have been that he was attracted by the 19-year-old Beryl. So it is not entirely inconceivable that some kind of intimacy developed between Christie and Beryl. If Hume was telling the truth, Evans seems to have thought that Christie and his wife became sexually intimate, or at least came close to it. The whole question could be regarded as irrelevant, except for one thing: the pubic hairs in the tin. These hairs bore a close resemblance to Beryl's. But Keith Simpson points out that they could not have been Beryl's, because the autopsy showed that Beryl's pubic hairs were intact; Simpson says that if the hairs in the tin were Beryl's, they must have been taken at least six months before, to allow Beryl's hair to regrow. Understandably, he dismisses this as an absurdity. Yet *if* there is any basis of truth in Hume's statement, then it becomes possible that the hairs in the tin *did* belong to Beryl, and not to some prostitute, or another unknown murder victim. The oddest thing—if Evans made such a statement—is that he failed to see that it also contradicted his assertion that Christie killed Beryl. Christie was a sex killer; if there was some "arrangement" between her and Christie, then Christie would have had no reason to kill her.

From this tangled mass of assertion and counter-assertion, one thing seems to emerge clearly: that whoever killed Geraldine, it seems relatively certain that Timothy Evans murdered his wife.

———————————— 15 ————————————

To criminologists of the future, the year 1960 may seem a watershed in the history of crime. Until that time, most crime could be conveniently classified in terms of motives, as Locard does in the *Traité de criminalistique*. But in his seventh volume (1940), Locard has a section entitled "Crime Without Cause." And although he begins by admitting, "this title is a decoy" *(leurre)*, he nevertheless goes on to raise the problem of apparently motiveless crimes, and cites a curious case in 1886, in which a young chemist's assistant named Pastré-Beaussier poisoned several people without apparent motive. The first victim was his employer, M. Decamp, who kept a pharmacy in Havre. Decamp suspected his assistant of petty theft, and in April 1886, Mme. Decamp died after drinking a cup of bouillon prepared by the assistant. The laboratory assistant, a youth named Perotte, was the next to fall ill; but as soon as he began eating his meals at home, the vomiting and nausea ceased. But his successor in the shop became equally ill. So did M. Decamp's mother, although her symptoms disappeared when she returned home.

M. Decamp was the next to die. His successor, M. Delafontaine, also came to suspect his assistant of stealing; soon afterwards, M. Delafontaine and two of his employees became ill with vomiting. One of these, the housekeeper Mme. Morisse, died. At this point, M. Delafontaine took an action against his landlord, alleging that the drains were a health hazard. This finally led the town council of Havre to send three experts to investigate. They found nothing wrong with the drains, but a post-mortem on Mme. Morisse revealed that she had died of arsenic poisoning. Further inquests revealed that M. Decamp and his wife had also died from arsenic.

The assistant, Pastré-Beaussier, was the only person who could have been responsible for the illnesses—this conclusion was reached by a simple process of elimination. Placed under arrest, he protested that he had no reason to poison anyone, and that the suspicion of petty theft was too trivial to be regarded as a motive. The jury believed him, and in spite of all the evidence of the experts, acquitted him.

Locard had no doubt whatsoever of his guilt; 13 poisonings could not be coincidence. But he adds, "Pastré killed for pleasure, and perhaps, after his first murders, from habit."

When Locard was writing in 1939, such cases were a rarity. (The only other one cited by Locard is that of the poisoner Jeanne Weber, which we shall consider in the next chapter.) By the late 1950s, their number was increasing. In 1958, a man named Norman Foose stopped his Land Rover in the town of Cuba, New Mexico, raised his rifle, and shot dead two children who were playing. He explained after his arrest that he was trying to do something about the population explosion. In 1959, a pretty blonde named Penny Bjorkland accepted a lift from a married man and shot him dead with a dozen shots; she explained that she wanted to see if she could kill someone "and not worry about it afterwards." In the same year, a man named Norman Smith left his caravan in Sarasota County, Florida, and went and shot dead a woman (who was watching television) through an open window. He had been watching a television program called "The Sniper."

By the mid-1960s, "motiveless murder" had become commonplace. In November 1966, an 18-year-old student named Robert Smith walked into a beauty parlor in Mesa, Arizona, made five women and two children lie on the floor, and shot them all in the back of the head. He explained, "I wanted to get known, to get myself a name."

In England, the "Moors murder case" of the mid-1960s, had this same strangely motiveless quality. Ian Brady and his mistress Myra Hindley—whose crimes will be considered more fully in the final chapter—abducted children in the Manchester area, killed them after sexual assault, and buried their bodies on the moors. They made a habit of going back to the moors to eat picnics on the graves of their victims, a kind of "gloating response" often associated with sex murder. They were caught after they tried to involve Myra Hindley's brother-in-law in the murder of a youth named Edward Evans; the brother-in-law went straight to the police. But at the subsequent trial (1966), it became clear that these could not be classified simply as sex crimes. Brady wanted to be a master criminal, a kind of Public Enemy Number One, and the crimes were partly a defiance of society; in this sense they had something in common with the Leopold and Loeb murder. Brady and Hindley were sentenced to life imprisonment, still refusing to admit their guilt.

In the early 1970s, the trial of the Charles Manson "family" caused much the same kind of sensation in America that the Moors trial had caused in Great Britain. The murder of film star Sharon Tate and three of her friends in a house in Hollywood had produced shock headlines all over the world. The murders of a supermarket owner and his wife the following night increased the sensation and led to panic over the whole Los Angeles area. In prison on another charge a few months later, one of the killers, Susan Aitkens, told a cellmate about her part in the murders; the cellmate passed it on to another prisoner, who talked to the police.

The result was one of the most widely publicized—and most expensive—trials in American history. Yet, as with the Moors trial in England, there was something oddly frustrating about it for those who hoped to understand exactly what motives could lead to such crimes. The Manson family seemed to have no motive, except a vague resentment of "society." Killing had become a casual habit, rather like lighting a cigarette.

Locard had commented about "motiveless murders":

> Crime is a physical phenomenon conditioned by psychological fact. Neither in physics nor in psychology is there an effect without a cause. In vain do modern novelists do their utmost to depict such acts which, in the minds of their authors, are purely gratuitous manifestations of "play," expressions of a consciousness which wants to be free of the Kantian axiom, and moreover, of all law. All punishable acts—in fact, all acts—have their cause.

There is obviously some truth in this; but Locard was leaving out of account the acts committed by people who live in a vacuum, who feel a sense of moral weightlessness, analogous to an astronaut floating in space. Such acts may not be "motiveless," but they are committed with a degree of casualness that comes very close to it. The English equivalent of the Pastré-Beaussier case occurred in 1971, at a photographic firm called John Hadlands, in Bovingdon, Hertfordshire. Two storemen died after severe stomach pains, and two more employees began to lose their hair and suffer pins and needles. A team of experts sent to investigate the "Bovingdon bug" became suspicious when a recent employee named Graham Young asked whether the symptoms were not consistent with thallium poisoning. They asked Scotland Yard whether Young had a record, and were electrified to learn that Young had spent some time in Broadmoor, the prison for the criminally insane, for administering doses of poison to his family and killing his mother—he had been 14 at the time. A fellow prisoner had died of poison while Young was in Broadmoor. Young was arrested and found to be in possession of thallium, and his diary contained his notes on the progress of his poisonings. Young apparently felt superior to his working-class family, and hated his boring environment. His habit of referring to himself as "your friendly neighborhood Frankenstein" makes it clear that murders were a kind of attempt at self-dramatization. Like Robert Smith, he wanted to "make a name for himself." His sister also spoke of his "craving for publicity and notice." But this could hardly be regarded as adequate motivation for murder. For his second series of poisonings, Graham Young was sentenced to life imprisonment.

It is precisely this "motiveless" element in sex crimes that makes them such a baffling challenge to detectives and criminalists.

16

Yet the increasing use of computers is in itself one of the most important responses to this challenge, as well as being perhaps the greatest advance in crime detection since the invention of fingerprinting. In one of the most widely publicized cases of the 1970s, the use of a computer would undoubtedly have led to the arrest of the killer at a far earlier stage of the investigation.

On an evening in late August 1969, a prostitute walking down St. Paul's Road, in the red-light area of Bradford, Yorkshire, was struck violently on the head by a brick in a sock. She followed her assailant, and noted the number of the van in which he drove away. The police soon traced the owner of the van, who told them that he had been in the red-light area with a friend, who had vanished down St. Paul's Road late at night. The police went to see the friend, whose name was Peter Sutcliffe. He was a shy, rather inarticulate young man, who insisted that he only struck the woman with the flat of his hand. Since he had no criminal record, he was let off with a caution. The attack was the first crime of the man who would become known as the Yorkshire Ripper.

This attack was not quite "motiveless." Two months earlier, Sutcliffe had become intensely jealous of his girlfriend, Sonia, who was seeing another man and—he believed—being unfaithful to him. To "get even," he picked up a prostitute—the first time he had ever done such a thing—but the encounter was not a success. The woman took his £10, then got her pimp to chase him away. Three weeks later, he saw the woman in a pub, and demanded his money back; instead, she jeered at him and made him a laughing-stock. Sutcliffe was a shy, sensitive man, and the experience filled him with rage and embarrassment. It festered until he became a sadistic killer of women—innocent housewives and schoolgirls as well as prostitutes.

Five years later, on July 4, 1975, Sutcliffe walked up behind a pretty divorcee named Anna Rogulskyj, and struck her three times on the head with the ball end of a ballpeen hammer. Then, as she collapsed, he raised her blouse and made several slashes with a knife. He was about to plunge it into her stomach when a man's voice called out to ask what was happening. Sutcliffe fled. Anna Rogulskyj recovered after a brain operation. Six weeks later, on August 15, 1975, he crept behind a 46-year-old office cleaner named Olive Smelt, and struck her to the ground with the hammer. Then he raised her clothes and made some slashes on her buttocks with a hacksaw blade before going to rejoin a friend who was waiting for him in a car. When the friend asked him what he had been doing, he explained in a mumble that he had been "talking to that woman." Olive Smelt also recovered after an operation to remove bone splinters from her brain.

On October 29, 1975, Sutcliffe picked up a 28-year-old prostitute named Wilma McCann, and went with her to a playing field near her home. But he found it impossible to achieve an erection at short notice. When the woman told him he was "fuckin' useless," he asked her to wait a moment, got the hammer from the toolbox of his car, and struck her on the head. Then he tugged down her white slacks and stabbed her nine times in the abdomen and five in the chest.

Wilma McCann was the first of 13 murder victims over the course of five years. Some of the victims were "amateur prostitutes," mothers of single-parent families trying to earn money. Some, like 16-year-old Jayne MacDonald, were schoolgirls who happened to be returning home late at night. Some were working women, like 47-year-old Marguerite Walls, a Department of Health official who had been working overtime. Although Sutcliffe was later to insist that he was interested only in killing prostitutes, his craving to kill and mutilate extended to all women.

By the late 1970s, the murder hunt for the Yorkshire Ripper (as the Press christened him) was the biggest in British criminal history. Thousands of people were interviewed—including Peter Sutcliffe—but all this information was not computerized, and so overwhelmed the investigators. Sutcliffe was interviewed in connection with the murder of a prostitute named Jean Jordan, a 20-year-old Scot, whom he had killed in the Southern Cemetery in Manchester, stripping her naked and stabbing her in a frenzy. After the murder, Sutcliffe looked for her handbag, which contained the £5 note he had given her—a new one he had been paid in his wage packet. In due course, this was found by the police, and all the employees of 23 firms in Bradford were interviewed, including Sutcliffe. His wife confirmed his alibi, and the police filed a report saying they had found nothing to arouse their suspicions.

In 1978 and 1979 the police received three letters signed "Jack the Ripper," which had led them to mount an extensive investigation in the Wearside area, 100 miles to the north of Bradford. And on June 26, 1979, the police received a recorded tape beginning with the words "I'm Jack," and taunting them for failing to catch him; the accent was "Geordie"—again, from the Wearside area. After Sutcliffe's arrest, the letters and the tape were recognized as hoaxes, but at the time, most police officers on the case assumed that the Ripper was from somewhere around Durham.

In December 1980, after the thirteenth murder, the police decided to set up an advisory team consisting of four police officers and a forensic expert, Stuart Kind. There had been 17 attacks in all—including the ones of Anna Rogulskyj and Olive Smelt, and two more in the autumn of 1979 when the victims survived. The main clues were three sets of tire tracks at three scenes of crime, three sets of footprints also found near three of the victims, and finally the new £5 note found in Jean Jordan's handbag. It will be recalled that this had been found far from the sites of the earlier Ripper murders, across the Pennines in Manchester, so it seemed highly likely that the "Ripper" had taken it with him from Bradford—Sutcliffe had received it in his pay packet two days before the murder. But if the Ripper lived in the Bradford area, then the search of Wearside was a waste of time. In that case, the tape was probably also a hoax, for although the "Geordie" Ripper might live in Bradford, the extensive police investigations had failed to pinpoint such a suspect. This is why, at the beginning of the investigation, the five-man team decided that the tape and letters should be dismissed as irrelevancies.

There was another reason. The team had gone to examine all the murder sites, including that of a Bradford University student, Barbara Leach, who was killed returning to her flat in the early hours of the morning. As they were looking at the site, one of the police officers, Commander Ronald Harvey, had one of those sudden hunches that come from years of experience, and he remarked, "Chummy lives in Bradford and he did it going home." What he was suggesting was that the Ripper lived in this area, and that he killed Barbara Leach on his way home, perhaps after an unsuccessful search for a victim.

The comment impressed Stuart Kind, for surely here was an important point: that a murder committed in the early hours of the morning indicated that the killer was not far from home, whereas a murder committed earlier in the evening suggested that he had driven far from home in search of a victim and had to get back. Anna Rogulskyj had been attacked in Keighley, close to Bradford, at 1:10 in the morning. But Olive Smelt, attacked at 11 p.m., had been in Halifax. Josephine Walker had been murdered in Halifax at 11:30 p.m. Helen Rytka had been attacked in Huddersfield—even further from Bradford—at nine in the evening. Vera Millward had been murdered in Manchester at nine in the evening. Admittedly, this pattern did not hold for all of the 17 attacks—Emily Jackson had been murdered in nearby Leeds at seven in the evening—but it held for most of them.

So it looked as if the Ripper was probably a local man living in Bradford or Leeds, where 10 out of 17 attacks took place. Next, the team took a map of the area, and computed the "center of gravity" of the attacks. The basic principle was to stick a pin in the 17 sites, then to take an eighteenth pin, and join it to the other 17 by lengths of thread, minimizing the amount of thread required. The eighteenth pin proved to be squarely in Bradford. (In fact, the "pin test" was carried out on the forensic laboratory computer.)

The team suggested that a special squad of detectives should concentrate their energies on Bradford. That would involve re-checking all the men in Bradford who had been interviewed. And since the £5 note was the most vital clue so far, the men who had been interviewed in this connection would have been top of the list. Since the police possessed samples of the tire tracks of the Ripper's car, it would have been a simple matter to check the tire tracks of each of these men.

It can be seen that this method should have led infallibly to Peter Sutcliffe, who was by then living with his wife Sonia at 6 Garden Lane, in the Heaton district of Bradford. That it did not do so was due to the simple circumstance that the Yorkshire Ripper was finally arrested within two weeks of the interim report being completed. On January 2, 1981, in the early evening, Peter Sutcliffe drove the 30 or so miles from Bradford to Sheffield, and in the red-light district there, picked up a black prostitute named Olive Reivers, and

backed into a drive. She removed her knickers and handed
him a condom; he unbuttoned his trousers and struggled
uncomfortably across her in the passenger seat. But he was
unable to obtain an erection. As he sat beside her again,
telling her about his wife's frigidity, they were dazzled by
the lights of a police car which pulled up with its nose to the
bonnet of Sutcliffe's old Rover. Sutcliffe told Olive Reivers
to back up his story that she was his girlfriend, and gave his
name as Peter Williams. One of the policemen went to the
nearest telephone and checked the car's number plates with
the national police computer at Hendon; within two minutes, he had learned that the plates on the Rover actually
belonged to a Skoda. Sutcliffe had stolen them from a car
scrap-yard and fixed them on with Sellotape, because he
knew the police were noting the number plates of cars in
red-light areas.

As both policemen escorted Olive Reivers to the police
car, Sutcliffe hurried behind a nearby oil storage tank,
explaining that he was "busting for a pee," and there
managed to dispose of the ballpeen hammer and knife that
had been concealed under his seat. The police then took him
to Hammerton Road police station. There he revealed that
his name was Sutcliffe, and explained that he was using
false number plates because his insurance had lapsed and he
was due to appear on a drunken driving charge. He was
placed in a cell for the night. And at eight o'clock the next
morning—Saturday—he was taken to the Ripper Incident
Room at Leeds. Here it was immediately noted that the size
of his shoe was the same as that of the footprint found at
three of the murder sites. When he volunteered the information that he had been among those questioned about the new
£5 note, and had also been questioned routinely as a regular
visitor to red-light areas, the investigators suddenly became
aware that this man could well be the Ripper. When they
learned that his car had also been logged in Manchester, it
began to look even more likely. Yet there was still no real
evidence against Sutcliffe, and after a long day of questioning, during which he had been pleasantly cooperative, the

police recognized this lack of evidence. But five and a half years of fruitless search for the Ripper had made them persistent; they decided to hold him for another night. And, back in Sheffield, the policeman who had arrested him heard that he was still being questioned by the Ripper squad. On an impulse, he went back to the oil storage tank where Sutcliffe had urinated. There he found the hammer and knife on a pile of leaves.

When Sutcliffe was told about the find, he admitted that he was the Yorkshire Ripper, then went on to dictate a statement describing his murders in detail.

Stuart Kind is inclined to take the view that the findings of the five-man team would inevitably have led to the arrest of the Yorkshire Ripper in the early part of 1981, and in the light of the team's deductions, it is hard to disagree with him. It should also be clear that the Ripper was caught by police work as much as by chance. He was one of hundreds of suspects who had been interviewed, and when he was taken into the Incident Room, the chance of his being the Ripper were hundreds to one. The size of his shoe shortened the odds; so did the fact that he had been involved in the £5 note inquiry, and that his name was on the computer as a "punter" seen in red-light areas. The finding of the hammer and knife clinched the matter; but even if they had not been found, the Rover's tire tracks would have narrowed the odds to a virtual certainty. So although, in terms of the history of crime detection, the Ripper inquiry must be labeled a police failure, closer analysis reveals that it deserves to be classified as a real—if belated—success.

——————————— **17** ———————————

Most crime writers who have discussed the Whitechapel murders of 1888 have posed the same question: would Jack the Ripper have been trapped by modern police methods? The answer has usually been a depressing negative. But the Yorkshire Ripper case demonstrates that the British police *were* finally mastering the art of trapping a serial sex killer through modern technology. Their chief problem was the sheer quantity of information accumulated over a five-year inquiry. If this had all been computerized, there can be no possible doubt that Sutcliffe would have emerged as the chief suspect at a far earlier stage. As far as the British police were concerned, this was the main lesson of the case. They lost no time in rectifying the omission, and the result was that the computer played a major role in the solution of Britain's next major case involving a serial sex killer.

In 1982, five women were raped by two men wearing balaclavas, one tall, one short. In the second half of 1984, the short rapist began to operate alone. In the following year, Detective Superintendent Ken Worker was placed in charge of an inquiry code-named Operation Hart to try to trap the rapist. Twenty-seven attacks had taken place in the London area, the majority around Camden Town and further north. It was observed that many of the attacks took place near railway lines, which led the team to formulate the theory that the rapist was a railway worker. He usually engaged the victims in conversation, then threatened them with a knife, tied their hands and raped them. He seemed to enjoy frightening them and committing the rapes with a great deal of violence.

On December 29, 1985, 19-year-old Alison Day set out to meet her boyfriend from his place of work in Hackney, east London. She never arrived. Seventeen days later, her body was found in the River Lea, which ran close to the printing factory where her boyfriend worked. She had been tied up, strangled and probably raped—the period in the river destroyed most forensic evidence. But her sheepskin coat was also found in the river, and when it was dried, revealed a number of fibers that might have come from her killer. The pathologist observed that she had been strangled with a tourniquet—a scarf knotted around her throat, then tightened with a stick. An additional knot in the scarf had obviously been tied to press on the victim's windpipe and cause unconsciousness.

Four months later, on April 17, 1986, 15-year-old Maartje Tamboezer, whose father—an oil executive—had only recently moved to Britain, set out on her bicycle to buy sweets in nearby Horsley. Cycling along a short cut near the railway line, she was forced to dismount by a fishing line stretched across the path. A man dragged her into the woods, battered her unconscious with blows to the head, and raped her. He then strangled her, and made an attempt to burn the body. Particularly strange was the fact that he rammed burning handkerchief tissues into the genitals—obviously an attempt to eliminate his sperm traces. For the Surrey police, whose team was led by Detective Superintendent John Hurst, this suggested that he had some previous experience with blood group identification, and might have a previous record as a sex offender. As Surrey's largest ever manhunt developed, hundreds of possible witnesses were interviewed. The picture of the rapist that began to emerge was of a smallish man wearing a blue parka. He had been seen running frantically to catch the 6:07 train from East Horsley to London. Two million train tickets were examined, in the hope that the rapist had left his fingerprints behind; but although a number of possible tickets were located, none had fingerprints.

At least the police were able to determine the murderer's blood group from traces of sperm left on the dead girl's clothing. It was group A, and since the scientists had determined it from his sperm, he was a "secretor"—one of those whose blood group can be determined from bodily fluids. One in three people are group A, so this was hardly a breakthrough. But an enzyme called PGM (phosphoglucomutase) enabled forensic scientists to make a closer determination that would eliminate four out of five suspects.

There was another important clue: Maartje Tamboezer's hands had been tied with a peculiar kind of brown string, which proved to be made of paper; it was called Somyarn, and the manager of the Preston factory which made it was able to say that the sample dated back to at least 1982, and that it had been made from an unusually wide "edge" strip of the paper. If they could locate the rest of that ball of string, there would be a strong possibility that its owner would be the killer.

A month later, on Sunday May 18, 1986, a 29-year-old secretary named Ann Lock worked late at London Weekend Television, and set out for her home in Brookmans Park, in Hertfordshire; she had been married only four weeks, and had just returned from her honeymoon in the Seychelles. She never arrived home, and an extensive police search failed to find the body. In fact, it was discovered in some undergrowth near the Brookmans Park station some 10 weeks later. She had been raped and allowed to suffocate, and there had again been an attempt to burn the body, apparently to eliminate traces of sperm. The blood group and the PGM reading pointed again to the "railway rapist."

By now it had struck Detective Chief Superintendent Vincent McFadden, who was in charge of the case, that the man he was looking for might also be the north London rapist, as well as the killer of Alison Day and Maartje Tamboezer. The various forces involved decided to link their computers to share information. Operation Hart—the team looking for the rapist—had started with a list of 4,900 sex offenders, which they had whittled down to 1,999. On this list, at number 1,594, was a man called John Duffy, an ex-British Rail carpenter, who was in trouble with the law for raping his ex-wife. This had happened in August 1985, two months after Margaret Duffy had left her husband because of his increasingly violent behavior, and gone to live with Hungarian-born Imre Lovas. Duffy had attacked them with a knife and raped his wife. The following day he appeared before West Hendon magistrates on a charge of causing grievous bodily harm. He was remanded in custody until September 19, when a judge granted him bail.

On May 17, the day before Ann Lock vanished, Duffy had been arrested on suspicion for loitering near a railway station, and had been found to be in possession of a sharp knife. He explained that he was a student of Zen Budo, a form of Japanese martial arts which combines ju-jitsu and weapons training. He needed the knife, he said, for his classes in Kilburn, where he lived. This explanation was accepted, but the computer recorded the arrest.

With the sex charge and his arrest on suspicion, Duffy now figured on the suspect list for the railway rapist. The police were working their way slowly through the remaining 1,999, taking blood samples, and in due course, called in Duffy for questioning. This was on July 17, 1986. Duffy arrived with a solicitor, and declined to give a blood sample. The interviewers instantly realized that this ginger-haired, pockmarked little man—about five feet three inches tall—corresponded to the description of the railway rapist (although earlier descriptions had given him fair hair). They disliked his manner, which was glib and a little *too* helpful. The following day, the detectives reported to Ken Worker, the head of Operation Hart, that they thought Duffy was a likely suspect. But when they tried to follow up the interview, they discovered that Duffy was now in the Friern Barnet Hospital, apparently suffering from amnesia. A few hours after being interviewed, he had gone to the Hampstead police station, looking bruised and battered, and explained that he had been mugged and lost his memory. When the Operation Hart team tried to interview him at Friern Barnet, doctors declined to allow it. This should have placed Duffy at the head of the list of suspects. But they still had more than 1,000 to interview, and for the moment, Duffy was allowed to remain in the security of the hospital.

The police were also mounting a massive surveillance operation on British Rail stations that were unmanned at weekends, hoping to catch the railway rapist; but a Sunday newspaper revealed the secret, and it had to be dropped—an example of the Press actively hindering the search for a killer.

Meanwhile, Duffy—who was now a part-time patient at the Friern Barnet Hospital—raped another schoolgirl. She described the rapist as a short pockmarked man, with a dog named Bruce. For a while, police even suspected that the man might be a jockey, and sent detectives to every racing stable. All these inquiries led nowhere.

But the police were now willing to try another interesting experiment. Possibly inspired by stories of the new technique of "psychological profiling" used in America (of which we shall speak in the last chapter), they asked a professor of psychology from the University of Surrey, Dr. David Canter, to set up a team to review all the information, and see if he could reach any general conclusions about the rapist. Canter studied the reports of the rapist, and reached some interesting conclusions. The "center of gravity" method, used by the team in the Yorkshire Ripper case, enabled him to conclude that the killer lived in the north London area, within three miles of Finchley Road. He also concluded that he was, or had been, a semi-skilled worker, that his relationship with his wife had probably been a turbulent one, and that he had two very close male friends. Seventeen points were listed. And when Canter's analysis was matched against the 1,999 suspects, the computer instantly threw up the name of John Duffy...

Duffy, who lived in Barlow Road, Kilburn, was placed under close surveillance; detectives reported on his activities from the moment he left his home to the moment he returned. But at some point, Duffy realized he was being watched, and the detectives realized that he was enjoying trying to give them the slip—for example, jumping on a train just a moment before the doors closed. And when Duffy shaved off his moustache one day, Chief Superintendent John Hurst decided that he could no longer take the risk of a killer rapist committing a murder while under police surveillance; he ordered Duffy's arrest.

The 30-year-old Irish-born suspect proved a difficult man to question. He would neither admit nor deny that he was the railway rapist; his attitude was that if the police thought so, it was up to them to prove it. He had a disconcerting way of staring with wide open eyes at the questioner, his face blank, trying to force him to drop his eyes. The rapist's victims had described the same cold, dominant gaze. Hurst's position was a difficult one. Now he had arrested Duffy, he had 36 hours to find evidence sufficient to convince a magistrate that he ought to be held in custody. Duffy's home was searched, and many knives found. Duffy's ex-wife was interviewed, and was able to tell them that her husband had once told her that he had raped a girl and that it was her fault because she was frigid. Margaret Duffy also told the police that her husband liked to tie her hands and rape her; the more she struggled, the more he enjoyed it. On the other hand, if she submitted passively, he lost interest . . .

In the home of Duffy's parents, police found a vital piece of evidence—a ball of brown string; it proved to be the unique Somyarn they were looking for. Yet even faced with this evidence, Duffy gazed back blankly, refusing to comment.

The clinching piece of evidence came from one of Duffy's closest friends, Ross Mockeridge, a fellow martial arts enthusiast. He went to the Romford Incident Room, and described how Duffy had persuaded him to punch him in the face and slash his chest with a razor—Duffy had explained that the police were trying to "frame" him for rape. Mockeridge finally obliged. And Duffy hurried off to the Hampstead police station to report that he had just been mugged and lost his memory.

When five of Duffy's rape victims unhesitatingly picked him out in an identity parade, he must have realized that there was now enough evidence to ensure a guilty verdict. Yet he continued to fix his questioners with what one of them described as his "laser beam stare" and to remain silent.

Detectives were confident that the string of evidence would link Duffy to the death of Maartje Tamboezer. But the Ann Lock case and the Alison Day case were more doubtful. Apart from similarity of method, there was nothing to link Duffy with either. Then, at the last minute, the forensic laboratory again came up with a vital piece of evidence. Seventy items of Duffy's clothing had been seized, and of these, 30 selected as the kind that might shed fibers when in contact with a rape victim. Under the microscope, 13 fibers taken from Alison Day's sheepskin coat—hurled into the river by her killer, with stones in the pockets—were matched with fibers from Duffy's garments, with such precision that one expert described the result as a "fingerprint."

Now, at last, the full story of the railway rapist had begun to emerge, largely with the help of his wife. The problem of the duo-rapes of 1982-1984 was never cleared up, although police are believed to know the identity of Duffy's fellow rapist. In 1983, Duffy and his wife were trying hard to have a child, but his sperm count proved to be too low; no rapes took place during that year. Duffy had lost his job as a British Rail carpenter, at Euston, in 1982, but had continued to use his free rail pass. His first attack as a solo rapist took place in November 1984, when a girl was raped at knife-point at Barnes Common, in southwest London. By this time, Duffy and his wife were quarreling all the time, and she left him in June 1985. Two months later he attacked her and raped her, also wounding her boyfriend. On December 2, 1985, Duffy appeared in Hendon magistrates court on the assault charge, and a member of the Operation Hart team took one of the rape victims to court to see if she recognized him. She did not; but Duffy undoubtedly recognized her, and realized suddenly the danger of leaving his victims alive. Three weeks later, he murdered Alison Day and carefully disposed of her body in the river, determined to leave no clues. Maartje Tamboezer and Ann Lock were murdered with the same ruthless efficiency. But after the death of Ann Lock, Duffy seems to have lost the stomach for murder—or perhaps decided that, after all, it was unnecessary.

In court, four rape victims gave evidence, all describing how Duffy had tied their hands behind them in a "prayer" position—just as the hands of the murder victims had been tied. The last victim, a 14-year-old schoolgirl, described how Duffy had tied her with her own tights before raping her against a tree; she burst into tears as she gave her evidence. A 16-year-old rape victim was in court when the jury found Duffy guilty of four rapes and two murders—those of Alison Day and Maartje Tamboezer. (As the police had expected, Duffy was found not guilty of the murder of Ann Lock for lack of evidence.) Duffy stared impassively in front of him as the judge sentenced him to a minimum of 30 years in prison. He was the first sex killer in England to be caught by computer.

But it is also interesting to reflect that, by the time of his trial, the police had a choice: they *could* have proved his guilt by DNA fingerprinting, using the sperm from his rape victims. And this in itself was a watershed in the history of forensic science. Since the days of Jack the Ripper, the random sex killer had posed an apparently insoluble problem for scientific crime detection. With the introduction of the computer and genetic fingerprinting, those days were finally over.

3

The Soul of the Criminal

1

The biggest manhunt in New York's history began on December 3, 1956; on the previous evening, a bomb had exploded in the Brooklyn Paramount cinema, injuring seven people, one of them so badly that doctors spent the night trying to save his life. The man who planted it had been christened by the newspapers "The Mad Bomber," and in the past 16 years he had planted 28 explosive devices in public places. Until the Brooklyn Paramount bomb, none of them had caused death, or even serious injury. But this was not because of any precaution on the bomber's part. In

March 1951, a bomb had destroyed a telephone booth at Grand Central Station; anyone who had been making a call would have been blown to pieces. The same thing applied to a bomb that destroyed a telephone booth at the New York Public Library on Fifth Avenue a month later. During the next five years, there were explosions at the Radio City Music Hall, the Paramount Theatre, the Capitol Theatre, the Port Authority bus terminal, the Rockefeller Center, and many other places, including the Consolidated Edison Plant on 19th Street.

To a Sherlock Holmes, the location of this latter might have presented a vital clue. For the first two bombs, both of them "duds," had been planted at Consolidated Edison plants, the first in November 1940, the second nine years later. It was after this that the real epidemic of bombing began in 1951. But by 1956, these two earlier episodes had been forgotten.

The result of the Brooklyn cinema bomb, the first to involve serious injury, was a wave of panic, and a sudden drop in attendances at theatres, cinemas, and museums. The police had few clues. On a few occasions, the Mad Bomber had tipped off the police by telephone, or by letters written in block capitals. But the voice was soft and anonymous, and the letters contained no fingerprints.

It was after the Brooklyn bomb that the editor of a New York newspaper, the *Journal-American,* decided to publish an open letter to the bomber. This appeared the day after Christmas 1956, and begged the bomber to give himself up, offering to give a full airing to his grievances. Two days later, a bomb was found in the Paramount Theatre, in an opening slashed in a seat; it was deactivated by the police bomb squad. Like the others, it was a home-made device consisting of a piece of piping with nuts at both ends. But on that same Friday afternoon, the *Journal-American* received a reply from the Mad Bomber. It was written in block capitals, and began:

> I read your paper of December 26—placing myself
> in custody would be stupid—do not insult my
> intelligence—bring the Con Edison to justice—start
> working on Lehmann—Poletti—Andrews . . .

It was signed "F.P."

The men named were the former Governor of New York State, a former Lieutenant-Governor, and a former Industrial Commissioner. The bomber went on to promise a truce until mid-January, and to list 14 bombs he had planted in 1956, many of which had not so far been discovered. The police later found eight pipe-bombs, five dummies, but three still live and unexploded—the crude chemical detonating mechanism had failed to work.

Police Commissioner Stephen P. Kennedy asked the newspaper not to print the letter, in case it caused public panic; instead, the editor inserted an advertisement in the personal column:

> We received your letter. We appreciate truce. What
> were you deprived of? We want to hear your views
> and help you. We will keep our word. Contact us
> the same way as previously.

But other newspapers spotted the item, and the secret was out. The *Journal-American* decided to print most of the bomber's letter, together with yet another appeal.

The result was another letter from the bomber, promising a "truce" until March 1, and offering an important piece of information:

> I was injured on a job at Consolidated Edison
> Plant—as a result I am adjudged totally and
> permanently disabled. I did not receive any aid of
> any kind from company—that I did not pay for
> myself—while fighting for my life—section 28
> came up.

* * *

Section 28 of the New York State Compensation Law limits the start of any legal action to two years after the injury. The letter went on to accuse the Edison company of blocking all his attempts to gain compensation, and to criticize Lehmann, Poletti, and Andrews for ignoring his letters. Like the previous letter, this was signed "F.P."

Here, then, were clues that could lead to the bomber's identity. But then, the Consolidated Edison company supplies New York with its electric light, and has many power plants; if the bomber had been injured before 1941—the date of the first bomb—the chances were that his records had been destroyed long ago or lost. The same problem applied to Lehmann, Poletti, and Andrews; they probably received a hundred letters a day during their terms of office, and most of them would have ended in the waste-paper basket. No politician files all his crank letters.

The police decided on a curious expedient—to consult a psychiatrist for his opinion on the bomber. This was the decision of Inspector Howard F. Finney of the crime laboratory. The man he chose was Dr. James A. Brussel, who had been working for many years with the criminally insane. Finney handed Brussel the file on the bomber, together with the letters. Brussel studied the letters, and his first conclusion was that the bomber was not a native American; the letters contained no Americanisms, while phrases like "they will pay for their dastardly deeds" suggested a member of the older generation.

The bomber, said Brussel, was obviously a paranoiac, a man far gone in persecution mania. The paranoiac has allowed himself to become locked into an inner world of hostility and resentment; everyone is plotting against him and he trusts no one. But because he is so close to the verge of insanity, he is careful, meticulous, highly controlled—the block-capital letters were beautifully neat. Brussel's experience of paranoia suggested that it most often develops in the mid-30s. Since the first bomb was planted in 1940, this suggested that he must now be in his mid-50s.

Brussel was a Freudian—like most psychiatrists of that

period—and he observed that the only letters that stood out from the others were the W's, which were made up of two rounded U's, which looked like breasts. From this Brussel deduced that the bomber was still a man with strong sex drives, and that he had probably had trouble with his mother. He also noted that the cinema bombs had been planted inside W-shaped slashes, and that these again had some sexual connotation. Brussel's final picture of the bomber was of a man in his 50s, Slavic in origin, neat and precise in his habits, who lived in some better part of New York with an elderly mother or female relative. He was—or had been—a good Catholic. He was of strong build. And finally, that he was the type who wore double-breasted suits. Some of these deductions were arrived at by study of the letters—the meticulousness, obsessive self-control—and others by a process of elimination: the bomber was not American, but the phrasing was not German, Italian, or Spanish, so the likeliest alternative was a Slav. The majority of Slavs are Catholic, and the letters sometimes revealed a religious obsession . . .

Meanwhile, the *Journal-American* had printed a third appeal, this one promising that if the bomber gave further details of his grievances, the newspaper would do its best to reopen his case. This brought a typewritten reply that contained the requested details:

> I was injured on September 5, 1931. There were over 12,000 danger signs in the plant, yet not even First Aid was available or rendered to me. I had to lay on cold concrete . . . Mr. Reda and Mr. Hooper wrote telling me that the $180 I got in sick benefits (that I was paying for) was ample for my illness.

Again, the signature was "F.P."

Now they had a date, all the clerical employees of the Consolidated Edison Company began searching the files. There was still no guarantee that a file dating back to 1931 would exist. But it was eventually located by a worker named Alice Kelly. The file concerned a man called George Metesky, born in 1904, who had been working as a generator wiper in 1931 at the Hell Gate power station of the United Electric and Power Company, later absorbed by Consolidated Edison. On September 5, 1931, Metesky had been caught in a boiler blowback and inhaled poisonous gases. These caused hemorrhages, and led to pneumonia and tuberculosis. He had been sent to Arizona to recuperate, but been forced to return to Waterbury—where he lived—because of lack of funds. He had received only $180 in sick benefits, and the file contained letters from the men called Reda and Hooper that he had mentioned . . .

The police lost no time in getting to Waterbury, taking a search warrant. The man who opened the door of the ramshackle four-storey house in an industrial area wore gold-framed glasses, and looked mildly at the policemen from a round, gentle face. He identified himself as George Metesky, and allowed the officers to come in. He lived in the 14-room house with two elderly half-sisters, May and Anna Milausky, daughters of his mother's previous marriage. On that matter, Brussel's "guess" had been remarkably accurate.

A search of the house revealed nothing, but in the garage police found a workshop with a lathe, and a length of the pipe used in the bombs. In a bedroom there was a typewriter that would later be identified through forensic examination as the one that had written the letters. An hour later, at the police station, Metesky confessed that he was the "Mad Bomber." A photograph of him taken immediately after his arrest showed that, as Brussel had predicted, he wore a double-breasted suit. The initials "F.P." stood for "fair play."

Psychiatrists at Bellevue found Metesky to be insane and incapable of standing trial; he was committed to Matteawan State Hospital for the Criminally Insane, where he spent the remainder of his life.

_____ 2 _____

The founding father of modern criminology—as noted earlier—was Cesare Lombroso, one of the most brilliant scientists of the nineteenth century. Born in Verona in 1835 into a Jewish family, Lombroso soon became an atheist and a materialist in reaction against the domination of the Catholic Church (Italy then being largely under the rule of the Catholic Austrians). After serving as an army surgeon in the war against the Austrians, he became Professor of Psychiatry at Pavia, as well as director of the lunatic asylum. He performed numerous dissections of the brains of madmen, hoping to establish some physical cause for insanity. This was unsuccessful, but in 1870 he was immensely excited when the German pathologist Rudolf Virchow announced that he had discovered certain "atavistic" features in the skulls of criminals. Lombroso began studying criminals in Italian prisons, and was asked to perform the post-mortem on the body of the famous brigand Vilella. What he found seemed to confirm Virchow's observation: Vilella's brain had a depression in the place where the spine is normally found—a depression found in animals, particularly rodents. This, says Lombroso, was a revelation. "At the sight of that skull, I seemed to see, all of a sudden, lighted up as a vast plain under a flaming sky, the problem of the nature of the criminal—an atavistic being who reproduces in his person the ferocious instincts of primitive humanity and the inferior animals." This seemed to be confirmed when he studied the sex killer Vincent Verzeni, "who showed the cannibalistic instincts of primitive anthropophagists, and the ferocity of beasts of prey." A new insight came when he studied a young soldier called Misdea, a decent, harmless young man who was an epileptic; one day Misdea lost his temper and killed eight fellow soldiers and officers. He then fell into a deep sleep, and remembered nothing when he woke up. This convinced Lombroso that "many criminal characteristics . . . were morbid characteristics common to epilepsy.''

Such "born criminals" Lombroso called—borrowing the terminology of his colleague Enrico Ferri—"criminals by passion," and distinguished these from people who might be driven to a crime through illness or difficult circumstances; these he called "occasional criminals."

These views were announced to the world in 1876 in a book called *Criminal Man (L'Uomo delinquente)*, which immediately made him an international reputation, as well as provoking bitter hostility. The attacks came from people who felt he was oversimplifying, and their view is now generally accepted. But it is important to realize that Lombroso had proposed a notion of profound importance, no matter how crude and simplistic. The notion of civilization is based on the concept of concern for other people, the Christian belief that all men are brothers. Nature, on the other hand, seems to know little of fellow feeling; most creatures regard other creatures as potential prey. So Lombroso is making a basic, if crude, distinction. It *is* true that criminals like Joseph Vacher, Peter Kürten, Albert Fish, behave exactly like animals in search of prey. Lombroso may have been mistaken in believing that the "born criminal" can be regarded as a "throwback" to the caveman, but he had nevertheless made an observation of immense significance to criminology.

In the year after *Criminal Man*, confirmatory evidence of Lombroso's view that criminal tendencies are inherited was provided by a book called *The Jukes* by the sociologist Richard Dugdale. The sire of the Jukes clan was born in New York in the early eighteenth century, and spent most of his time drinking and whoring. Two sons married their illegitimate sisters, and Dugdale traced over 700 descendants of the clan, and discovered that all but half a dozen were prostitutes or criminals. Another sociologist, Henry H. Goddard, studied the descendants of a soldier named Martin Kallikak, who had fathered a baby by a feeble-minded girl, then married a Quaker of an honest and intelligent family.

Nearly 500 of the Quaker girl's descendants were traced, and none were criminals. Of the same number of descendants of the feeble-minded girl, only 10 per cent were normal.

Alexandre Lacassagne was among those who criticized Lombroso; he went to the opposite extreme and took the view that crime is caused by society, and that "every society has the criminals it deserves." And the Dutchman Willem Bonger, a Marxist, took the predictable view that crime is entirely due to capitalism. Lombroso was open minded enough to take note of these criticisms, and to modify his views. In a later work, *Crime: Its Causes and Remedies* (1899), he made the immensely interesting observation that when food is easy to obtain, crimes against property decreased while crimes against the person, particularly rape, increased. He had recognized, in effect, that crime may be the outcome of a kind of boredom. Like a heat-seeking missile, it seeks out experiences that will produce a feeling of being "more alive." (The Leopold and Loeb murder remains the classic instance of this type of crime.) In the last decade of his life, Lombroso had begun to recognize that crime may be far more "mental" than he had supposed.

Perhaps the most important of Lombroso's critics was Dr. Charles Goring, whose book *The English Convict* (1913) argued that the main characteristic of most criminals is defective intelligence, not Neanderthal attributes. Yet, in some respects, his findings support those of Lombroso. He noted, for example, that the majority of the population of burglars in prison were physically inferior to the average man, and suggested that they were trying to compensate for physical inferiority with crime. He also talked about the type of criminal he called the "lone wolf," the man who feels no social loyalty. To some extent, he is speaking of what we would now call the psychopath. (The researches of zoologists like Konrad Lorenz have revealed that if young animals receive no affection within the first few days of their lives, they become permanently incapable of affection.) But he is also speaking of the type of person Karl Marx called the "alienated man" (and whom I was later to label "the Outsider"). Dostoevsky produced a remarkable portrait of such a man in *Crime and Punishment:* one who feels cut off from society because he feels no one understands him, and who therefore feels that he has the right to make his own rules. In fact, such "alienated men" seldom turn to crime since, in spite of their alienation, their sense of fellow feeling is too strong. Yet the rise of the "high IQ killer" since the 1960s—individuals like Ian Brady, Charles Manson and Ted Bundy—indicates that, in a civilization with a high level of technical achievement, "alienation" becomes an increasingly important element in serious crime.

Goring's "defective intelligence" theory certainly seems more convincing than Lombroso's caveman theory, but it is open to a basic objection. When convicts in Sing Sing were tested, their average mental age was found to be 13, which appears to bear out Goring's theory. But when American soldiers were subjected to the same tests, their average mental age was found to be 13½. And at the trial of the child-murderer John Thomas Straffen in 1952, Dr. Alexander Leitch testified that, while Straffen's mental age was only 9½, that of the average person is 15. And since only a tiny proportion of "average people" are criminals, the defective intelligence theory has obvious drawbacks.

The connection between crime and sex received an interesting new emphasis in the researches of Professor Max Schlapp, a New York neuropathologist. One of his patients in the early 1920s was a wealthy woman who had a compulsion to steal handbags. Schlapp discovered that she had an abnormally high metabolic rate, and that her adrenal glands were hyperactive. Since these are closely associated with the sex glands, she was flooded with adrenalin whenever she began to menstruate. Under treatment with sedatives and gland extracts, her kleptomania vanished. Another patient, Arnold Anderson, was a member of a stable and religious family whose members were "superior types," yet

Anderson was a compulsive thief and burglar. Schlapp again discovered that he had overactive adrenals, which affected his sexuality. But Anderson grew tired of treatment and threw away his pills. In 1924, in the course of a burglary, he murdered a householder, and was sentenced to life imprisonment. Schlapp's book *The New Criminology* (1928) came at a time when enlightened prison governors were preaching reform of the harsh penal system. One of them, Thomas Mott Osborne, had actually got himself incarcerated in Auburn jail as a normal prisoner, and was horrified by what he found; as governor of Sing Sing, he instituted a humanitarian regime and an ''honor'' system among the convicts which was immensely successful.

One of the most remarkable successes of this system came to light in the year *The New Criminology* appeared. One of the most violent and ruthless criminals of the century, Carl Panzram, produced an autobiography which uncovered the motivations behind his life of robbery and mass murder. Panzram had started life as an underprivileged child, the son of a farmer who deserted his family, and he began committing robberies as a kind of protest against his poverty. In prison he was always violent and rebellious, and suffered endless beatings and periods in solitary confinement— sometimes strung up by the hands from the ceiling. There was nothing intelligent about his revolt; it was motivated by resentment and sheer willpower. (Nietzsche would certainly have admired him.) He was simply determined to continue to fight back, and became one of the toughest troublemakers the guards had ever encountered. He burned down the prison workshop and wrecked the kitchen with an axe. Then a new warden, Charles A. Murphy, tried a new approach; he told Panzram that he would trust him to walk out of the prison, and be back for suppertime. Panzram promised—with every intention of breaking his word. Yet once outside, he experienced a compulsion to keep his promise, and returned. Murphy began to allow him increasing freedom—until one night, Panzram got drunk and absconded. He was recaptured after a gun battle and thrown into the punishment cell; Murphy's humanitarian regime came to an end. Panzram realized that his own weakness was to blame, and was plunged into an attitude of sullen defeatism. When he escaped in the following year—1918—he began committing murders. The motive was usually robbery and sex—he had acquired a taste for sodomy in jail—but sometimes the crimes were motiveless, as when he hired a canoe with six natives to take him on a trip in the Belgian Congo, then shot them all in the back and threw them to the crocodiles. Back in America he began raping and sodomizing boys—bringing the number of his murders up to 20. Caught after a robbery, he was sent to America's toughest prison, Dannemora, and the cycle of beating and defiance began all over again.

At this point, a young Jewish guard, Henry Lesser, felt sorry for Panzram, and after a particularly brutal bout of torture, sent him a dollar by a "trusty." At first Panzram thought it was a joke; when he realized it was a gesture of sympathy, his eyes filled with tears. He told Lesser that if he would get him writing materials, he would write his autobiography. The book, with its descriptions of rape and murder, was far too horrifying to be published at the time; yet it revealed a man of remarkable intelligence and honesty. As the book was shown to American publishers and intellectuals, there was a movement to try to get Panzram out of jail. He refused; he felt that he could never lose the habit of violence. Panzram finally murdered a guard, with the deliberate intention of getting himself sentenced to death; he succeeded, and was hanged in 1930, at the age of 38.

Perhaps one of the most significant episodes in Panzram's life was an occasion when Lesser went into his cell to check the bars, and turned his back on Panzram. Panzram was shocked: "Don't ever do that again." Lesser said: "But you wouldn't harm me." And Panzram replied: "You're the one man I wouldn't want to kill. But I'm so erratic, I might do anything." He was admitting that he had "lost control." He had become, in a sense, a wild animal—or rather, a part of him had become a wild animal that the human part could no longer control. This insight seems remarkably close to Lombroso's "atavistic" theory, and makes us aware that Lombroso's basic intuition remains, in a sense, the foundation of all later criminology.

After the Second World War, criminological theories became increasingly "liberal." Dr. Fredric Wertham, the man who had studied Albert Fish, wrote a number of influential books, including *Dark Legend* and *The Show of Violence*. *Dark Legend* is a study of an Italian boy, Gino, who murdered his mother with a breadknife, making an attempt to cut off her head. Wertham discovered that, after the death of the boy's father—when Gino was a child—the mother allowed the family to starve, and took a series of lovers. Wertham saw many parallels between Gino's crime and that of Orestes in Greek mythology, who murdered his mother because she had dishonored his father. He also argues that Shakespeare is portraying the same symbolic situation in *Hamlet,* and that it is rooted in the child's incestuous desire for the mother. So Gino's crime becomes symbolic, like the Freudian Oedipus complex; in a sense, Gino is as much a victim as his mother. The same idea runs through *The Show of Violence* (1948) with its studies of murderers; these people are trapped in the tentacles of an invisible octopus. Like Lacassagne, Wertham feels that society gets the criminals it deserves, because "in our society respect for human life is only a professed theoretical ideal."

In 1961, another liberal American psychiatrist, Samuel Yochelson, decided to begin a program of study of criminals in St. Elizabeth's Hospital in Washington DC, starting out from "the compassionate view that these people were the way they were because of deep-seated psychologic problems." He worked with a younger colleague, Stanton E. Samenow. And the conclusions at which they began to arrive dismayed them both: that the central traits of the criminal personality were weakness, immaturity, and self-delusion, mixed with a strong desire to deceive other people. Moreover, the rapists, murderers, and child-molesters they studied seemed to have no *desire* to change; the moment they left the doctor's office, they went straight back to their previous criminal pattern. They had amazing skill in self-justification, and in appealing to the humanitarian sympathies of the doctors. They also had a "shut-off mechanism" that enabled them to ignore or forget anything they preferred to ignore or forget; they might admit to something at one session, and then deny that they had ever said it at the next. They lacked self-discipline and were often cowards— for example, allowing their teeth to rot rather than face the pain of the dentist's drill. And "the greatest fear of these criminals was that others would see some weakness in them." They were hypersensitive to what was said to them and reacted very angrily when "put down." One of the few child-molesters who changed his pattern of behavior did so "because he applied choice, will, and deterrence to a pattern that offended him"—in other words, because he suddenly developed the insight that his behavior was simply the wrong way to achieve what he wanted to achieve. He was like a gambler who had adopted a "system" that caused him to lose repeatedly, and who one day decided to abandon it and try another system.

Yochelson and Samenow recognized that what they wanted to achieve was something not unlike religious conversion: to activate a certain *insight* in the criminal, a desire to change himself. They realized, for example, that criminals were particularly susceptible to change when about to suffer a period of confinement for some offense, and when they were in a phase of inner conflict and self-disgust. Then they would be reminded that the three options open to a criminal are crime, suicide, or change, and that it was up to them to choose.

Yochelson's view may be illustrated by an earlier case, that of Canada Blackie, described by Thomas Mott Osborne, the reforming governor of Sing Sing. Blackie was a bank robber, and his tendency to sudden violence alarmed the guards. After shooting a guard with a home-made gun, he was thrown into solitary confinement for a year and eight months, sleeping on the stone floor without covers. He contracted tuberculosis and went blind in one eye. Then he was placed in a normal cell, but still in solitary confinement, for several more years. When Canada Blackie heard about Osborne's reforms, he asked to see him. Then he drew out a tin containing a key to his cell, which he had filed, and a home-made knife. These he handed over to Osborne telling him: "I want the warden to know that he need have no further anxiety about me...I'm going straight." Next day, Blackie was allowed out into the open air. Then he was made a "trusty," and became assistant of the Mutual Welfare League, achieving immense popularity with the other prisoners because of his sufferings. When Osborne moved to Sing Sing, he took Blackie with him and gave him a comfortable bedroom overlooking the river instead of a cell. But Blackie was a sick man, and died in 1915, praying for three men who were to be electrocuted that day. What is clear is that Blackie's sufferings had made him ready to change, and that when the change came, it was basically a form of religious conversion. It all sounds like a story out of Dostoevsky's *House of the Dead*, and reminds us that that profound psychologist also understood that the springs of "conversion" lie in man's recognition that he is free.

But perhaps the deepest insight into the criminal mentality was achieved by an American penologist named Dan MacDougald. MacDougald began, in fact, as a lawyer, and in the mid-1950s he was approached by farmers who wanted him to stop the Federal authorities in Georgia from overloading the Buford dam, which was flooding their land and drowning their cattle. Their case seemed so reasonable that MacDougald had no doubt it would be easily accomplished. To his astonishment, the authorities seemed literally deaf to his arguments, and it took three years and a cost of $46,000 to change things. Then one day, MacDougald heard of an experiment performed at Harvard by Dr. Bernard Jouvet, and it seemed to throw a flood of light on the problem. Jouvet had connected a cat's aural nerve to an oscilloscope, so when a sharp click sounded in its ear, the oscilloscope registered the vibration. But if a jar with white mice was placed in front of the cat, it not only ignored the click, but the needle failed to move. This was preposterous, for even if the cat was too fascinated by the mice to hear the sound, it should nevertheless have traveled from its eardrum to the oscilloscope. The cat was somehow *cutting out* the sound at the eardrum, just as if it had put its paws over its ears. And this, MacDougald realized, was exactly what the Federal authorities had been doing. It struck MacDougald that this was also what criminals do. It was Yochelson's "shut-off mechanism." For example, when a swindler deliberately deceives someone, he keeps his human feelings in a separate compartment. To begin with, he may be two persons: a "human being" with his wife and family and a swindler with his dupes. But if he carries on long enough, he is bound to become less human with everyone. This is what H. H. Holmes meant when he said he had "come to resemble the Evil One."

According to MacDougald, the criminal is dominated by negative *attitudes* towards society; for example, he may feel that everyone is as dishonest as it suits them to be, that the basic law of life is "Look after number one," and that society is a rat-race anyway. He literally *sees* things this way. He is blind and deaf to all things that contradict his negative view of existence. Dickens's Scrooge is an example of what MacDougald called "negative blocking." He has got himself into a state of general negativity and mistrust in which he has totally ceased to enjoy life. The three ghosts of Christmas cause him to *open up*, so he once again begins to appreciate life.

Now it is obvious that we are *all* in this condition, to some extent—for, as Wordsworth says, "shades of the prison house" begin to close around us as we learn to "cope" with the complexities of existence. So we are all in the position of the criminal. But criminals do it far more than most people—to such an extent that, when we read of a man like Holmes, we can suddenly *see* that he was an idiot to waste his own life and that of his victims. As strange as it sounds, studying criminality has much the same effect on most of us that the ghosts of Christmas had on Scrooge—of making us more widely aware of the reality we ignore. This is the ultimate justification of a book such as this.

MacDougald could see that his problem was to make criminals aware of their "faulty blocking mechanisms," and cause them to "open up." If he could do this, they would cease to be criminals. MacDougald reasoned that the faulty blocking mechanism would become apparent if you studied the criminal's use of words, and got him to explain what he meant by certain words—such words as "law," "honesty," "neighbor," "love," "self," and so on. The method he devised was basically Socratic: that is, the criminal was made to explain himself until he began to see where he was going wrong.

In 1967, Dr. C. D. Warren, medical director of Georgia's maximum security prison near Reidesville, was told that he was going to be visited by MacDougald and another colleague from the "Yonan Codex Foundation"—the name MacDougald had selected for his enterprise (he subsequently changed it to "Emotional Maturity Instruction"), because they believed they had developed a method for rehabilitating "hard-core psychopaths" in two or three months by "specialized instruction." Deeply skeptical to begin with, he was amazed by the success of the venture. "Gentlemen, it worked. It worked so well it changed the attitudes of those . . . in contact with the technique, and for the better . . . You would not believe the results. In two weeks with the 22-man group, the constructive changes were impressive . . . In eight weeks they had successfully rehabilitated 63 per cent of the men under instruction." Moreover, the rehabilitated criminals became instructors to others, and showed the same rate of success. The "unblocking" process had the effect of raising the subject's self-esteem, so he ceased to be a criminal—for MacDougald recognized that criminality is essentially an *undervaluation of oneself*. (We can see what he means in the case of Panzram, who hated himself as much as he hated everyone else, and whose self-hatred drove him virtually to suicide.) According to MacDougald, the New Testament invocation to love one's neighbor as much as oneself means that one *should* love oneself.

He gives an interesting example of what his method means in practice. One prisoner had come to hate another so much that he decided that, in order to live up to his code of honor, he had to kill him. He knew this meant life imprisonment, but he could see no alternative. So he stole a hacksaw blade from the prison workshop and fashioned himself a stiletto. But on the day he intended to use it, he attended one of MacDougald's sessions, and began to understand that his feeling that he had *no alternative* to murder was an example of what MacDougald meant by a faulty blocking mechanism. After the session, he saw his "enemy" in the canteen, walked over to him, and offered to buy him a cup of coffee. The man looked astonished, but accepted, and the two became friends. The whole problem had dissolved away. In effect, he had seen his way out of the cul-de-sac that led Panzram to self-destruction.

The psychologist William Sheldon once remarked: "To read Lombroso is to feel the strike of a powerful and dangerous game-fish. Lombroso hooked something of tremendous importance, but the tackle he had was insufficient to land it." We can see that criminologists like Yochelson and MacDougald have begun to develop tackle that is strong enough to land it. We can also see that when MacDougald learned to diagnose the extent of a man's criminality from his "word blindness," he was developing a technique that might also be as potentially useful as a lie-detector, and which could be compared with Dr. Brussel's ability to form a clear picture of the Mad Bomber from his communications, or Dr. David Canter's amazingly accurate assessment of the Railway Rapist from the crimes themselves—an assessment which actually led to the arrest of the rapist when Canter's "portrait" was fed into the computer. This "psychological dimension" is perhaps the most interesting development in crime detection in the second half of the twentieth century.

—————————————— 3 ——————————————

In November 1979, the New York police decided to ask the FBI for help in the case of a sex murder of a New York schoolteacher. On October 12, 1978, 26-year-old Francine Elveson, a graduate student at Fordham University, was on her way to work when she was accosted on the stairs of the apartment building—Pelham Parkway Houses, in the Bronx—and forced up to the roof at knifepoint. There she was stripped and raped, then strangled with the strap of her handbag. The police doctor discovered that she had been badly beaten about the face, and that her nipples had been cut off and placed on her chest. A pendant in the form of a Jewish good luck sign (Chai) was missing from around her neck, and her body had been spreadeagled in the form of the pendant. Her nylons had been tied around her wrists and ankles, and her knickers placed over her head. The earrings she had been wearing had been placed neatly and symmetrically on either side of her head. Her umbrella and a pen had been forced into her vagina, and a comb placed in her pubic hair. The words "Fuck you" and "You can't stop me" had been scrawled on her thighs and abdomen. There were clear teeth-marks on the victim's legs.

All the tenants of the building were interviewed, but there seemed to be no obvious clues, and after a few weeks, the investigation stalled; this was when it was referred to the FBI, who in turn referred it to their new "psychological profiling team" at the FBI Academy in Quantico, Virginia. The team, consisting of nine men, was officially known as the Behavioral Science Unit, and its job was to try to apply the techniques originally developed by Dr. James Brussel.

Agent John Douglas was able to make a number of immediate deductions from the scene-of-crime evidence. The ritualistic nature of the crime—the arrangement of the body in the form of a Chai, the neat arrangement of the earrings, the words scrawled on thighs and abdomen, the comb in the pubic hair—all these indicated a killer who was taking his time, and who was therefore relatively certain that he would not be disturbed. This in turn suggested that he knew the place well, and was therefore on his "home territory." So recommendation number one was: look for the killer in the building, or for someone who was thoroughly familiar with the building.

Douglas was also virtually certain that the killer was white. This was simply a matter of experience and statistics; in most mutilation murders, the victim is of the same race as the killer.

The face battering indicated to Douglas that the killer knew his victim. Again, this rule had emerged from a study of dozens of cases. The face of the stranger-victim is anonymous, so there is no point in battering it. But in the case of someone known to the killer, the same impulse that leads to the attack also leads to a desire to obliterate the *person;* the closer the relationship, the more violent the battering.

The killer's age, Douglas decided, was between 25 and the early 30s. Teenage killing tends to be violent and impulsive; this attack seemed measured and deliberate, a sign of an older man. Douglas ruled out the notion that the killer was a man in his late 30s or 40s, simply because such a man would probably be in prison. The urge to sexual attack manifests itself early—in some cases even before the rapist enters his teens—and when such men go on committing sex attacks, they usually get caught.

Douglas ventured another deduction based on experience: the killer would probably live alone; the crime had the characteristics of an alienated "Outsider" type, not of someone integrated into a family. Moreover, the detailed nature of the ritual—the knickers covering the head, the umbrella in the vagina, and writing on the thigh—all indicated someone who fantasized a great deal about sex, and who therefore was an avid reader of pornography.

A clear picture was beginning to emerge—of someone who, assuming he was not actually a tenant, visited the

building regularly, and often saw the schoolteacher; he had
fantasized about attacking her for some time before doing
so. He was also familiar with her movements, and had
probably been waiting for her on the morning she was
forced up to the roof.

Since the police had interviewed everyone in the area, it
seemed fairly certain that they had already talked to the
killer. Homicide detective Thomas Foley re-checked his list,
and saw that the profile fitted an unemployed actor named
Carmine Calabro, whose father had an apartment in the
building. Calabro, who was 32, often visited his father, and
must have known Francine Elveson. Foley had eliminated
Calabro as a suspect because he had been in a mental
hospital at the time of the murder. But further checks
revealed that hospital security was lax enough to allow
patients to come and go as they pleased. Calabro proved to
be a high school dropout—as Douglas had predicted—and
he shared a pornography collection with his father. Calabro
was asked for his tooth-prints, and three dental experts
testified that they matched those on the victim's legs. He was
found guilty of the murder, and sentenced to 25 years in jail.

Douglas applied the same technique to a case involving
the kidnapping and murder of a baby-sitter, Betty Shade, in
Logan, Pennsylvania, in June 1979. Her mutilated body was
found on a rubbish dump, and there was evidence that she
had been raped after death. The injuries to her face convinced Douglas again that the killer knew the victim well,
and had killed her in a fury of resentment; but the mutilations had been performed after death, suggesting that the
killer was too frightened to inflict them while she was alive.
This indicated a young and nervous killer. Yet the girl had
been driven from her baby-sitting job to the dump in a car,
requiring a degree of organization. The rape after death also
suggested a killer who was taking his time. To Douglas, all
this pointed unmistakably to two killers. Again, his "profile"
pointed the police in the right direction. The girl lived with
her boyfriend, and it seemed unlikely that he would rape her
after death, which is why he had originally been eliminated

from the inquiry. But the boyfriend had an elder brother who owned a car. Both men were eventually convicted of the murder. The younger man had killed and mutilated her; the brother had raped her after death.

Such accuracy is the result of long experience. In the 1960s, "psychological profiling" had been altogether more haphazard. Between June 1962 and January 1964, 13 women were strangled and raped in Boston, with the result that the killer became known as the Boston Strangler. The result was a police operation similar to that of the Jack the Ripper investigation in 1888, but far bigger. A psychiatric team which included Dr. James Brussel was set up to try to create a "profile" of the Strangler. Their conclusion was that there were two stranglers, one a man who lived alone and was probably a schoolteacher, one a homosexual with a hatred of women. On January 4, 1964, 19-year-old Mary Sullivan was strangled and raped; the killer bit her all over her body, masturbated on her face, and left her with a broom handle thrust into her vagina. But then, suddenly, the killings stopped. Rapes continued in the Boston area, but the rapist seemed to be a polite and gentle sort of person; he always apologized before he left, and if the woman seemed too distressed, even omitted the rape. The descriptions of this "gentle rapist" reminded the police of an offender who had been jailed for two years in 1960. He had become known as "the measuring man," because he talked his way into apartments, posing as an executive from a modeling agency, and persuaded young women to allow him to take their measurements. Occasionally he ventured a few indecent caresses. Some of the women allowed him to make love to them as a bribe—the modeling jobs, of course, never materialized. The "measuring man" was a husky young ex-soldier named Albert DeSalvo, and he was sentenced for "lewd and lascivious behavior," as well as for attempted breaking and entry.

DeSalvo was identified by the rape victims, and sent to the Bridgewater mental institution for observation; there he was found to be schizophrenic and not competent to stand trial. Soon after his permanent committal to Bridgewater, DeSalvo confessed to a fellow patient that he was the Boston Strangler, and the patient informed his lawyer, who happened to be the controversial F. Lee Bailey. In taped interviews with Bailey, DeSalvo confessed in detail to the 13 murders in Boston; the police were at first inclined to be skeptical, but soon became convinced by DeSalvo's detailed knowledge of the crimes. As a result, DeSalvo was sentenced to life imprisonment; he had served only six years when he was found stabbed to death in his cell by a fellow prisoner who was never identified.

In fact, nothing about the "psychological profile" corresponded to the real Albert DeSalvo. DeSalvo was not a homosexual, or a schoolteacher who lived alone; he was a married man with children. His real problem was hypersexuality—a sex drive so powerful that his wife complained that he often wanted intercourse six times a day. There was no Freudian hatred of his mother; on the contrary, he loved her deeply. His father had been a brutal man who ill-treated his mother—on one occasion he broke her fingers one by one—and who brought home prostitutes, with whom he had sex in front of the children. Albert DeSalvo had incestuous relations with his sisters. The DeSalvo home, like the Kürten home, was permeated with an overpowering atmosphere of sex. The real key to the Boston Strangler was not that he was a neurotic driven by a hatred of women, but a man who wanted sex with *every* woman he saw. Several of the murders should have given the investigators a clue, for the women were often raped more than once in a brief period. But then, when the police have dozens of possible suspects and hundreds of possible leads, it is often difficult to see the wood for the trees.

Even Brussel was hopelessly wrong about the Strangler. Misled by the fact that some of the victims had been elderly women, he theorized that the Strangler had an Oedipus complex, and was "searching for his potency." (We may note that the one part of Brussel's profile of the "Mad Bomber" that was totally wrong was the Freudian part—

W's shaped like breasts, etc.) In the early murders he had often assaulted the victims with bottles or broom handles—a confession of impotence. Then he had attacked a 20-year-old girl, Sophie Clark, and "found his potency." This was why the murders stopped; he was "cured." The simple truth was that, in spite of his manic sex drive, DeSalvo was basically a "nice guy," and he later admitted that talking with his intended victims made it hard to go through with the killing. In the last case, Mary Sullivan, the girl had been so open and trusting that killing her produced a powerful revulsion; after that he went back to straightforward rape. What seems to have misled Brussel—and all the other psychiatrists— about the Strangler was that his crimes seemed to be those of a madman; in fact, DeSalvo was not a psychotic, only a "satyr," a man who can never get enough sex.

Fourteen years after the Strangler came the Son of Sam case. In July 1976, an unknown man began shooting couples in cars in the New York area, killing six and wounding seven. A letter addressed to the police captain in charge of the case declared "I am the Son of Sam," and explained he liked to hunt women because they were "tasty meat." One year later, after shooting a courting couple in Brooklyn, the killer jumped into his car and drove away; but he had parked near a fire hydrant, and a policeman had stuck a parking ticket on his windscreen. A woman saw him drive off and reported the incident when she heard of the shootings—one victim died and the other was blinded—and the police checked on the four parking tickets that had been issued that night, and found that one of them bore the registration number of David Berkowitz, of Pine Street, Yonkers. Arrested three days later, Berkowitz proved to be a pudgy little man with a beaming smile, a paranoid schizophrenic who lived alone in a room lit by a naked light bulb, and slept on a bare mattress.

In the Berkowitz case, a team of 45 psychiatrists was assembled at Creedmore Hospital, but in a three-hour meeting all that emerged was that they all had their individual theories about the killer. But the final police theory was remarkably close to Berkowitz: describing him as neurotic, schizophrenic, and paranoid, it continued: "He is probably shy and odd, a loner, inept in establishing relationships, especially with women." The major problem was that Berkowitz was not on any list of suspects, so a profile was of no practical value.

But the case made the police aware of the importance of learning as much as possible about such random killers. FBI agent Howard Teten, who taught a course in applied criminology at the Academy, seemed to have a natural talent for "profiling" random killers, which he had been applying since the early 1970s. On one occasion, a Californian policeman had contacted him about a case in which a young woman had been stabbed to death by a frenzied killer. The frenzy suggested to Teten that the murderer was an inexperienced youth, and that this was probably his first crime, committed in a violently emotional state. And, as in the later case of the Bronx schoolteacher, Teten thought the evidence pointed to someone who lived close to the scene of the crime. He told the policeman that he should be looking for a teenager with acne, a loner, who would probably be feeling tremendous guilt and would be ready to confess. If they ran across such a person, the best approach would be just to look at him and say "You know why I'm here." In fact, the teenager who answered the door said: "You got me" even before the policeman had time to speak.

With Teten as an adviser, the FBI Behavioral Science Unit was set up with a grant of $128,000 from the National Institute of Justice. It began by building a file of taped interviews with mass murderers and assassins, such as Charles Manson, Richard Speck—the killer of eight nurses in a Chicago hostel in 1966—David Berkowitz, Sirhan Sirhan (assassin of Robert Kennedy) and the necrophile killer Ed Gein who ate parts of corpses from the local graveyard and made a waistcoat from the skin of one of them. It was a project that had been foreshadowed by Karl Berg's study of Peter Kürten in the early 1930s, but which, unfortunately, had never been followed up. (I myself had been recommending such a study project since *An Encyclopedia of Murder* in 1960). Now, with over 100 tapes of interviews with mass murderers and assassins, the FBI team began placing the similarities on computer. Some of this information could have been gathered from Berg's study of Kürten—for example, the discovery that when Son of Sam was unable to find a suitable victim, he went back to the scene of a previous murder and fantasized about it. They also discovered that Berkowitz, like the Yorkshire Ripper, thought that demons were urging him to kill.

The FBI's new insight into the mind of the killer and rapist began to pay dividends almost immediately. In 1979, a woman reported being raped in an east-coast city; the police realized that the *modus operandi* of the rapist was identical to that of seven other cases in the past two years. They approached the FBI unit with details of all the cases. The deliberation of the rapes seemed to indicate that the attacker was not a teenager or a man in his early 20s, but a man in his late 20s or early 30s. Other details indicated that he was divorced or separated from his wife, that he was a laborer whose education had not progressed beyond high school, that he had a poor self-image, and that he was probably a Peeping Tom. In all probability he had already been interviewed by police, since they had been questioning men wandering the streets in the early hours of the morning. This "profile" led the police to shortlist 40 suspects living in the neighborhood, and then gradually, using the profile, to narrow this list down to one. This man was arrested and found guilty of the rapes.

It soon became clear that psychological profiling could also help in the interrogation of suspects. The agency began a program of instructing local policemen in interrogation techniques. Their value was soon demonstrated in a murder case of 1980. On February 17 the body of a girl was found in a dump area behind Daytona Beach Airport in Florida; she had been stabbed repeatedly, and the body was in a state of decomposition which indicated that she had been dead for a matter of weeks. The girl was fully dressed and panties and bra were apparently undisturbed; she had been partly covered with branches, and laid out neatly and ritualistically on her back, with her arms at her sides. The FBI team would immediately have said that this indicated a killer in his late 20s or early 30s. From missing persons reports, Detective Sergeant Paul Crowe identified her as Mary Carol Maher, a 20-year-old swimming star who had vanished at the end of January, more than two weeks previously. She had been in the habit of hitching lifts.

Towards the end of March, a local prostitute complained of being attacked by a customer who had picked her up in a red car. She had been high on drugs, so could not recollect the details of what caused the disagreement. Whatever it was, the man had pulled a knife and attacked her—one cut on her thigh required 27 stitches. She described her assailant as a heavily built man with glasses and a moustache, and the car as a red Gremlin with dark windows. She thought he had been a previous customer, and that he might live in or near the Derbyshire Apartments.

Near these apartments an investigating officer found a red Gremlin with dark windows; a check with the vehicle licensing department revealed that it was registered to a man called Gerald Stano. And the manager of the Derbyshire Apartments said that he used to have a tenant called Gerald Stano, who drove a red Gremlin with dark windows. A check revealed that Stano had a long record of arrests for attacking prostitutes, although no convictions; he apparently made a habit of picking up prostitutes who were hitchhiking. A photograph of Stano was procured, and shown to the prostitute, who identified the man as her attacker.

It was at this point that Detective Crowe heard about the case, and reflected that Mary Carol Maher had also been in the habit of hitching lifts—she had been an athletic girl who was usually able to take care of herself. Crowe's observations at the crime scene told him that Mary Maher's killer had been a compulsively neat man; he was now curious to see Stano.

The suspect was located at an address in nearby Ormond

Beach, and brought in for questioning. Crowe stood and watched as Stano was interrogated by a colleague, whom he had primed with certain questions. But his first encounter with Stano answered the question about compulsive neatness; Stano looked at him and told him that his moustache needed a little trimming on the right side.

What Crowe wanted to study was Stano's "body language," which can be as revealing as a lie detector. And he soon discovered that Stano was an easy subject to "read." When telling the truth, he would pull his chair up to the desk or lean forward, rearranging the objects on the desktop while talking. When lying, he would push back his chair and cross his legs, placing his left ankle on his right knee.

It was not difficult to get Stano to admit to the attack on the prostitute—he knew that she could identify him. Then Crowe took over, and explained that he was interested in the disappearance of Mary Carol Maher. He showed Stano the girl's photograph, and Stano immediately admitted to having given her a lift. "She was with another girl," he said, pushing back his chair and placing his left ankle on his right knee. After more conversation—this time about the fact that Stano was an orphan—Crowe again asked what had happened with Mary Maher. Pushing his chair back and crossing his legs, Stano declared that he had driven her to a nightclub called Fannie Farkel's—Crowe knew this was one of Mary's favorite haunts, a place frequented by the young set—but that she had not wanted to go in. Crowe knew that the truth was probably the opposite: Stano had not wanted to mix with a young crowd (he was 28). He asked Stano if he had tried to "get inside her pants." Stano pulled the chair up to the desk and growled "Yeah." "But she didn't want to?" "No!" Crowe recalled being told by Mary's mother that her daughter had, on one occasion, "beaten the hell" out of two men who had tried to "get fresh." "She could hit pretty hard, couldn't she?" "You're goddamn right she could," said Stano angrily. "So you hit her?" Stano pushed back his chair and crossed his legs. "No, I let her out. I haven't seen the bitch since."

Crowe knew he now had the advantage. As he pressed Stano about the girl's resistance, it visibly revived the anger he had felt at the time. And when Crowe asked: "You got pretty mad, didn't you?" Stano snorted: "You're damn right I did. I got so goddamn mad I stabbed her just as hard as I could." Then he immediately pushed back his chair, crossed his legs, and withdrew his statement. But when Crowe pressed him to tell how he stabbed her, he pulled his chair forward again and described stabbing her back-handed in the chest, then, as she tried to scramble out of the door, slashing her thigh and stabbing her twice in the back—Crowe had already noted these injuries when he first examined the body. After this admission, Stano drove with Crowe to the dump behind the airport, and showed where he had hidden the body.

It was after Stano had signed a confession to killing Mary Carol Maher that one of Crowe's fellow detectives showed him a photograph of a missing black prostitute, Toni Van Haddocks, and asked: "See if he knows anything about her." When Crowe placed the photograph in front of Stano, Stano immediately sat back in his chair and placed his left ankle on his right knee. But he persisted in his denials of knowing the woman. Two weeks later, on April 15, 1980, a resident of Holly Hill, near Daytona Beach, found a skull in his back garden. Local policemen discovered the scene of the murder in a nearby wooded area—bones scattered around by animals. When Crowe went to visit the scene, he immediately noted that four low branches had been torn off pine trees surrounding the clearing, and recognized Stano's method.

Back at headquarters, he again showed Stano the photograph, asking: "How often do you pick up black girls?" Stano pushed back his chair. "I hate them bastards." "But you picked her up." Stano stared at the photograph, his legs still crossed. "That's the only one I ever picked up." It was at this point that Crowe realized that he was talking to a multiple killer.

Stano persisted in denying that he had killed Toni Van

Haddocks. Crowe stood up to leave the room. "I know you did because you left your signature there." Stano stared with amazement, then called Crowe back: "Hey, wait. Did I really leave my name there?" Then, realizing that he had virtually admitted killing her, he went on to confess to the crime. But these two murders, he insisted, were the only ones he had ever committed.

Crowe did not believe him. Now he knew that Stano was a ritualistic killer, and that ritualistic killers often kill many times. There had been no more recent disappearances in Daytona Beach, so Crowe studied the missing persons files and records of past murders. He found many. In January 1976, the body of Nancy Heard, a hotel maid, had been discovered in Tomoka State Park, near Ormond Beach, where Stano lived. Reports said the death scene looked "arranged." She had last been seen alive hitchhiking. Ramona Neal, an 18-year-old girl from Georgia, had been found in the same park in May 1976, her body concealed by branches. In Bradford County, 100 miles away, an unknown young woman was found concealed by tree branches, while in Titusville, to the south, another girl had been found under branches—a girl who had last been seen hitchhiking on Atlantic Avenue in Daytona Beach.

When Stano had moved to Florida in 1973—from New Jersey—he had lived in Stuart. A check with the Stuart police revealed that there had been several unsolved murders of girls there during the period of Stano's residence.

Stano's adoptive parents told Crowe that they had fostered Gerald Stano even after a New York child psychiatrist had labeled him "unadoptable." He had been taken away from his natural mother as a result of "horrible neglect." In all probability, Stano had never received even that minimum of affection in the first days of his life to form any kind of human bond. He had never shown any affection, and he had been compulsively dishonest from the beginning, stealing, cheating, and lying. He preferred associating with younger children—a sign of low self-esteem—and preferred girls who were deformed or crippled—he had got a retarded girl pregnant once. He had married a compulsive over-eater, but the marriage quickly broke down.

Crowe traced Stano's wife, who was living with her parents in a house of spectacular untidiness—Crowe admitted that it reminded him of the home of the TV character Archie Bunker, who spends most of his time in his undershirt. There Stano's ex-wife answered questions as she rested her huge breasts on the kitchen table. Stano's sexual demands had been normal, as was only to be expected "with his itty-bitty penis." But he *had* a peculiar habit of going out late at night, and returning, exhausted, in the early hours of the morning . . .

What had now emerged about Stano convinced Crowe of the need for more psychological "profiling," and he called in an Ormond Beach psychologist, Dr. Ann MacMillan, who had impressed police with her "profile" of a mass killer called Carl Gregory. The result of tests on Stano revealed a psychological profile almost identical with those of Charles Manson and David Berkowitz; she believed that it meant that his crimes were virtually predictable—or, in other words, that he was one of Lombroso's "born killers."

Over many months, Crowe's interrogation of Stano continued. At some point, Stano realized that Crowe was "reading" his physical "signals," and changed them. But his compulsive nature made it inevitable that he developed new ones, and Crowe soon learned to read these. Eventually, Stano confessed to killing 34 women; then, typically, he declared that this had been a strategem to make him appear insane. As with Peter Kürten, his memory of his crimes was remarkably detailed—for example, he was able to describe a prostitute whom he had picked up in Daytona Beach as wearing a brown leather jacket, brown shoes, and a shirt with an inscription: "Do it in the dirt." When he led them to the woman's skeleton—covered with branches—the police found that it was wearing precisely these clothes.

With plea-bargaining, Stano finally agreed to admit to six murders: Mary Maher, Toni Van Haddocks, Nancy Heard,

Ramona Neal, Linda Hamilton, and an unidentified girl. On
September 2, 1981, Stano was sentenced to three consecu-
tive terms of 25 years—75 years in all—and was taken to
the Florida State prison. But a later trial resulted in a death
sentence.

4

Lombroso may be regarded as the father of "psychological
profiling." He noticed that when people tell lies, they often
blush or lower their eyes. A good liar can disguise such
reactions; even so, he becomes slightly more tense, so that
blood pressure and pulse rate increase. And since doctors
are able to detect blood pressure and pulse rate mechanically,
should it not be possible to construct a machine that would
detect lies? Lombroso designed a machine that would measure the pulse, and cause it to register as a line on a
revolving drum; he called it the hydrosphygmograph. This
consisted of a glass bulb filled with water, and the fist of the
suspect, grasping a short rod, was sealed in by a rubber
membrane. Pulsations of the heart visibly lowered and
raised the water level in the bulb, and these fluctuations
were transferred to a column of air in a graduated glass
tube. Changes in the pulse rate could be clearly seen. An
opportunity to try it out came when a thief named Bersone
Pierre was arrested on a charge of robbing railway passengers of 20,000 francs. He was also found to be in possession of a passport belonging to a man named Torelli.
Lombroso looked at Pierre and decided that he conformed to
his "criminal type." He then connected him up to the
machine and questioned him about the railway robbery.
Pierre denied it, and his pulse remained steady. But when
Lombroso questioned him about Torelli, the pulse revealed
that Pierre was nervous. Lombroso reported that Pierre had
nothing to do with the railway theft, but that he had almost
certainly robbed the owner of the passport. The police later
discovered both these assertions to be true.

It was at about this time (1905) that a young man named August Vollmer was appointed Town Marshal of Berkeley, in California; he was only 29 at the time, and the crooks dubbed him "the boy marshal." But, like Allan Pinkerton 40 years earlier, he proved to have a brilliant natural talent for detection and organization, as well as a bravery that made him widely respected. On one occasion, a call from Alameda told him that a murderer named Browne had escaped from the jail there, and was thought to be heading for Berkeley, where his father lived. Vollmer had the father's telephone tapped, and that night, Browne rang and arranged to meet him at the corner of 62nd Street and San Pablo Avenue at midnight. When Vollmer and some officers arrived, they saw that it was a well-lit spot. "If I were a murderer I wouldn't wait here," said Vollmer, "I'm going to take a look down that dark alley." He had only walked a block when a man stepped out of the shadows and pointed a gun at him: "Beat it quick, or I'll plug you." Vollmer had his hands in his pockets, and he took the risk of walking straight towards the man. "I just want to talk to you." The man backed away. Then, as Vollmer came close, the man turned and ran. Vollmer pulled his gun, shouting "Stop or I'll shoot." Then, as the running man raised his gun, he pulled the trigger at the same moment the other fired. The man dropped, and the police came running up. Browne was dead, shot through the head. "But I aimed at his legs" said Vollmer. An autopsy showed that Vollmer's bullet had gone through Browne's right leg, and that the bullet in his brain was from his own pistol.

Vollmer was the first man to introduce a signal system into police work. In the days before portable radios, there was no way of relaying messages to his men on the beat. Then he heard of a private detective in Los Angeles who had devised his own method of protecting a wealthy neighborhood: to attach small telephone boxes to poles around the neighborhood, each box being wired back to his own home. Vollmer went to see for himself, and accompanied the detective—a man named Foster—on his beat. A red light flashed, and Foster and Vollmer rode off on bicycles. Foster's wife had received a telephone call reporting a prowler. Within minutes, Foster and Vollmer had caught the prowler hiding in a large dustbin.

Vollmer was impressed, and decided to have similar red lights suspended at intersections throughout the town. His board of trustees vetoed the idea as too expensive—it would cost $25,000. Vollmer insisted on demanding a vote of all the citizens, and they supported him; the money was raised by a bond issue, and Vollmer now had a way of signaling to individual policemen to get to the nearest telephone and ring headquarters.

But Vollmer was not simply a good Chief of Police; he never ceased to ask *why* men became criminals. One of his best known remarks was: "Attempting to make folks good by law is the height of imbecility. What we need is a study of the factors underlying delinquency rather than bigger, better laws." This is why he created the first Crime Prevention Bureau, as well as the first Police School. And he kept Hans Gross's *Criminal Investigation* on his desk. It was when reading the chapter on liars in Gross's *Criminal Psychology* that Vollmer began to wonder whether it might not be possible to build a machine to detect lies. His curiosity finally led him to Lombroso's researches, and those of Lombroso's colleague Vittorio Benussi. And in 1921, Vollmer read an article by William Marston, of Fordham University, in the Bronx, about his own researches into a lie detector. Marston and his colleague Father Walter Summers believed that the most significant thing about the liar is that his blood pressure rises, and they were working on a machine that would detect even small increases.

Vollmer sent for Sergeant John Larson, who happened to be a University of California graduate as well as a policeman, and explained the problem. Larson had already devised a better method of fingerprinting. It took Larson some weeks to build his first model. It was a simple variation on the device doctors still use for testing blood pressure—an inflatable rubber tube wrapped around the arm where the pulse beats, and a needle that would register the pressure on a roll of paper. Vollmer was the first person on whom it was tried. Larson told him that he had to answer a simple yes or no to various questions, and began by asking if he had had lunch today. Vollmer said yes.

"Do you like to swim?"

"Yes."

"Did you go to bed after midnight last night?"

"No."

"Do you like roast beef?"

"No."

"Do you like ice cream?"

"Yes."

"Do you live on Bonita Street?"

"Yes."

"Did you go to bed after midnight last night?"

"No."

And at this point Vollmer could no longer contain his enthusiasm; he had been watching the needle tracing a line on the soot-blackened paper. "It registered every time I lied—about not liking roast beef and about going to bed before midnight."

Larson called his machine the cardio-pneumo-psychogram, but this ponderous label was soon dropped in favor of lie detector. Tramps were picked up in boxcars, and brought in for testing; the result was some confessions. Two youths were brought in for questioning regarding hold-ups on automobiles, and their nervousness soon convinced Larson that they were lying. Faced with this apparently omniscient machine, they broke down and admitted that they were members of a gang of eight, who had begun by frightening courting couples, and when they realized how easy it was, began robbing them at gunpoint. All eight were charged with a series of robberies.

The lie detector soon achieved wider publicity when it solved one of the most publicized cases of 1921. On the evening of August 2, the housekeeper of Father Patrick E. Heslin answered an urgent knocking at the door of the priest's residence in Colma, just outside San Francisco, and found herself confronted by a man wearing motorists' goggles and a long overcoat with the collar turned up; his car was idling at the curb behind him. The man explained that a friend had been badly injured in a motor accident, and that he wanted Father Heslin. The priest, a burly man of 60, lost no time in pulling on his own coat and clambering into the car. That was the last his housekeeper saw of him.

The housekeeper—Marie Wendel—decided to inform the archbishop, Edward J. Hanna. Soon after this telephone call, Hanna received a kidnap note demanding $6,500 for the return of Father Heslin. That afternoon, the newspaper headlines announced the kidnapping.

The note was partly handwritten, partly typewritten, and it declared that the priest was being held in a cellar. On the table there was a candle, and when this burned to the bottom, it would ignite a mass of chemicals that would fill the room with deadly poison gas. This candle would be lit when the kidnapper went to collect the ransom money, so there must be no attempt to trap him . . . A further message specifying the exact spot would be sent at nine o'clock that evening.

In fact, this letter never arrived; the kidnapper was obviously alarmed by the newspaper publicity. Mass searches were organized, but at the end of eight days, nothing had been found. A second ransom note reiterated the demand for $6,500, but again failed to specify how the money should be delivered.

On the afternoon of August 10, 1921, a reporter named George Lynn went to call on Archbishop Hanna, and as he waited for the door to be opened, a round-faced stranger walked up and stood beside him. A Filipino houseboy opened the door and asked them to come in and wait. And as the reporter and the stranger sat in the parlor, the stranger explained that his name was William A. Hightower, and that he thought he knew where the priest could be found. He had learned it via a prostitute named Dolly

Mason, who had heard it from a client. A man who fries pancakes all the time was watching over him . . .

The reporter did not jump to the conclusion that Hightower was insane, for he knew that there was a vast billboard displaying just such a sign above Salada Beach. Further questioning elicited the explanation that Hightower had learned of a cache of bootleg liquor buried beneath the billboard, and had gone to dig it up; as he was digging, he had uncovered a black scarf, such as that which had been worn by the priest (according to the newspapers). So he was certain the priest would be buried there. "And now," asked Hightower, "do you think I'm eligible for the reward?"

A few hours later, policemen carrying shovels and lights accompanied Hightower to Salada Beach. The talkative Hightower had by now told them most of his life story—how he had once been a successful baker, but had gone bankrupt; how he had invented a machine-gun and a candied-fruit substitute . . . He was still talking as he pointed to the black scarf. "Start digging there . . ." He seized a shovel and thrust it vigorously into the sand. "Be careful," said Police Chief O'Brien, "you might damage his face." "That's all right," said Hightower, "I'm digging at his feet." O'Brien stared at him. "I thought you hadn't uncovered the body?" "That's right" said Hightower, still digging. A moment later, one of the policemen said: "I've found him."

Father Heslin, it seemed, had been knocked unconscious by a tremendous blow which had crushed the back of his skull, then shot twice.

In the San Mateo county jail, Hightower stuck to his story that he had found the priest accidentally when looking for a cache of bootleg liquor. Nothing would shake his story, and he was obviously more interested in the reward than in answering questions. Chief O'Brien remembered Vollmer's lie detector, and telephoned the Berkeley headquarters. Within an hour, John Larson was on his way over with his lie detector.

Hightower submitted cheerfully to being attached to the

machine. Then Larson began to question him about his story of the bootleg liquor. Again and again, the needle leapt upward, indicating a rise in systolic blood pressure. And Hightower, who could see this, began to look less euphoric. When the test was over, Larson was able to tell O'Brien with confidence that Hightower had murdered the priest.

Hightower's guilt was confirmed by other evidence. Handwriting experts said that his block-printing was identical with that of the kidnap note, while a typewriter in his hotel room matched the typed part.

Hightower was found guilty, but sentenced only to life imprisonment—probably because both judge and jury had strong doubts about his sanity. He spent the rest of his life in jail, where his megalomania flourished, and died in the early 1960s.

Another young recruit to the Berkeley police force, Leonarde Keeler, built a portable lie detector in 1923. This quickly proved its value when a girl in a sorority house was accused of thieving. She denied it, and Keeler's portable lie detector established that she was telling the truth. He tried it on all the other girls, and eliminated them from the inquiry. Then, in order to be thorough, he tested the woman who ran the place; the needle immediately began to jump wildly; the woman became increasingly confused, and finally confessed.

In 1926, Keeler decided to try a new idea. His machine already registered blood pressure, pulse, and breathing rate; he decided to add a device for measuring skin resistance to electricity. The theory was that when a suspect lies, his pores exude tiny quantities of sweat, and his skin resistance drops. This proved to be the best idea so far, and the basic principle of the modern polygraph was established.

In 1930, a young recruit named Albert Riedel joined the Berkeley force, and became fascinated by the lie detector. Riedel soon realized the machine was far from foolproof. To begin with, a tired suspect would often cease to react when he told a lie; he had used up all his adrenalin. Riedel made it a rule never to question a suspect for more than three minutes without allowing him a break. He also realized that other kinds of tension—such as heat or the sound of a telephone—could confuse the issue, so he always insisted that a suspect should be questioned in a comfortable, well-lit, well-ventilated room, with no telephone and no one allowed to enter. He learned the importance of getting to know about the suspect's background and social standing, for these could offer important clues on how he should be handled. It was also of vital importance that a question should be quite unambiguous. Finally, Riedel made a habit of mixing relevant and irrelevant questions, so he could note the difference in response. His technique was taught at the Berkeley Police School, and finally became the standard method all over the world.

There were, nevertheless, still problems. A madman who was asked whether he was Napoleon said no, and the machine registered a lie. Clearly, the mind could influence the reading. And in 1935, a widely publicized murder caused a loss of confidence in the efficiency of the lie detector. On June 17, the body of a girl was found in a ditch in the cemetery of Peoria, Illinois. She was identified as 19-year-old Mildred Hallmark, and her neck had been broken in the course of violent strangulation; lying near the body was underwear that had been cut off with a pair of scissors. As a result of newspaper publicity, 25 girls came forward to say that they had been raped by a man who was young, good-looking, and very strong.

Five days after the murder, another girl came to the police headquarters with the same story. She had been waiting for a bus when a charming and clean-cut young man offered her a lift; he seemed so polite that she felt sure she could trust him. He chatted as they drove along, and he said that his name was Lee Bridges. But in a quiet lane, he stopped and grabbed her. She fought back and he hit her under the jaw again and again, holding her neck with the other hand; finally, when she was stunned and submissive, he raped her, cutting off her clothes with scissors. Sobbing, she told him that she would go to the police as soon as he released her; at this, Bridges dragged her in front of the car, threw her down on the road, turned on the headlights, and took photographs of her with a box camera. He told her that if she reported the rape, he would send copies to her friends and neighbors. Then he allowed her to dress in her torn clothes, and dropped her off a block from her home.

This was six months ago, and she had never reported the rape. But two months later, at a dance, she had been introduced to a man who looked just like the rapist. When she asked him if they had met before, he denied it, and gave his name as Jerry Thompson, and said that he lived with his grandparents in East Peoria. But the girl was sure he was the rapist. And now she had decided to come to the police.

The police called on Mildred Hallmark's father, who worked in a caterpillar tractor factory, and asked him if he knew a Lee Bridges or Jerry Thompson. "Oh sure I know Jerry—I work next to him." They asked him if Mildred also knew him. "Yes, he used to live a couple of blocks away."

The police lost no time in interviewing Gerald Thompson, a handsome, curly-haired man of 25. He flatly denied the rapes, even when the girl picked him out unhesitatingly in a line-up. Asked if he would take a polygraph test, Thompson agreed readily. Fred Imbau, the lie detector expert, wired him up to his machine. Asked if he had killed Mildred, Thompson replied "No," and the needle remained steady, indicating that he was telling the truth.

But a search of the house where Thompson lived with his grandparents left no doubt of his guilt. The police not only found the photographs of naked girls that proved he was the Peoria rapist; they also found a bloodstained car cushion and bloodstained trousers. Tested in the laboratory, they proved to be of the same blood type as Mildred Hallmark. Faced with this evidence, Thompson finally confessed. He had offered Mildred a lift, and she had accepted because she knew him. When he took her to the cemetery where he had taken so many previous victims, she fought savagely, scratching his face—scratches he still bore when questioned. He had beaten and throttled her into submission, then realized that he had broken her neck. So he tossed the body into a ditch and drove off. When a collection was taken at the factory for the dead girl's funeral, Thompson gave generously.

Public outrage led the police to transfer Thompson out of town to prevent him from being lynched. On July 30, 1935, he was sentenced to death, and on October 15, he was electrocuted. But before he died, he told how he had deceived the lie detector. When asked if he had murdered Mildred, he had simply thought of another Mildred, and the polygraph had registered that he was telling the truth . . .

In fact, Leonarde Keeler admitted that he had learned to deceive his own lie detector by various techniques. It demanded, obviously, a remarkable degree of self-control. But it could be done. (In 1960, a multiple killer named Chester Weger, who had murdered three women in a state park, passed lie detector tests twice by washing down aspirins with Coca Cola before he took the tests.) What was altogether more serious was that innocent suspects might well register as guilty because they were so nervous. This happened in the 1950s in the case of a suspect named Paul Altheide, convicted of murdering a tailor in Phoenix, Arizona, although he protested that he was in Texas at the time. His polygraph test so clearly proclaimed his guilt that the police did not bother to check his alibi. But a reporter named Gene McLain went to Texas, and discovered that the alibi was genuine; Altheide was released after serving four months of his sentence. Cases such as this led J. Edgar Hoover to denounce the lie detector as thoroughly unreliable, and after 1923—when a man named Frye tried to introduce his polygraph test to prove his innocence of murder, and was refused—polygraph evidence became inadmissible in most American courts. (It can be used only if both sides agree, or the judge demands it.)

Chris Gugas, founder of the National Board of Polygraph Examiners, argues passionately that this is unfair. In *The Silent Witness* (1979), he points out that modern leaps in technology mean that the polygraph is now almost infallible; a study of 4,280 criminals in the 1950s revealed that the accuracy of the polygraph—provided it was used by a trained expert—was 95 per cent.

Gugas's casebook makes fascinating reading because it becomes clear that the lie detector is as important in the establishment of innocence as of guilt. He tells, for example, the story of a well-known actor who was charged with exposing himself to schoolgirls. The schoolgirls claimed that he had parked near their school—in Hollywood—opened the car door, and masturbated himself. The actor agreed that he had driven around the school that day, looking for the home of a friend. But he had not stopped the car. The police had shown the schoolgirls several photographs, including that of the actor, and two of them had immediately picked him out. There could be no doubt that it looked bad.

Gugas was approached by the actor's lawyer, and submitted him to a polygraph test. It showed him that the actor was telling the truth. He was, in fact, a rather prudish man, with almost Victorian morals, and this accusation had shattered him.

Gugas reasoned that the girls who had identified him had seen his face on the television or in movies; he was not a famous star, but one of those faces that everyone knows in secondary roles. And when Gugas learned that the actor always had to wear glasses when driving, he asked him to accompany him to the homes of the girls. At the first one, he introduced the actor as his associate, then questioned the young girl about the man who had exposed himself. Would she recognize him if she saw him again? She was emphatic: she would never forget that face . . . Gugas pointed to his associate. "Was he anything like Mr. Jones?" The girl shook her head. "No. He was like that photograph the police showed me." The photograph was without the driving glasses that the actor was now wearing.

The result at two more homes was the same; the girls failed to recognize Gugas's bespectacled associate as the "flasher." The fourth girl's mother refused to allow them to see her.

Gugas had recorded the interviews; when he played them to the public prosecutor the next day, the case was dropped.

Gugas makes it clear that the lie detector can do far more than detect lies. After the Second World War, he was sent to a Greek seaport to train local police in the new methods of crime detection (Gugas is Greek by birth). The Chief of Police was convinced that the lie detector was a waste of time. Gugas agreed to demonstrate, and set out to make it as dramatic as possible. He chose three men at random and told them that one of them was to play the part of a pickpocket and steal a wallet. Another three men were to agree privately on a certain color. Finally, he told the police chief that the polygraph would tell him the name of his mother. Then Gugas left the room for five minutes. When he returned, he tested the first group of three, then the second—in this case simply running through a list of colors. In neither case did he reveal his results. Then he attached the machine to the police chief, and read out a list of the names of Greek women. He got a strong reaction to two names—although one was weaker than the other. When it was over, he pretended to be unsure of himself. The police chief chuckled. "The Nazis could get nothing out of me. How could I be intimidated by a few knobs and wires? Now give us your results."

Gugas pointed at one of the first group. "You stole the wallet." The man nodded. Gugas turned to the second group. "The color was red, wasn't it?" There was a murmur of superstitious astonishment as they admitted it. Then Gugas turned to the police chief. "Your mother's name is Helena." The chief stared with incredulity. Finally he said: "But I thought only of the name of my grandmother." "Oh, I know that too. It was Maria, wasn't it?" He was right. After that, he encountered no more incredulity.

At the end of his term in the seaport, Gugas produced his most conclusive demonstration. A powerful local politician named Petroklos was making life difficult for the police because his wife had disappeared. Gugas learned, to his astonishment, that they had not even questioned the politician—

the man was too powerful and respected. He persuaded some police officers to accompany him to Petroklos's house, where the man agreed to answer some innocuous questions about his wife's habits, but announced: "The interview is at an end" when Gugas asked whether they had quarreled.

Gugas learned that Petroklos had a mistress, and went to interview her. The result was an angry call from Petroklos's lawyer, and an interview with the American consul in which Gugas was warned to "lay off." He ignored the warning, and went on probing. When he learned that Petroklos's wife had owned a remote estate, now deserted, he sent police photographers out to take as many pictures as possible. Then he asked Petroklos's lawyer if he could interview his client again. The lawyer refused. But Petroklos finally came of his own accord when Gugas promised to get off the case. When Gugas held out the photographs, Petroklos tried to take them; Gugas refused, saying that he first wanted to connect him up to the polygraph. Petroklos finally agreed, on condition that he would be asked no questions. Gugas said he had no intention of asking questions. And when Petroklos was connected to the machine, he showed him the photographs one by one. When they came to the stable building, there was an unmistakable reaction. Gugas completed the test, shook Petroklos by the hand, and said he would be in touch when he had analyzed his results. He restrained an impulse to say "I think we have solved your wife's disappearance," sensing that this would be dangerous as well as reckless.

Hours later, the police were digging up the half-decomposed body in the stable. Petroklos was charged with the murder of his wife, and later convicted. Gugas kept in the background, allowing the full credit to go to the local police.

————————— 5 —————————

Gugas's evidence makes one thing very clear: that as an instrument of scientific crime detection, the polygraph is as important as the microscope or the spectroscope. It is not 100 per cent reliable; but then, as we have seen in the course of this book, neither is any other technique of forensic science. But a machine that, in the hands of a skilled operator, is 95 per cent reliable is as valuable—in the all-important department of labor saving—as the police computer or the fingerprint file.

There is, admittedly, a purely practical problem. Even in the mid-1970s, the cost of a lie detector from the Leonarde Keeler Institute in Chicago, and of training an operator to use it, was a minimum of $5,000; a decade later it had more than doubled. This is why, in the winter of 1972, Police Chief Raymond Beary of Winter Park, Florida, requested two of his lieutenants to attend a seminar which a Los Angeles hypnotist, Dr. William Bryan, would be conducting in Tampa.

In deciding to send them, Beary was undoubtedly recalling a remarkable case of 1956 which had been solved by hypnosis. On February 2, a patrolman in a radio car on Biscaya Island, near Miami Beach, saw a body on a vacant lot near the sea. It proved to be that of an attractive brunette in her late teens or early 20s; she wore a bright red dress, and had been stabbed repeatedly. The pathologist established that she had died at about 3 a.m., although she may have been stabbed much earlier, and slowly bled to death. The first problem was to identify the body, and this was solved when her fingerprints were found in the files; she had once been detained in connection with a stolen car. She was 22-year-old Ruth Downing, a divorcee who had come to Florida looking for work. But even this failed to help the investigators. Her friends knew of no one who might have killed her, no regular boyfriends. Recently released sexual deviates were interviewed as a matter of course, but still no lead developed.

Lieutenant T. A. Buchanan of the homicide squad suspected that the killer was a man who had become known as the ''kiss or kill murderer,'' because he had approached a pretty secretary standing at a bus stop and asked for a kiss; when she refused, he had stabbed her in the throat. The man was obviously a mental case, since the incident had occurred at a busy street corner. A man of the same description—young and unshaven—had raped a young mother in the Miami area.

For two months police visited bars with a photograph of Ruth Downing. Finally, in April, a tavern employee recognized her. He had seen her leaving the bar with a young man some time around the night of the murder. The description of the youth reminded the officers of an occasional sex offender called Rudolph Valentino Herring, one of whose habits was to try to induce unwilling girls to fellate him. He was known to be mentally unbalanced. Suddenly, it struck Buchanan that Herring sounded exactly like the man they were looking for. The next problem was to find him, since he had no fixed address. It took days of old-fashioned sleuthing before he was finally located living in an abandoned shack. When asked if he had murdered Ruth Downing, he shrugged and replied that he did not remember. But this was not just an excuse. He insisted that his mind was a blank, and that if the police could help him to restore his memory, he would willingly tell them anything he knew. Buchanan asked if he was willing to be hypnotized, and Herring agreed.

The hypnotist chosen was Dr. Julien Arroyo, head of the Arroyo Academy of Advanced Hypnosis. The following morning, Arroyo succeeded in hypnotizing Herring, who proved to be a cooperative patient. And under hypnosis, Herring readily admitted his murder of Ruth Downing, whom he knew as Renée. He had met the divorcee casually, and the two had done some drinking together. On the evening of the murder, they had left the bar where her photograph had been recognized, and gone out to the vacant lot, known as a "lovers' lane." The girl had obviously been willing to have normal sexual intercourse, but when Herring demanded fellatio, she refused indignantly; he had pulled out a knife and stabbed her, then hitchhiked back home.

Herring went on to confess to the rape of the young

mother, and to stabbing the secretary in the throat when she refused to kiss him. In fact, he admitted that he had committed between 30 and 40 rapes, and that he had an inexplicable hatred of women.

Herring had a long police record for burglary, robbery, and attempted rape, and had been a patient in the Chattahoochee State Hospital. A month earlier, an attempt had been made to return him there, but a judge had decided he was mentally competent.

For the police, the chief problem was that, now they had a confession, they still had only half a case. Florida had no cases in which a confession had been obtained by hypnosis; like the lie detector, such evidence would probably be inadmissible in court. After all, it might be argued that Herring was simply highly suggestible, and had agreed to whatever the hypnotist had wanted him to say. The problem was eventually solved by having him examined by a panel of psychiatrists, who decided that his mental state warranted a re-committal to the Chattahoochee State Hospital.

Such a result was obviously unsatisfactory, and probably explained why there was no further attempt to use hypnosis in Florida until Dr. William Bryan came to lecture in Tampa in 1972. Two police lieutenants, Avery and Aurbeck, were asked to attend. And, to Police Chief Beary's surprise, they returned in a state of enthusiasm. Bryan had lectured on the use of hypnosis to solve certain plane crashes; when the pilot and some passengers had been hypnotized, they had been able to provide vital information which had been blotted from their memories by the trauma of the crash. Bryan had also revealed that he had played a vital part in the case of the Boston Strangler. When a patient in the Bridgewater State Hospital had told a fellow patient that he was the Strangler, the authorities were dubious; they thought it could be fantasy. The fellow patient's lawyer, F. Lee Bailey, interviewed the self-confessed Strangler, Albert DeSalvo, and persuaded the hospital authorities to allow him to be hypnotized. Dr. Bryan was the man chosen. Before an audience of psychiatrists and detectives, he had placed his hands gently on DeSalvo's powerful shoulders, and spoken softly and coaxingly, until DeSalvo's eyes closed. Then he had told him that, as soon as he entered the trance, his right arm would become rigid and lose all feeling. Suddenly, DeSalvo's arm stiffened, the outstretched fingers pointing at the ceiling. Bryan ran a needle into the flesh; DeSalvo did not flinch, and when the needle was withdrawn, no blood came out. That convinced the audience he was not shamming. Then Bryan began asking DeSalvo about the eleventh murder victim, 68-year-old Evelyn Corbin. DeSalvo described how he had entered the apartment by posing as a building superintendent sent to repair a broken bathroom fixture, how he had coaxed the woman onto the bed, how she had refused to allow him to have sexual intercourse, and how he had strangled her. After this, Dr. Bryan took DeSalvo back to the beginning, and extracted a confession that was so full of detail that was unknown to the general public that his guilt was established beyond all doubt . . .

Police Lieutenants Avery and Aurbeck had no doubt that hypnosis could help to solve crime; Police Chief Beary was more skeptical; how could they be sure that a subject was under hypnosis and not shamming, how could they be sure that a ''confession'' was not the result of suggestion? The lieutenants begged to try it out, and Ron Avery began experimenting on his family and colleagues until everyone was sick of hearing about hypnosis. He attended a hypnosis training course in Orlando. And finally, he had a chance to try his skill. A young man had been arrested, accused of sexual assault on a 14-year-old girl. She claimed that she had been on her way to work in a local hamburger restaurant when the youth had forced her into his car, driven her to a remote spot, and forced her to perform fellatio. He had also beaten her and thrown her out of the car near her home. Her story was reinforced by the fact that she *had* been beaten.

The youth, who was 18, had a different story. He claimed that he knew the girl as a ''hot little number,'' and had offered her a lift when he saw her at a bus stop. They had driven to a quiet spot and engaged in heavy petting; but the girl had refused to allow him sexual intercourse, and slapped him when he offered her money. He had then hit her, and she began crying. Eventually, as he apologized and comforted her, she softened and they began petting again; this time she performed fellatio. When he dropped her off at home, she was worried that she had missed work and it was late; he advised her to invent some story.

Avery talked to the girl's mother, and asked her permission to hypnotize her daughter; the mother agreed. Then Avery placed her under hypnosis and asked her if she was a virgin; she said no. He asked how many times she had had intercourse, and she admitted she didn't know. When Avery went on to question her about the incident in the car, her story tallied exactly with that of the boy. She had invented the story about the rape to excuse her lateness and the fact that she had missed work. The result was that the boy received a six-month suspended sentence for intercourse with a minor, while the girl was subjected to stricter parental supervision.

-------- **6** --------

Doubts about the use of hypnosis in criminal cases are understandable; for more than a century now, there has been a widespread belief that a person cannot be hypnotized to do something that he or she finds disagreeable. In that case, it seems obvious that a criminal could not be induced to confess "against his will." In fact, this notion is based on a failure to understand the nature of hypnosis. When a patient is hypnotized, a part of the mind goes to sleep, and so do certain inhibitory mechanisms. But normal "defense mechanisms" remain active. A medical student who was a pupil of the great Charcot once placed a girl under hypnosis in front of a class, and ordered her to remove her clothes; she immediately came out of the trance. But if he had told her that she was in her bedroom, and ordered her to prepare herself for sleep, she would almost certainly have undressed. The hypnotist's problem is simply to find a way of slipping below the patient's "threshold of resistance." It has been proved repeatedly that a hypnotized subject can be induced to harm other people. In the mid-1930s, a crook named Franz Walter hypnotized a woman he met on a train, induced her to work for him as a prostitute, and finally ordered her to kill her husband by tampering with the brakes on his car. The husband became suspicious after her sixth attempt and went to the police. Dr. Ludwig Mayer, a psychologist, placed the woman under hypnosis, and learned that the previous hypnotist had imposed certain "blocks" to prevent her confessing. With skill and patience, he succeeded in slipping below this "resistance threshold" and getting the full story; Walter was sentenced to 10 years in jail.

The strangest of post-war murder cases began on March 29, 1951, when a young man in overalls entered a Copenhagen bank and in the course of a hold-up shot dead the cashier and manager; he then walked out and escaped on a bicycle. An alert youth leapt on his own bicycle and followed him; within an hour, the police had arrested a 29-year-old man named Palle Hardrup, who immediately confessed to the robbery, and insisted that he had acted completely alone. But the police soon received a tip-off to the effect that Hardrup was completely under the domination of an older man, Bjorn Nielsen, whom he had met in prison when Hardrup was serving a sentence as a Nazi collaborator. The police psychiatrist, Dr. Max Schmidt, slowly came to the conclusion that Hardrup had been hypnotized, and the police learned that, while he was in jail, Nielsen could place him in a hypnotic trance simply by making an X-sign in chalk. When Nielsen was brought in for questioning, the police made the mistake of putting both men in the same room; Nielsen leaned forward on the desk, crossing his forearms, whereupon Hardrup instantly went into a blank, passive state and confirmed everything that Nielsen said.

Little by little, the police accumulated evidence that Nielsen had planned the robbery, as well as a previous one in which Hardrup had walked out of a bank with $61,000.

And in prison, Hardrup finally broke down and wrote a full confession revealing how Nielsen had achieved total hypnotic domination over him, and ordered him to commit the bank robberies—the profits of which went entirely to Nielsen. The task of studying the minds of both men was placed in the hands of Dr. Paul J. Reiter, whose work on the subject, *Antisocial or Criminal Acts and Hypnosis* (1958) has become a classic of psychology. Nielsen was sentenced to life imprisonment, Hardrup to detention in a criminal lunatic asylum.

The science of psychology has still failed to achieve a full understanding of hypnosis; the only thing that seems to be clear is that the normal conscious ego—the ''you''—is lulled into a form of sleep, while normal physical actions—walking, talking, and so on—become mechanical. The phenomenon was first recognized in 1780, when Armand Chastenet, the Marquis de Puységur—who happened to be a disciple of the celebrated Dr. Mesmer—was trying to cure a young peasant named Victor Race; he had tied him to a tree and was making passes with a magnet over his head (the theory being that Race's ''vital energies'' needed to be moved around his body). Suddenly, Race's gaze became blank, then his eyes closed. Yet when Puységur ordered him to untie himself, he did so. Puységur discovered that Race was an excellent hypnotic subject; moreover, when he was hypnotized, he would respond to Puységur's thoughts—for example, singing a song that Puységur was singing ''in his head.'' This seemed to show that while hypnosis placed the conscious ''self'' in a state of trance, it could enhance the powers of the unconscious part of the mind—for example, enabling the subject to retrieve forgotten memories.

This was the aspect of hypnosis that Police Lieutenant Ron Avery found most useful. In many rape cases, the trauma causes the victim to ''block out'' the details, so that she may not even be able to recall how many men were involved. Avery discovered that, under hypnosis, rape victims could often supply precise descriptions of the attacker, as well as recalling small details that helped to identify him.

A burglary victim was able to provide vital details about a burglar under hypnosis. Victims of car crashes were able to describe the cause of the crash in detail, although they had unconsciously repressed them. When a 17-year-old girl named Karen Chitwood was murdered in her apartment, Avery obtained precise descriptions of the suspected killer from witnesses under hypnosis, and as a result, was able to arrest Cecil Floyd, who confessed to the murder.

But it was not Avery, but two fellow investigators, who solved, by hypnosis, one of Florida's worst cases of mass murder. On February 22, 1972, two corpses were found in the cemetery at Wildwood, Florida, both victims of a violent knife attack. Detectives Don Plummer and Wayne Pierce—from Gainesville—were summoned to the scene. The victims lay near a parked car; the youth had been stabbed 43 times, the girl—who was naked from the waist down—had 31 knife wounds. The girl had apparently been stabbed on the nearby road, and had fled back to the car, chased by her attacker.

The girl was identified as a cashier and clerk in a truckers' overnight stop; her name was Shirley Whiddon, and she was 19. Her companion was an assistant truck driver named Roger Higgins. There seemed to be few clues. The man's trouser pocket had been ripped off, and the inside handle of the driver's door was bent. When the police tried to raise the bonnet of the car, it seemed to be stuck, and it took three men to raise it; they then discovered that it was held down by a home-made catch. The car tires were also slashed badly, demonstrating that the killer had been in a kind of frenzy. Shirley Whiddon had taken a break at three o'clock that morning, and gone off with Roger Higgins, who was regarded as her boyfriend.

Three weeks later, Plummer had followed up every lead, and the investigation was at a standstill. At this point, he opened the morning's mail, and saw a wanted notice from Charlotte, North Carolina. The wanted man had murdered the man and woman with whom he was boarding, shooting them with a pistol. His name was Karl de Gregory, and he was believed to be living in Ormond Beach. What struck Plummer was that the killer had shown the same kind of maniacal frenzy in killing the Charlotte couple that the Wildwood cemetery murderer had displayed. Plummer drove to Ormond Beach, made enquiries, and finally located Karl de Gregory, a man of 27 who spoke with a French accent. He was a salesman for a chemical firm in Daytona Beach, a married man with a wife and two children. He flatly denied any knowledge of either the Charlotte crime or the Wildwood cemetery murders. Since he seemed a pleasant and open young man, Plummer was half-inclined to believe him.

But nine days after his arrest, de Gregory suddenly changed his mind. He admitted that he had killed the couple in the cemetery. According to de Gregory, he had left home after a quarrel with his wife, driven aimlessly for hours, and ended at the truck-stop at Wildwood. He saw a couple embracing in a corner of the building; then they climbed into a car and drove off. De Gregory followed them to the cemetery, and stabbed them both to death.

Plummer was not entirely happy about this story. There were some internal discrepancies. Could it be that de Gregory was *not* the murderer of the young couple, but was merely confessing to it for his own advantage? North Carolina law makes no allowance for "temporary insanity," so the charge there could lead to life imprisonment or a death sentence. In Florida, he might succeed in getting himself committed to an institution for the criminally insane . . .

Plummer's first thought was the lie detector. The nearest one was in Tallahassee, and an expert came over to interview de Gregory. As he left the room he said: "He's your man." But lie detector evidence was inadmissible in court. Plummer called upon the Ormond Beach psychologist Dr. Ann MacMillan—who was later to play an important part in the case of Gerald Stano—and asked her to examine de Gregory. She spent two hours talking to de Gregory, and when she left his cell, her face was pale. "He's a killer all right. He may be guilty of as many as twenty-two murders."

But for the moment, Plummer had no desire to get

sidetracked into any other crimes de Gregory might have committed. He could think of only one solution: to try hypnosis. Dr. Joe B. McCawley agreed to undertake the case. And in front of Don Plummer, Wayne Pierce and de Gregory's attorney, he set out to place the accused killer in a trance. The detectives knew he had succeeded when McCawley asked de Gregory his name. The voice that replied no longer had a French accent; instead, a deep southern drawl replied: "Carl D. Gregory." He went on to tell how he had run away from home at the age of 16, had taught himself French (although he was a high school dropout) and acquired foreign papers which showed him to be a French national who was discharged from the American Air Force with the rank of captain; this had enabled him to obtain an excellent job with the Daytona Beach chemical company. He explained that he had shot the couple in Charlotte because the woman had kissed him, and that proved she was a "bad woman."

His description of the cemetery murder left Plummer in no doubt that Gregory was the killer. He described how he had halted at the truck-stop at Wildwood, left his car, and seen the young couple kissing. This, he said, proved that she was also a "bad woman." In fact, it seemed clear that he had followed them with the intention of playing the part of a Peeping Tom. It was, Gregory claimed, his "brother" who took over when he went into a maniacal frenzy. He had watched the two kissing and "fooling around," then pulled open the driver's door and started to stab the boy. As he dragged him out of the car, Higgins's pocket had caught on the inside handle, and bent it, tearing off the pocket—just as the detectives had observed. The girl had run away screaming, with Gregory stalking her. She ran back to the car, and, afraid that she might drive away, Gregory tried to raise the bonnet to disable the engine. It refused to move, so he decided to slash the tires. After that, he chased the girl to the road, where he stabbed her repeatedly. Then he dragged her body back to the car, leaving it by the body of Roger Higgins.

Ann MacMillan had mentioned a possible 22 other murders. Under hypnosis, Gregory confessed to only three, but in such detail that there could be no doubt of his guilt. After all this, he was extradited back to North Carolina, where he was indicted for the double killing, and received two life sentences, to run consecutively. It was the first mass murder case in Florida history in which hypnosis had played a vital part.

7

Such cases make it clear that the modern detective is faced with a completely new type of problem. From Fielding to Bertillon, the criminal pursued his uncomplicated ends with uncomplicated animal cunning, and the problem of the detective was simplified by the straightforwardness of the motive. Until the late nineteenth century, most crimes were committed for profit—with the exception of the occasional *crime passionnel*. With the Jack the Ripper murders, this ceased to be true; the Whitechapel killer was the first of a new type of sadistic mass murderer. Fortunately, the Joseph Vachers, Earle Nelsons, and Peter Kürtens remained a rarity; their victims comprised an insignificant percentage of the murder statistics. But in the 1970s, the American police suddenly became aware that this had ceased to be true. The proportion of random killings had risen from 6 per cent in the mid-1960s to 18 per cent in the mid-1970s, a total of more than 4,000 cases a year. Moreover, the solution rate for homicides, which had been about 90 per cent immediately after the Second World War, continued to fall until it was down to 76 per cent by 1983. This was not due to the inefficiency of the police, but to the fact that, as we have seen, a murder is solved by tracing a link between victim and killer. If no such link exists, then the case can be solved only by chance. The rise in the rate of unsolved murders suggested an increasing number of crimes in which there was no connection between killer and victim.

It is difficult to name any specific case that alerted police

to the existence of the new problem. The crimes of the
Boston Strangler, the Manson family, "Zodiac," John Linley
Frazier, and Herb Mullin were treated as the individual
aberrations of "wierdos." But in 1973, the murder of a
homosexual named Dean Corll by his 17-year-old lover
Elmer Wayne Henley led to the discovery of the bodies of
27 teenage boys in Houston, Texas, and to the realization
that Corll had been raping and murdering boys for the past
three years. The sheer number of victims—more than 30 in
all—suggested that for Dean Corll, murder had ceased to be
a catharsis, a release of tension, and had become a *habit*,
like smoking. And throughout the 1970s, it became clear
that this applied to an increasing number of killers. In June
1972, a supermarket hold-up in Santa Barbara resulted in
the arrest of a man named Sherman McCrary, his teenage
son Danny and his son-in-law Carl Taylor; as police investigated the activities of this "nomadic" family—which included McCrary's wife, daughter, and three grandchildren—
they realized that they had left a trail of at least 22 bodies
from Texas to California, most of them shop assistants and
waitresses who had been abducted in the course of robbery,
then raped and murdered. A murderer who raped and
mutilated more than 40 teenage boys, then dumped their
bodies beside California highways, became known as the
Freeway Killer; in December 1981, a man named William
Bonin, who admitted that he "threw away bodies like
garbage," was sentenced to death. Randall Woodfield,
known as the "I.5 killer," raped and murdered an unknown
number of girls as he traveled up and down the Interstate 5
highway between California, Oregon, and Washington State.
And in Chicago in 1978, police found the bodies of 27
teenage boys under the floors in the house of a contractor
named John Wayne Gacy, who later confessed to murdering
and raping 31 young men. Such killings were not confined
to North America. In April 1980, a swollen river near
Ambato, in Ecuador, overflowed its banks and uncovered
the corpses of four pre-pubescent girls; a few days later, a
31-year-old vagrant named Pedro Alonzo Lopez was arrested

when trying to abduct an 11-year-old girl; Lopez later confessed to the murder of about 350 girls between 1978 and 1980, most of them Indians. In 1983, discovery of decaying flesh in a drain in Muswell Hill, north London, led to the arrest of an employment officer named Dennis Nilsen, and to his confession to the murder and dismemberment of 16 young men in the past five years. In 1986, a Colombian named Daniel Camargo Barbosa was arrested in Quito, Ecuador, with blood on his clothing, and subsequently admitted to killing 72 pre-pubescent girls in the past year; he was sentenced to 16 years, the maximum penalty in Ecuador. At about the same time the Soviet news agency Tass announced that a Soviet man would go on trial for the murders of 33 women around the Byelorussian city of Vitebsk.

The case that made the American public aware of the existence of serial killers began in June 1983, when a preacher named Reuben Moore—who ran a small fundamentalist sect called the House of Prayer in Stoneberg, Texas—reported to the police that a member of his flock was in possession of a gun; since the man in question— Henry Lee Lucas—was an ex-convict, this was a felony. Lucas was an unprepossessing individual with a glass eye and a downturned mouth, who looked as if he had stepped out of a horror movie, and it was probably his appearance as much as his subsequent confession to 360 murders, that led to the widespread morbid interest in his career. In the following months he often retracted and then repeated his confession, leading to widespread doubts about the precise figure; but the recovery of several bodies at sites indicated by Lucas demonstrated that it was not entirely fantasy.

It became clear that, from the beginning, Lucas had been a "loser." The child of alcoholic parents, he was continually beaten and abused by his mother, a Chippewa Indian who was also a prostitute; she had once hit him so hard with a piece of wood that she caused brain damage. His father had lost both legs in a railway accident, and had subsequently been thrown out of his home and left to freeze to death. In

1960, when he was 23, Lucas had stabbed and raped his mother, then left her to die; for this he was sentenced to 40 years in prison. But he had committed his first murder at the age of 15, when he tried to rape a 17-year-old girl at a bus stop, and strangled her when she resisted.

After several suicide attempts, Lucas was committed to a mental hospital; recommended for parole in 1970, he warned the prison authorities that he would go on killing after his release; they nevertheless discharged him. Lucas told them: "I'll leave you a present on the doorstep" and on the day he was released, he killed a woman in Jackson, only a few miles down the road—a murder that remained unsolved until his subsequent confession. For the next 13 years Lucas went on a killing spree—during the latter years accompanied by another vagrant named Ottis Elwood Toole, whose own sexual preference was for children, whom he raped, tortured, and murdered; Lucas later claimed that he had crucified some victims and "filleted others like a fish." His statements about motive bring Carl Panzram to mind: "I was bitter at the world," said Lucas, "I had nothing but pure hatred. Killing someone is just like walking outdoors. If I wanted a victim, I'd just go get one."

Newspaper accounts of Lucas and Toole led to a spate of publicity about "serial killers," and one police officer speculated that there could be as many as 35 killers at large in America, and that the number could be increasing at the rate of one a month. In 1984 the FBI admitted that there was an "epidemic" of serial murders in America. When a psychologist, Joel Norris, began to study the case of Wayne Williams, the black youth accused of 28 child murders in Atlanta, he realized that there were no fewer than six other less publicized cases of serial murder in Georgia alone, and dozens throughout America. And in a subsequent book on serial killers, Norris admitted that he could see no obvious solution to the problem. He noted that the majority of serial killers are "physically and psychologically damaged people . . . Almost all of them had scars on their bodies, missing fingers, evidence of previous contusions and multiple abrasions on and around the head and neck area." And he points out that demands for vengeance and retribution are counterproductive. "Perversely, he wishes for death, and the threat of the gas chamber, the electric chair or the lethal injection is only an inducement to keep committing murders until he is caught and put to death." For: "he is suffering from a disease that is terminal, not only for his numerous victims but also for himself. He is his ultimate victim. On his own initiative, the serial killer can no more stop killing than a heroin addict can kick the habit."

All this would seem to suggest that the problem of serial killers is virtually insoluble—at least, until some great social transformation has created a society in which there are no alcoholic parents or abused children. Yet Norris and his associates believe that "most forms of episodic aggression— including serial murder—could be prevented through an organized program of testing and diagnosis and intervention." This is because "as our understanding of the serial killer syndrome developed, we realized that these profiles could lead to the development of a diagnostic or prediction instrument that would identify individuals who might be at risk. . . ." Many serial killers, he points out, have sustained severe head injuries (Earle Nelson is an obvious example); most have had emotionally traumatic childhoods, with lack of maternal affection; many are the unwanted children of alcoholic or drug-addicted parents. And, oddly enough, many have "obvious physical and congenital defects such as webbed fingers, attached ear lobes, elongated limbs, and other abnormalities," an interesting, if belated, confirmation of some of Lombroso's observations.

Yet Norris goes on to undermine his own theory by asking: "Do all people who sustain head traumas become murderers? Do all people who hate women become murderers? Do all people who sustain chronic physical abuse as children become murderers?" The obvious answer is no. Then wherein lies the difference? Norris touches upon an important clue when he speaks of what he calls "the mask of sanity," "manifested through grandiosity or a belief in his own superhuman importance.'' But this makes it sound as though such individuals are paranoiacs who suffer from delusions of grandeur. The truth is simpler: that many serial killers not only appear to be normal members of society, but even seem to be model citizens of more-than-average achievement. John Gacy was a highly successful building contractor who canvassed for the Democrats and was photographed shaking hands with Mrs. Jimmy Carter. Wayne Williams ran his own advertising agency and was featured in local newspapers and television programs. Gerald Schaefer, a Florida serial killer suspected of the murder of 28 girls, was a high school teacher, a deputy policeman and a member of the local golf club. And Ted Bundy, one of the most widely publicized serial killers of the 1970s, was a law student who had worked for the Crime Commission and the Office of Justice Planning, and had been a highly regarded volunteer on the staff of the local Democratic candidate. The Bundy case offers an important insight into this aspect of the psychology of the serial killer.

_____ 8 _____

On January 31, 1974, a student at the University of Washington, in Seattle, Lynda Ann Healy, vanished from her room; the bedsheets were bloodstained, suggesting that she had been struck violently on the head. During the following March, April, and May, three more girl students vanished; in June, two more. In July, two girls vanished on the same day. It happened at a popular picnic spot, Lake Sammanish; a number of people saw a good-looking young man, with his arm in a sling, accost a girl named Janice Ott and ask her to help him lift a boat onto the roof of his car; she walked away with him and did not return. Later, a girl named Denise Naslund was accosted by the same young man; she also vanished. He had been heard to introduce himself as "Ted."

In October 1974 the killings shifted to Salt Lake City;

three girls disappeared in one month. In November, the police had their first break in the case: a girl named Carol DaRonch was accosted in a shopping center by a young man who identified himself as a detective, and told her that there had been an attempt to break into her car; she agreed to accompany him to headquarters to view a suspect. In the car he snapped a handcuff on her wrist and pointed a gun at her head; she fought and screamed, and managed to jump from the car. That evening, a girl student vanished on her way to meet her brother. A handcuff key was found near the place from which she had been taken.

Meanwhile, the Seattle police had fixed on a young man named Ted Bundy as a main suspect. For the past six years, he had been involved in a close relationship with a divorcee named Meg Anders, but she had called off the marriage when she realized he was a habitual thief. After the Lake Sammanish disappearances, she had seen a photofit drawing of the wanted "Ted" in the *Seattle Times* and thought it looked like Bundy; moreover, "Ted" drove a Volkswagen like Bundy's. She had seen crutches and plaster of Paris in Bundy's room, and the coincidence seemed too great; with immense misgivings, she telephoned the police. They told her that they had already checked on Bundy; but at the suggestion of the Seattle police, Carol DaRonch was shown Bundy's photograph. She tentatively identified it as resembling the man who had tried to abduct her, but was obviously far from sure. (Bundy had been wearing a beard at the time.)

In January, March, April, July, and August 1975, more girls vanished in Colorado. (Their bodies—or skeletons— were found later in remote spots.) On August 16, 1975, Bundy was arrested for the first time. As a police car was driving along a dark street in Salt Lake City, a parked Volkswagen launched into motion; the policeman followed, and it accelerated. He caught up with the car at a service station, and found in the car a pantyhose mask, a crowbar, an icepick and various other tools; there was also a pair of handcuffs.

Bundy, 29 years old, seemed an unlikely burglar. He was a graduate of the University of Washington, and was in Utah to study law; he had worked as a political campaigner, and for the Crime Commission in Seattle. In his room there was nothing suspicious—except maps and brochures of Colorado, from which five girls had vanished that year. But strands of hair were found in the car, and they proved to be identical with those of Melissa Smith, daughter of the Midvale police chief, who had vanished in the previous October. Carol DaRonch had meanwhile identified Bundy in a police line-up as the fake policeman, and bloodspots on her clothes—where she had scratched her assailant—were of Bundy's group. Credit card receipts showed that Bundy had been close to various places from which girls had vanished in Colorado.

In theory, this should have been the end of the case—and if it had been, it would have been regarded as a typical triumph of scientific detection, beginning with the photofit drawing and concluding with the hair and blood evidence. The evidence was, admittedly, circumstantial, but taken all together, it formed a powerful case. The central objection to it became apparent as soon as Bundy walked into court. He looked so obviously decent and clean-cut that most people felt there must be some mistake. He was polite, well-spoken, articulate, charming, the kind of man who could have found himself a girlfriend for each night of the week. Why *should* such a man be a sex killer? In spite of which, the impression he made was of brilliance and plausibility rather than innocence. For example, he insisted that he had driven away from the police car because he was smoking marijuana, and that he had thrown the joint out the window.

The case seemed to be balanced on a knife-edge—until the judge pronounced a sentence of guilty of kidnapping. Bundy sobbed and pleaded not to be sent to prison; but the judge sentenced him to a period between 1 and 15 years.

The Colorado authorities now charged him with the murder of a girl called Caryn Campbell, who had been abducted from a ski resort where Bundy had been seen by a witness. After a morning courtroom session in Aspen, Bundy succeeded in wandering into the library during the lunch recess, and jumping out the window. He was recaptured eight days later, tired and hungry, and driving a stolen car.

Legal arguments dragged on for another six months— what evidence was admissible and what was not. And on December 30, 1977, Bundy escaped again, using a hacksaw blade to cut through an imperfectly welded steel plate above the light fixture in his cell. He made his way to Chicago, then south to Florida; there, near the Florida State University in Tallahassee, he took a room. A few days later, a man broke into a nearby sorority house and attacked four girls with a club, knocking them unconscious; one was strangled with her pantyhose and raped; another died on her way to hospital. One of the strangled girl's nipples had been almost bitten off, and she had a bite mark on her left buttock. An hour and a half later, a student woke up in another sorority house when she heard bangs next door, and a girl whimpering. She dialed the number of the room, and as the telephone rang, someone could be heard running out. Cheryl Thomas was found lying in bed, her skull fractured but still alive.

Three weeks later, on February 6, 1978, Bundy—who was calling himself Chris Hagen—stole a white Dodge van and left Tallahassee; he stayed in the Holiday Inn, using a stolen credit card. The following day a 12-year-old girl named Kimberley Leach walked out of her classroom in Lake City, Florida, and vanished. Bundy returned to Tallahassee to take a girl out for an expensive meal—paid for with a stolen credit card—then absconded via the fire escape, owing large arrears of rent. At 4 a.m. on February 15, a police patrolman noticed an orange Volkswagen driving suspiciously slowly, and radioed for a check on its number; it proved to be stolen from Tallahassee. After a struggle and a chase, during which he tried to kill the policeman, Bundy was captured yet again. When the police learned his real name, and that he had just left a town in which five girls had been attacked, they suddenly understood the importance of their capture. Bundy seemed glad to be in custody, and began to unburden himself. He explained that "his problem" had begun when he had seen a girl on a bicycle in Seattle, and "had to have her." He had followed her, but she escaped. "Sometimes," he admitted, "I feel like a vampire."

On April 7, a party of searchers along the Suwanee River found the body of Kimberley Leach in an abandoned hut; she had been strangled and sexually violated. Three weeks later, surrounded by hefty guards, Bundy allowed impressions of his teeth to be taken, for comparison with the marks on the buttocks of the dead student, Lisa Levy.

Bundy's lawyers persuaded him to enter into "plea bargaining": in exchange for a guarantee of life imprisonment—rather than a death sentence—he would confess to the murders of Lisa Levy, Margaret Bowman, and Kimberley Leach. But Bundy changed his mind at the last moment and decided to sack his lawyers.

Bundy's trial began on 25 June 1979, and the evidence against him was damning; a witness who had seen him leaving the sorority house after the attacks; a pantyhose mask found in the room of Cheryl Thomas, which resembled the one found in Bundy's car; but above all, the fact that Bundy's teeth matched the marks on Lisa Levy's buttocks. The highly compromising taped interview with the Pensacola police was judged inadmissible in court because his lawyer had not been present. Bundy again dismissed his defense and took it over himself; the general impression was that he was trying to be too clever. The jury took only six hours to find him guilty on all counts. Judge Ed Cowart pronounced sentence of death by electrocution, but evidently felt some sympathy for the good-looking young defendant. "It's a tragedy for this court to see such a total waste of humanity. You're a bright young man. You'd have made a good lawyer... But you went the wrong way, partner. Take care of yourself..."

Bundy was taken to Raiford prison, Florida, where he was placed on Death Row. On July 2, 1986, when he was due to die a few hours before Gerald Stano, both were granted a stay of execution.

The Bundy case illustrates the immense problems faced by investigators of serial murders. When Meg Anders—Bundy's mistress—telephoned the police after the double murder near Lake Sammanish, Bundy's name had already been suggested by three people. But he was only one of 3,500 suspects. Later Bundy was added to the list of 100 "best suspects" which investigators constructed on grounds of age, occupation, and past record. Two hundred thousand items were fed into computers, including the names of 41,000 Volkswagen owners, 5,000 men with a record of mental illness, every student who had taken classes with the dead girls, and all transfers from other colleges they had attended. All this was programmed into 37 categories, each using a different criterion to isolate the suspect. Asked to name anyone who came up on any three of these programs, the computer produced 16,000 names. When the number was raised to four, it was reduced to 600. Only when it was raised to 25 was it reduced to 10 suspects, with Bundy seventh on the list. The police were still investigating number six when Bundy was detained in Salt Lake City with burgling tools in his car. Only after that did Bundy become suspect number one. And by that time, he had already committed a minimum of 17 murders. (There seems to be some doubt about the total, estimates varying between 20 and 40; Bundy himself told the Pensacola investigators that it ran into double figures.) Detective Robert Keppel, who worked on the case, is certain that Bundy would have been revealed as suspect number one even if he had not been arrested. But in 1982, Keppel and his team were presented with another mass killer in the Seattle area, the so-called Green River Killer, whose victims were mostly prostitutes picked up on the "strip" in Seattle. Seven years later, in 1989, he has killed at least 49 women, and the computer has still failed to identify an obvious suspect number one.

The Bundy case is doubly baffling because he seems to contradict the basic assertions of every major criminologist from Lombroso to Yochelson. Bundy is not an obvious born criminal, with degenerate physical characteristics; there is (as far as is known) no history of insanity in his family; he was not a social derelict or a failure. In her book *The Stranger Beside Me*, his friend Ann Rule describes him as "a man of unusual accomplishment." How could the most subtle "psychological profiling" target such a man as a serial killer?

The answer to the riddle emerged fairly late in the day, four years after Bundy had been sentenced to death. Before his conviction, Bundy had 'indicated his willingness to co-operate on a book about himself, and two journalists, Stephen G. Michaud and Hugh Aynesworth, went to interview him in prison. They discovered that Bundy had no wish to discuss guilt, except to deny it, and he actively discouraged them from investigating the case against him. He wanted them to produce a gossipy book focusing squarely on himself, like bestselling biographies of celebrities such as Frank Sinatra. Michaud and Aynesworth would have been happy to write a book demonstrating his innocence, but as they looked into the case, they found it impossible to accept this; instead, they concluded that he had killed at least 21 girls. When they began to probe, Bundy revealed the characteristics that Yochelson and Samenow had found to be so typical of criminals: hedging, lying, pleas of faulty memory, and self-justification: "Intellectually, Ted seemed profoundly dissociative, a compartmentalizer, and thus a superb rationalizer." Emotionally, he struck them as a severe case of arrested development: "he might as well have been a twelve year old, and a precocious and bratty one at that. So extreme was his childishness that his pleas of innocence were of a character very similar to that of the little boy who'll deny wrongdoing in the face of overwhelming evidence to the contrary." So Michaud had the ingenious idea of suggesting that Bundy should "speculate on the nature of a person capable of doing what Ted had been accused (and convicted) of doing." Bundy embraced this idea with enthusiasm, and talked for hours into a tape recorder. Soon Michaud became aware that there were, in effect, two "Teds"—the analytical human being, and an entity inside him that Michaud came to call the "hunchback." (We have encountered this "other person"—Mr. Hyde—syndrome in many killers, from William Heirens and Peter Sutcliffe to Carl Gregory.)

After generalizing for some time about violence in modern society, the disintegration of the home, and so on, Bundy got down to specifics, and began to discuss his own development.

He had been an illegitimate child, born to a respectable young girl in Philadelphia. She moved to Seattle to escape the stigma, and married a cook in the Veterans' Hospital. Ted was an oversensitive and self-conscious child who had all the usual daydreams of fame and wealth. And at an early stage he became a thief and something of a habitual liar—as many imaginative children do. But he seems to have been deeply upset by the discovery of his illegitimacy.

Bundy was not, in fact, a brilliant student. Although he struck his fellow students as witty and cultivated, his grades were usually Bs. In his late teens he became heavily infatuated with a fellow student, Stephanie Brooks, who was beautiful, sophisticated, and came of a wealthy family. Oddly enough, she responded and they became "engaged." To impress her he went to Stanford University to study Chinese; but he felt lonely away from home, and his grades were poor. "I found myself thinking about standards of success that I just didn't seem to be living up to." Stephanie wearied of his immaturity, and threw him over—the severest blow so far. He became intensely moody. "Dogged by feelings of worthlessness and failure," he took a job as a busboy in a hotel dining-room. And at this point, he began the drift that eventually turned him into a serial killer. He became friendly with a drug addict. One night, they entered a cliffside house that had been partly destroyed by a landslide, and stole whatever they could find. "It was really thrilling." He began shoplifting and stealing "for thrills," once walking openly into someone's greenhouse, taking an eight-foot tree in a pot, and putting it in his car with the top sticking out of the sunroof.

He also became a full-time volunteer worker for Art Fletcher, the black Republican candidate for Lieutenant-Governor. He enjoyed the sense of being a "somebody" and mixing with interesting people. But Fletcher lost, and Bundy became a salesman in a department store. He met Meg Anders in a college beer joint, and they became lovers—she had a gentle, easy-going nature, which brought out Bundy's protective side. But she was shocked by his kleptomania.

In fact, the criminal side—the "hunchback"—was now developing fast. He acquired a taste for violent pornography—easy to buy openly in American shops. Once, walking round the university district, he saw a girl undressing in a lighted room. This was the turning point in his life. He began to devote hours to walking around, hoping to see more girls undressing. He was back at university, studying psychology, but his night prowling prevented him from making full use of his undoubted intellectual capacities. He obtained his degree in due course—this may tell us more about American university standards than about Bundy's abilities—and tried to find a law school that would take him. He failed all the aptitude tests and was repeatedly turned down. A year later, he was finally accepted—he worked for the Crime Commission for a month, as an assistant, and for the Office of Justice Planning. His self-confidence increased by leaps and bounds. When he flew to San Francisco to see Stephanie Brooks, the girl who had jilted him, she was deeply impressed, and willing to renew their affair. He was still having an affair with Meg Anders, and entered on this new career as a Don Juan with his usual enthusiasm. He and Stephanie spent Christmas together and became "engaged." Then he dumped her as she had dumped him.

By this time, he had committed his first murder. For years, he had been a pornography addict and a Peeping Tom. ("He approached it almost like a project, throwing himself into it, literally, for years.") Then the "hunchback" had started to demand "more active kinds of gratification." He tried disabling women's cars, but the girls always had help on hand. He felt the need to indulge in this kind of behavior after drinking had reduced his inhibitions. One evening, he stalked a girl from a bar, found a heavy piece of wood, and managed to get ahead of her and lie in wait. Before she reached the place where he was hiding, she stopped at her front door and went in. But the experience was like "making a hole in a dam." A few evenings later, as a woman was fumbling for her keys at her front door, he struck her on the head with a piece of wood. She collapsed, screaming, and he ran away. He was filled with remorse, and swore he would never do such a thing again. But six months later, he followed a woman home and peeped in as she undressed. He began to do this again and again. One day, when he knew the door was unlocked, he sneaked in, entered her bedroom, and jumped on her. She screamed and he ran away. Once again, there was a period of self-disgust and revulsion.

This was in the autumn of 1973. On January 4, 1974, he found a door that admitted him to the basement room of 18-year-old Sharon Clarke. Now, for the first time, he employed the technique he later used repeatedly, attacking her with a crowbar until she was unconscious. Then he thrust a speculum, or vaginal probe, inside her, causing internal injuries. But he left her alive.

On the morning of February 1, 1974, he found an unlocked front door in a students' rooming-house and went in. He entered a bedroom at random; 21-year-old Lynda Healy was asleep in bed. He battered her unconscious, then carried the body out to his car. He drove to Taylor Mountain, 20 miles east of Seattle, made her remove her pajamas, and raped her. When Bundy was later "speculating" about this crime for Stephen Michaud's benefit, the interviewer asked: "Was there any conversation?'' Bundy replied: ''There'd be some.'' ''Since this girl in front of him represented not a person, but again the image of something desirable, the last thing we would expect him to want to do would be to personalize this person.''

So Lynda Healy was bludgeoned to death; Bundy always insisted that he took no pleasure in violence, but that his chief desire was ''possession'' of another person.

Now the ''hunchback'' was in full control, and there were five more victims over the next five months. Three of the girls were taken to the same spot on Taylor Mountain and there raped and murdered—Bundy acknowledged that his sexual gratification would sometimes take hours. The four bodies were found together in the following year. On the day he abducted the two girls from Lake Sammanish, Bundy ''speculated'' that he had taken the first, Janice Ott, to a nearby house and raped her, then returned to abduct the second girl, Denise Naslund, who was taken back to the same house and raped in view of the other girl; both were then killed, and taken to a remote spot four miles northeast of the park, where the bodies were dumped.

By the time he had reached this point in his ''confession,'' Bundy had no further secrets to reveal; everything was obvious. Rape had become a compulsion that dominated his life. When he moved to Salt Lake City and entered the law school there—he was a failure from the beginning as a law student—he must have known that if he began to rape and kill young girls there, he would be establishing himself as suspect number one. This made no difference; he had to continue. Even the unsuccessful kidnapping of Carol DaRonch, and the knowledge that someone could now identify him, made no difference. He merely switched his activities to Colorado. Following his arrest, conviction, and escape, he moved to Florida, and the compulsive attacks continued, although by now he must have known that another series of murders in a town to which he had recently moved must reduce his habitual plea of ''coincidence'' to an absurdity. It seems obvious that by this time he had lost the power of choice. In his last weeks of freedom, Bundy showed all the signs of weariness and self-disgust that had driven Carl Panzram to contrive his own execution.

Time finally ran out for Bundy on January 24, 1989. Long before this, he had recognized that his fatal mistake was to decline to enter into plea bargaining at his trial; the result was a death sentence instead of life imprisonment. In January 1989, his final appeal was turned down and the date of execution fixed. Bundy then made a last-minute attempt to save his life by offering to bargain murder confessions for a reprieve—against the advice of his attorney James Coleman, who warned him that this attempt to "trade over the victims' bodies" would only create hostility that would militate against further stays of execution. In fact, Bundy went on to confess to eight Washington murders, and then to a dozen others. Detective Bob Keppel, who had led the investigation in Seattle, commented: "The game-playing stuff cost him his life." Instead of making a full confession, Bundy doled out information bit by bit. "The whole thing was orchestrated," said Keppel, "We were held hostage for three days." And finally, when it was clear that there was no chance of further delay, Bundy confessed to the Chi Omega Sorority killings, admitting that he had been peeping through the window at girls undressing until he was carried away by desire and entered the building. He also mentioned pornography as being one of the factors that led him to murder. Newspaper columnists showed an inclination to doubt this, but Bundy's earlier confessions to Michaud leave no doubt that he was telling the truth.

At 7 A.M., Bundy was led into the execution chamber at Starke State prison, Florida; behind Plexiglass, an invited audience of 48 people sat waiting. As two warders attached his hands to the arms of the electric chair, Bundy recognized his attorney among the crowd; he smiled and nodded. Then straps were placed around his chest and over his mouth; the metal cap with electrodes was fastened onto his head with screws and the face was covered with a black hood. At 7:07 A.M. the executioner threw the switch; Bundy's body went stiff and rose fractionally from the chair. One minute later, as the power was switched off, the body slammed back into the chair. A doctor felt his pulse and pronounced him dead. Outside the prison, a mob carrying "Fry Bundy!" banners cheered as the execution was announced.

_____ 9 _____

The Bundy case makes it clear that, in one respect at least, the science of criminology needs updating.

It seems to be the general consensus among criminologists that the criminal is a social inadequate, and that the few exceptions only underscore the rule. Faced with difficulties that require courage and patience, he is inclined to run away. He lacks self-esteem; he tends to see himself as a loser, a failure. Crime is a "short cut" to achieve something he believes he cannot achieve through his own merit. But everyone who reads this description must be aware that, to some extent, it fits himself. Being undermined by self-doubt is part of the human condition. Which of us, faced with problems, has not at some time chosen a judicious retreat?

The Bundy case underlines the point. Even as a schoolboy he was witty and amusing, and in his early 20s he developed a poise and confidence that were the envy of other males. Michaud quotes a fellow office worker: "Frankly, he represented what it was that all young males ever wanted to be . . . I think half the people in the office were jealous of him . . . If there was any flaw in him it was that he was almost too perfect."

If Yochelson and Samenow are right about the criminal personality, then Bundy should now have reached a point in his life where the criminal phase should have been left behind like a childhood ailment. According to them, criminality is closely connected to inadequacy, laziness, and self-pity; it is another name for defeat-proneness. By the time he was in his mid-20s, Bundy had tasted enough success to stand outside this definition. Then what went wrong?

Ann Rule's book contains the vital clue. She comments that Bundy became violently upset if he telephoned Meg Anders from Salt Lake City—where his legal studies were foundering—and got no reply. "Strangely, while he was being continuously unfaithful himself, he expected—demanded—that she be totally loyal to him."

In 1954, the science fiction writer A. E. Van Vogt had encountered this same curious anomaly when he was studying male authoritarian behavior for a novel called *The Violent Man*. He was intrigued by the number of divorce cases in which habitually unfaithful husbands had expected total fidelity from their wives; such a husband might flaunt his own infidelities, while erupting into murderous violence if his wife so much as smiled at another man. Such men obviously regarded women with deep hostility, as if they expected to be deceived or betrayed—this is why they chose to marry gentle and unaggressive women. Their "conquests" were another form of aggression, the aim being to prove that they were masterful seducers who could have any woman they liked. Their whole unstable structure of self-esteem was founded upon this notion that women found them irresistible; so it was essential for the wife to behave like a slave in a harem. This also explained another characteristic of such men: that they could not bear to be contradicted or shown to be in the wrong; this also threatened their image of themselves as a kind of god or superman. If confronted with proof of their own fallibility, they would explode into violence rather than acknowledge that they had made a mistake. For this reason, Van Vogt labelled this type "the Right Man" or "the Violent Man." To his colleagues at work he might appear perfectly normal and balanced; but his family knew him as a kind of paranoid dictator.

Only one thing could undermine this structure of self-delusion. If his wife walked out on him, she had demonstrated beyond all doubt that she rejected him; his tower of self-delusion was undermined, and often the result was mental breakdown, or even suicide.

Expressed in this way, it seems clear that the Right Man

syndrome is a form of mild insanity. Yet it is alarmingly common; most of us know a Right Man, and some have the misfortune to have a Right Man for a husband or father. The syndrome obviously arises from the sheer competitiveness of the world we are born into. Every normal male has an urge to be a "winner," yet he finds himself surrounded by people who seem better qualified for success. One common response is boasting to those who look as if they can be taken in—particularly women. Another is what the late Stephen Potter called "One-upmanship," the attempt to make the other person feel inferior by a kind of cheating— for example, by pretending to know far more than you actually know. Another is to bully people over whom one happens to have authority. Many "Right Men" are so successful in all these departments that they achieve a remarkably high level of self-esteem on remarkably slender talents. Once achieved, this self-esteem is like an addictive drug and any threat of withdrawal seems terrifying. Hence the violence with which he reacts to anything that challenges it.

It is obvious that the Right Man syndrome is a compensatory mechanism for profound self-doubt, and that its essence lies in convincing others of something he feels to be untrue; in other words, it is a form of confidence-trickery. It is, that is to say, a typically criminal form of "short-cut," like cheating on an exam, or stealing something instead of saving up to buy it.

Now the basic characteristic of the criminal, and also of the Right Man, is a certain lack of self-control. Van Vogt writes that the Right Man "makes the decision to be out of control"—that is, makes the decision to *lose* control at a certain point, exploding into violence rather than calling upon a more mature level of his personality. But he is adept at making excuses that place the blame for this lack of self-control on other people for provoking him. One British sex killer, Patrick Byrne, explained that he decided to terrorize women "to get my own back on them for causing my nervous tension through sex."

But the lack of self-control brings its own problems. Every time it happens he is, in effect, lowering his own bursting point. Carl Panzram told Henry Lesser never to turn his back on him: "You're the one man I don't want to kill. But I'm so erratic I'm liable to do anything." He is like a man who has trained an Alsatian dog to leap at people's throats, and finally realizes that the dog is stronger than he is. A 22-year-old sex killer named Stephen Judy begged the judge in Indianapolis to sentence him to death. He had been committing rapes and sex crimes since he was 12, and was on trial for killing a young mother and her three children. Aware that he would never be able to stop committing sex crimes, he told the jury: "You'd better put me to death. Because next time it might be one of you or your daughter." They agreed, and Judy was executed in 1981. Just before his death he told his stepmother that he had killed more women than he could remember, leaving a trail of bodies across the United States.

It should now be possible to see that the Right Man syndrome is the key to the serial killer, and that Bundy is a textbook case. From the beginning, he was obsessed by success: "I found myself thinking about standards of success that I just didn't seem to be living up to." The affair with Stephanie Brooks made it seem that success was within his grasp; he went to Stanford to study Chinese. But he lacked the application and self-confidence and she threw him over. This was the turning point; his brother commented: "Stephanie screwed him up . . . I'd never seen him like this before. He'd always been in charge of his emotions." It was after this rejection that Bundy became a kleptomaniac. This may seem a strange response to the end of a love affair. But stealing is a way of making a gesture of defiance at society. And this is what Bundy's thieving amounted to—as when he stole an eight-foot tree from a greenhouse and drove off with it sticking out of the roof of his car. It was essentially a symbolic gesture.

Seven years later, Bundy took his revenge on Stephanie Brooks. When she rang him to ask why he had not contacted her since their weekend together, he said coldly: "I have no idea what you're talking about," and hung up on her. "At length," says Ann Rule, "she concluded that Ted's high-power courtship in the latter part of 1973 had been deliberately planned, that he had waited all these years to be in a position where he could make her fall in love with him, just so he could drop her, reject her as she had rejected him." Stephanie Brooks wrote to a friend: "I escaped by the skin of my teeth. When I think of his cold and calculating manner, I shudder." The Right Man had escaped his feeling of vulnerability; he had established his dominance. Oddly enough, he committed his first violent sexual attack immediately after the weekend with Stephanie. He had proved that he was the conqueror; now, in this mood of exultation, he broke into the bedroom of a female student, battered her unconscious, and thrust a speculum into her vagina. Three weeks later he committed his first murder. It was also completely typical of the Right Man that, when eventually caught, he should continue to deny his guilt, even in the face of overwhelming evidence.

Henry Lee Lucas might seem an altogether less obvious example of a Right Man. But his confessions immediately make it clear that one of his most basic characteristics was "the decision to be out of control." He committed his first murder at the age of 15—the 17-year-old girl he attacked at the bus stop. *She resisted;* so he killed her, raped her, then buried her. Resistance aroused all his violence. (Gerald Stano, we may recall, had the same characteristic; he killed only those girls who fought back.) In appearance, he was mild and self-effacing, one of society's losers. One middle-class couple trusted him sufficiently to pay him to look after the wife's 80-year-old mother, Kate Rich. But one evening, after an argument, Lucas stabbed her to death, raped her, then hid the body in a culvert. When anyone opposed him, he was like a striking snake.

The parents of his fellow murderer, Ottis Toole, also trusted him enough to appoint him the guardian of their two youngest children, Frank and Becky Powell. Becky was 9, and Lucas cared for her like a father, sent her to school, and taught her the craft of burglary. Inevitably, he began to have sex with her. They began to disagree when both joined the House of Prayer sect, and Becky announced her desire to return to Florida to serve out a period of juvenile detention; she was longing for a stable life. Lucas started to hitchhike back to Florida with her, but one night they quarreled, and she slapped his face. Without even thinking, he stabbed her to death. Then he dismembered her body and buried it. But he was overwhelmed by remorse, and from then on, ceased to show the instinct for self-preservation that had so far kept him out of the hands of the police. He was arrested nine months later, and almost immediately confessed. Becky's brother Frank had to be committed to a mental home.

Charles Manson provides another example of the apparently mild and self-effacing Right Man. In a prison interview, he told Joel Norris that he saw himself as the ultimate victim of society, and the impression he made on his disciples in the Haight-Ashbury district of San Francisco was of a gentle, slightly comic figure, a mixture of Christ and Charlie Chaplin. Most of these disciples were teenagers—Manson was in his mid-30s—and he became a father figure. As his success as a cult leader increased in 1968, disciples handed over money and property. One of his followers, Susan Atkins, declared that he was the king, the "visible proof of God," and that his name meant "son of man." "All he ever does is to give, and if you watched him you could see the love he suggests with everything he does" said another follower, Patricia Krenwinkel. Permanently high on psychedelic drugs, Manson was convinced that the confrontation between blacks and whites in the 1960s would finally lead to open warfare and mutual annihilation, a prospect he welcomed. Manson also played guitar and wrote songs, and believed that he could become as successful as the Beatles or Bob Dylan. He developed a murderous resentment for those he felt had slighted him or ignored his talent, and drew up a "death list" that included Warren Beatty and

Julie Christie, as well as Doris Day's son Terry Melcher, whom he believed responsible for causing a recording contract to fall through. And on the evening of August 18, 1969, Manson told his disciples that "now was the time for Helter Skelter," his code-name for the war between blacks and whites, and four members of the gang went to the house in which Terry Melcher had lived, and murdered film star Sharon Tate and four other people, including a delivery boy. The following evening, Manson entered the nearby home of a couple called LaBianca, and tied them up at gunpoint; then his followers went in and killed them.

The solution of the case came through an unrelated piece of crime detection. In September 1969, rangers in the Death Valley National Park discovered that someone had set fire to a skip-loader, a kind of bulldozer. They followed tire tracks along the road, and some miles farther on, found a wrecked car that had been driven into a tree. Its tires corresponded to the tracks near the vandalized bulldozer; nearby were more tire tracks from another car. This car was located in a valley, and was found to be a stolen Toyota. A man who lived nearby told the police about a family of "hippies" who were living on a deserted ranch, and who were probably responsible for the theft and the destruction of the bulldozer. The police raided the ranch and arrested a crowd of hippies, including several girls.

It was one of these girls, Susan Atkins, who told a cellmate that she had taken part in the Sharon Tate killings. Manson and his followers were interrogated, and eventually charged with the murders.

What was so strange about the trial was that Manson seemed determined to turn it into an indictment of the authorities. "You make your children what they are . . . These children—everything they have done, they have done for the love of their brothers." The jury found all this incomprehensible. Was Manson saying that his "children" had not really committed the murders? When Susan Atkins was asked if she thought the murders of eight people were unimportant, she countered by asking if the killing of thousands of people with napalm was important, the implication being that two wrongs somehow made a right. What no one in the courtroom understood was that they were encountering the inverted logic of the Right Man, who is incapable of admitting that he is to blame. Eventually, Manson and four followers were sentenced to death, the sentences later being commuted to life imprisonment.

It should be clear by now that the Right Man syndrome is a mild form of insanity. The usual definition of insanity is a certain loss of contact with the real world, so that a person ceases to be able to distinguish between what is subjective and what is objective. In the case of Manson and many other serial killers (and it seems clear that the Manson family committed many more murders than those with which they were charged) this confusion was increased by drugs. The difference between the Right Man syndrome and clinical psychosis is that the psychotic is the victim of his delusions while the Right Man's separation from reality is to some extent voluntary; it is a form of self-deception. But when alcohol or drug abuse become involved, the dividing line becomes increasingly blurred. Van Vogt recognized that "most Right Men deserve some sympathy, for they are struggling with an almost unbelievable inner horror..." It is as if a kind of inner dam threatened to collapse, leaving them at the mercy of all their worst fears. "If they give way to the impulse to hit or choke," says Van Vogt, "they are losing the battle, and are on the way to ultimate disaster." But the serial killer *has* given way to his impulse to hit and choke. He is stranded in a kind of nightmare, faced with a deep, intuitive recognition that he has destroyed his potentialities as a human being and reached the end of the line. This explains why Panzram committed the murder that led to his execution, why Stephen Judy demanded to be electrocuted, and why so many serial killers have made obvious mistakes that led to their arrest.

—————————————— **10** ——————————————

A case of the mid-1980s provides a particularly clear example of this self-destructive mechanism. On June 2, 1985, a young Asian named Charles Ng tried to steal a vise from South City Lumber in San Francisco, but was caught after he had dropped it into the boot of his car. His companion, a man named Leonard Lake, offered to pay for the vise, but was told that the police were already on their way. Ng escaped, and a search of Lake's car revealed a handgun with a silencer. Taken to the police station, he asked for a glass of water, and swallowed a cyanide capsule. He died four days later without regaining consciousness. His car and identity papers were found to belong to a missing car salesman named Paul Cosner. When police searched a property belonging to Lake in Wilseyville, Calaveras County, they discovered an underground bunker with prison cells, and the remains of eight victims buried nearby. There were also two videotapes which made it clear that Lake and Ng tortured and raped their female victims. Ng was arrested a month later in Calgary, Canada, and sentenced to four and a half years for shoplifting; California applied for his extradition.

Lake had been a Vietnam veteran and a maker of pornographic films; his collection of videos was found to include "snuff movies" with actual scenes of murder; he also kept photographs of his victims' bodies, which included seven men, three women, and two children. Lake had apparently been inspired by a novel by John Fowles called *The Collector*, in which a man kidnaps a girl and holds her captive; Lake believed that a nuclear war was unavoidable, and had stockpiled food and weapons in his underground bunker. The cells were intended for "sex slaves."

The picture that began to emerge was of a man who spent most of his life living in a world of fantasy, a man who indulged in grandiose dreams of success without any realistic attempt to make them come true, and who boasted of imaginary heroic exploits in Vietnam. Like so many serial killers, he had been rejected by his parents at an early age, and brought up by a grandfather who imposed a military-style discipline. He was jealous of his younger brother Donald, who was favored by their parents. But Donald himself was mentally disturbed, indulging in sadistic cruelty to animals—one of the basic characteristics of the serial killer—and attempting to have sexual intercourse with his younger sisters. (Lake obtained their sexual favors in exchange for protecting them from Donald—and eventually Donald was to become one of his victims.)

Lake also took nude photographs of his sisters and cousins— the beginning of a lifelong preoccupation that led him to make pornographic movies (starring his wife) and the "snuff videos" of his victims. And in spite of his dominant role in relation to sisters and cousins, Lake had the Right Man's characteristic hatred and distrust of women, and the need for power over them. His fantasies were all about domination over women and their total submission to him.

So, as with so many Right Men, Lake's self-esteem was based on fantasies in which he was a kind of Haroun Al Raschid or Ivan the Terrible, with the power of life and death. He showed considerable skill at concealing his abnormality, teaching grade school, working as a volunteer firefighter, and donating his time to a company that provided free insulation in old people's homes. Slowly, the fantasies took over and he began to rape and kill. One video shows these fantasies in action. Eighteen-year-old Kathy Allen went searching for her boyfriend Michael Carroll, a drug dealer, and one of the many who made the fatal mistake of going to Lake's home to do business. The video shows Ng ordering her to undress, then shows Lake removing her handcuffs and clamping on leg irons. She is then ordered to take a shower. "You'll wash for us, clean for us, fuck for us." A later scene shows her strapped down to a bed, while Lake tells her that her boyfriend is dead.

The video cuts to another girl, Brenda O'Connor, who is handcuffed, and who asks about her baby. She is told that the baby is "sound asleep like a rock," then offered the choice of being a "sex slave" or dying. She agrees to cooperate. It emerges that Lake has invited the whole family—Brenda, common law husband, and 2-year-old child—over for dinner, then has taken them prisoner. Brenda asks: "Why do you guys do this?" and Lake replies: "We don't like you. Would you like me to put it in writing?" "You two are crazy." "The whole neighborhood's crazy." Ng starts to undress her saying: "Let's see what we're buying." "Don't cut my bra off." "Nothing is yours now." As she undresses she begs: "Give my baby to me. I'll do anything you want..." "You're going to do anything we want anyway." "He can't live without me." "He's gonna learn." And the naked girl is made to enter the shower with Ng as a preliminary to becoming a "sex slave" and then being killed.

What has happened is clear: Lake has taken the fatal step beyond most Right Men: he has decided he will *become* Haroun Al Raschid or Ivan the Terrible. But when fantasy comes into contact with reality, it melts away like fairy gold; the dreamer is left facing his own naked reality. Moreover, as Lake and Ng humiliate their victims, we sense that, in spite of the bravado and brutality ("Nothing is yours now"), they are still human enough to feel that they are outraging their own humanity. Like Panzram, Judy, and Bundy, they have delivered themselves into the power of the "hunchback," the killer Alsatian, and in so doing, have resigned from the human race. Lake admits in his diary that his dreams of success have eluded him and that his boasts of heroic deeds in Vietnam were delusions. He has become morally and spiritually bankrupt. Norris comments penetratingly: "By the time he was arrested in San Francisco, Lake had reached the final stage of the serial murder syndrome: he realized that he had come to a dead end, with nothing but his own misery to show for it." This is why Lake committed suicide when, if he had kept his head, he could probably have bluffed his way to freedom. His freedom had become meaningless.

——————————————— **11** ———————————————

It should be clear now that the Right Man syndrome is basically a matter of "dominance." This notion first came to general notice as a result of the work of students of animal behavior like Konrad Lorenz and Niko Tinbergen, who noticed that the "pecking order" of barnyard fowl has its counterpart in all human and animal societies. The psychologist Alfred Adler suggested that the "will to power" is the basic human drive—and not, as Freud suggested, the sex urge. This was confirmed by Abraham Maslow when he was studying the behavior of apes in the Bronx Zoo in the 1930s; their activities made him at first conclude that their main interest in life was sex, since they spent all their time mounting one another; yet as he observed that females sometimes mounted males, and that both males and females mounted members of their own sex, it dawned on him that they were actually expressing dominance: the more aggressive apes asserted themselves by mounting the less aggressive ones, without regard to sex.

As a result of this observation Maslow decided, in 1936, to study dominance behavior in human beings. Because he thought women tended to be more truthful about such matters, he began a series of interviews with college women, and soon made the interesting discovery that his subjects fell into three distinct dominance groups: high, medium, and low. High dominance women tended to enjoy sex for its own sake—in a manner that is usually regarded as distinctly male—and to be sexually experimental. Medium dominance women enjoyed sex, but it had to be with someone with whom they were romantically involved; they were looking for "Mr. Right," the kind of man who would take them to restaurants with soft lights and present them with bouquets. Low dominance women thought sex was rather frightening and disgusting: they preferred the kind of man who would admire them from a distance for years without daring to speak. Maslow also made another interesting observation: that the high dominance females were exactly 5 per cent of the total—one in twenty. This also confirmed an observation already known to zoologists: that there is a "dominant 5 per cent" in all animal groups. (Shaw once asked the explorer Stanley how many men could take over the leadership of his expedition if he himself fell ill; he replied: "One in twenty." "Is that approximate or exact?" asked Shaw, and Stanley replied: "Exact.")

Maslow made another significant observation: for the most part, men and women form close relationships within their own dominance group. Highly dominant males preferred highly dominant females, and so on. A high dominance male *would* sleep with a medium dominance female, but there was nothing "personal" about it; only in cases of "sexual drought" would he form a permanent relation with such a woman. Maslow also noted that the male–female relation worked best in all groups if the male was slightly—but not too much—more dominant than the female.

It should now be clear that "dominance" is the key to Right Man behavior. Among apes, lions, bison, dominance is easily established: the two contenders simply fight one another. In human society, it is far more complex. The king is not necessarily more dominant than his prime minister, the colonel than the sergeant major, the manager than the foreman—he may not even be more intelligent or better qualified for the job. It can obviously be intensely frustrating for a high dominance individual to be the subordinate of someone of lower dominance—sometimes of dozens of people of lower dominance—particularly if the low dominance individual tries to make up for it by bullying. Some high dominance individuals, placed in this situation of subordination, attempt to express their dominance in the only way that is left open to them: the family situation. This is, in a sense, a confession of defeat: he has made fantasy a substitute for reality, and if something undermines the fantasy— such as the woman leaving him—the result may be suicidal despair.

It is impossible to grasp the motivations of a serial killer like Ted Bundy, Charles Manson, or Leonard Lake without recognizing the basic role of dominance and fantasy-fulfillment. His crimes are fantasy-fulfillment, a substitute for the kind of real achievement to which he feels his dominance entitles him. The paradox is that the crimes cause the fulfillment to recede farther into the distance as if he is the victim of some magic spell.

One of the clearest examples is provided by the Moors murder case, which occurred in England in the mid-1960s; it also illustrates another curious aspect of the Right Man syndrome. Ian Brady, the illegitimate son of a waitress, was born in a tough Glasgow slum in 1938, and was farmed out to foster parents. He was intelligent and a good student; but at the age of 11 he won a scholarship to an expensive school where many of the students came from well-to-do families, and—like Panzram—he began to develop a fierce resentment of his own underprivileged position. He began committing burglaries, and at 13 was sentenced to two years' probation for housebreaking; as soon as this ended he was sentenced to another two years for ten burglaries. He also practiced sadistic cruelty to animals. When his mother moved to Manchester with a new husband, he found a job in a brewery, but was dismissed for stealing, and sent to a Borstal institution. At 21, he became a clerk in Millwards, a chemical firm in Gorton, and began collecting books on the Nazis, and reading the Marquis de Sade.

De Sade is virtually the patron saint of serial killers. His books give expression to their basic belief that the individual owes nothing to society, and has the right to live in it as a kind of outlaw—the philosophy of the fox in a poultry farm. Brady experienced a kind of religious conversion to these ideas. So far he had seen himself merely as a criminal; now—like Leonard Lake—he began to see himself as the heroic outcast, the scourge of society.

It was at about this point that Myra Hindley entered the story. She was a completely normal working-class girl, not bad-looking, inclined to go in for blonde hair-dos and bright lipstick, interested mainly in boys and dancing. She was a typical medium dominance female, who would have been perfectly content with a reasonably hard-working boy next door. When she came to work at Millwards, she was fascinated by Brady's sullen good looks and moody expression. But Brady was undoubtedly one of the dominant 5 per cent; he recognized her as a medium dominance type and ignored her; at the end of six months he had not even spoken to her. Without encouragement Myra filled her diary with declarations of love: "I hope he loves me and will marry me some day." Finally, Brady decided it would be a pity not to take advantage of the maidenhead that was being offered, and invited her out. Soon after this Myra surrendered her virginity on the divan bed in her gran's front room.

In the criminally inclined, the combination of high and medium dominance egos usually produces an explosive mixture—as can be seen, for example, in the Leopold and Loeb case. What seems to happen is that the high dominance partner finds himself regarded with admiration that acts as a kind of super-fertilizer on his ego; in no time at all he becomes a full-blown case of the Right Man syndrome. Brady found it intoxicating to have an audience; he talked to Myra enthusiastically about Hitler, and nicknamed her "Hessie" after Myra Hess. He also paid her the high compliment of telling her that she looked like Irma Grese, the concentration camp guard. But her sexual submission was not enough; it only intensified his craving to be a "somebody." He announced that he was planning a series of payroll robberies, and induced her to join a local pistol club to gain access to guns. He also took photographs of her posing in the nude and, using a timing device, of the two of them having sexual intercourse. In some of the photographs— which Brady tried to sell—she has whip marks across her buttocks.

Some time in 1963—when he was 25 and she was 21—he induced her to join with him in the murder of children. It is hard to understand how a typical medium dominance girl, who loved children and animals, allowed herself to be persuaded. But the answer undoubtedly lies in Brady's obsessive need to taste the delights of dominating another person, and in the sadism that had developed in him since childhood. The pleasure of completely dominating Myra aroused visions of dominating ''sex slaves.'' Brady and Hindley kidnapped children by offering them lifts in Myra's car, then took them back to Myra's home, where they were subjected to bondage, sexual abuse, and torture. They were photographed and their cries for mercy tape-recorded. Sixteen-year-old Pauline Reade, who knew Myra, was picked up on her way to a dance, taken up to the moor, and probably raped; then Brady cut her throat.

After four child murders—possibly more—Brady attempted to involve Myra Hindley's brother-in-law, a teenager named David Smith. He was still dreaming of bank robberies. On October 6, 1965, Brady picked up a teenage homosexual, Edward Evans, and took him back to the flat; then, with Smith looking on, he killed Evans with an axe. But he had overestimated Smith's callousness. (The FBI profiling team could have told him that a teenager would panic.) Smith lost no time in telling his wife what had happened, and together they telephoned the police. The corpse was still in the front room, wrapped in a polythene sheet, when Brady and Hindley were arrested the next day. Photographs of the graves led the police to uncover the bodies of a boy and a girl on Saddleworth Moor. In the typical manner of the Right Man, Brady refused to confess; to have done so would have been an admission that he was wrong. In May 1966, both were sentenced to life imprisonment.

_____ **12** _____

The problem of the serial killer is one of the most perplexing and frightening that has so far confronted the criminologist. Yet our survey of the history of crime detection has at least shown us how to place it in perspective. We know that human beings have been murdering one another in various appalling ways for thousands of years. H. G. Wells defined the cause of the problem when he wrote:

> Five hundred generations ago, human beings were brought together into a closeness of contact for which their past had not prepared them. The early civilizations were not slowly evolved and adapted *communities*. They were essentially jostling *crowds* in which quite unprecedented reactions were possible . . . With the first cities came the first slums, and ever since then the huge majority of mankind has been living in slums.*

These conditions, as Marx pointed out, produce "alienation," a state in which human beings have no more fellow-feeling for one another than they have for the birds and animals they slaughter for sport. Plutarch speaks of a Greek brigand who used to make travelers jump off a high cliff, and describes the tyrant Alexander of Pherae who liked to bury men alive or watch them being torn to pieces by dogs. Every schoolboy has shuddered at the story of the Sicilian tyrant Phalaris who roasted men alive in a brazen bull. The Wallachian ruler Vlad the Impaler—the original Dracula—derived such pleasure from watching impaled victims dying in agony that he had pointed stakes set up in his dining-hall. Ivan the Terrible—another typical "Right Man"—spent five weeks presiding over the torture of the inhabitants of Novgorod, taking special delight in torturing husbands and wives before one another. Gilles de Rais raped and dismembered more than 50 children. The Hungarian countess Elizabeth Bathory was tried in 1610 for murdering more than 80 servant girls in order to bathe in their blood. Clearly, then, cruelty has been with us down the ages, and the behavior of the serial killer is no proof that our civilization is going to

* *'42 to '44, A Contemporary Memoir,* Secker & Warburg, London, 1944, p. 15.

the dogs. What *is* unusual is that we are so shocked by cruelty. The present high regard for human life appeared only in the nineteenth century; before that, cruelty was accepted casually as one of the facts of life.

In the course of this book we have seen that it was not until the early nineteenth century that police forces became efficient enough to halt the more-or-less permanent crime waves that flourished in most major cities. And this was not due to some technological or sociological advance, but simply to the fact that men suddenly began to confront the problem in a new *spirit of optimism*. Instead of torturing men to make them confess, or crushing them under a series of 50 lb. weights, the police began to pay attention to the importance of clues; they began to use reason and logic to understand the ways of criminals just as Isaac Newton had used reason and logic to understand the ways of the planets. The result was the rise of the science of crime detection— and prevention—as recounted in this book. Slowly, little by little, this turned the war between the police and the criminal into something like an equal battle. By the beginning of the twentieth century, prophets like H. G. Wells and Bernard Shaw could look forward to the day when crime would simply disappear, like all the other "teething troubles of humanity." The invention of the telephone meant that crimes could be reported so quickly that the burglar or the footpad could often be caught before he had time to escape. (We have seen how Police Chief August Vollmer used the latest scientific advances to bring law and order to the streets of Berkeley.) The 1920s and 1930s were the golden age of crime detection, when civilized countries had less unsolved crime than at any other point in history.

And then, it seemed, the situation changed overnight. The rise of the dictators made it seem that prophets like Wells had been far too optimistic about human nature. The invasion of Abyssinia, the Stalin show-trials, the Spanish Civil War, the Second World War, all seemed to demonstrate that civilization was no more than a veneer. Wells was so shocked by the atomic bomb and by the revelations of

Buchenwald and Belsen that he wrote his most deeply pessimistic work, *Mind at the End of its Tether,* shortly before his death, prophesying some ultimate catastrophe that would bring an end to all life in the universe. And the steady rise in postwar crime seemed to justify his pessimism about human nature.

Yet such a view is hardly justified by the facts. It is true that the increase in drug abuse has caused a crime problem in the major cities. But modern London, Paris, Rome, New York, or Los Angeles are oases of law and order compared with London and Paris in the early eighteenth century. What has happened is that man has realized that even the most intractable problems can be solved with the use of patience, reason, and common sense. It was this new faith in reason and common sense that made all the difference between social chaos and social order. In 1750, most Londoners had come to accept that they had to live with footpads, pickpockets, and highwaymen; at this point, Henry Fielding demonstrated that the problem could be brought under control with surprising ease by a fairly small number of dedicated men. The same general truth applies today, but with even greater force, since the police can now utilize the results of two centuries of scientific crime detection.

The problem of the serial killer—and the closely related problem of the sexual criminal—is a case in point. The examples discussed in the last two sections make it clear that the phenomenon is not as chaotic and unpredictable as it appears. On the contrary, the serial killer is a recognizable type; in case after case, the same patterns repeat themselves with almost monotonous regularity: deprivation of affection in childhood, sadism towards animals, fear and distrust of women, alcohol and drug abuse, resentment towards society, high dominance, and the tendency to escape into a world of fantasy. It is the combination of these last two that tends to produce the Right Man syndrome which is so characteristic of serial killers. The main problem so far has been that police and medical authorities have failed to recognize that they are dealing with a clearly defined type. Yet as soon as

Joel Norris and his colleagues began to apply statistical methods to serial killers, they recognized "profiles that could lead to the development of a diagnostic or prediction instrument." Moreover, the recognition that the serial killer is almost invariably a "Right Man" adds a vitally important element to the "profile." During his studies of dominance in women, Maslow developed tests for determining the precise level of dominance, and these would obviously be of use to psychologists dealing with potential serial killers. It is true that the notion of a "diagnostic or prediction instrument" tends to strike us as vague and unrealistic; but it should be borne in mind that this is precisely how Bertillon's proposals for a new system of identification struck *his* contemporaries at the Sûreté.

In fact, there are altogether more down-to-earth possibilities for solving the problem of the serial killer. A retired Los Angeles homicide detective, Pierce Brooks, has created a program known as VICAP, the "violent criminal apprehension program." He pointed out that such killers as Sherman McCrary, Stephen Judy, Henry Lee Lucas, and Ted Bundy remained unapprehended for so long because they moved on before state authorities had reason to suspect a multiple killer. But this presents no problem to the computer, which can transmit information on "unsolved homicides, violent or deviant sexual assaults, and kidnappings or disappearances" to every other computer in the United States, and alert police to the activities of habitual criminals. In 1982, patient detective work led to the arrest of two hold-up men, Duane and Harley Willett (a father and son), who had killed a night manager of a discount store in Provo, Utah. Information from an accomplice made the police aware that the Willetts were responsible for 50 armed robberies in the western United States, and that in a dozen cases they had killed their victims as the easiest method of overcoming their resistance. In such a case, the VICAP computer would have revealed the similarities in their *modus operandi* at a far earlier stage and saved the lives of many victims.

At the time of writing, genetic fingerprinting offers the

most important hope for the solution of serial killings and sex crimes. Most sexual criminals leave behind a sample of their sperm; many also leave samples of blood and skin under the fingernails of their victims. This means, in effect, that they have left behind a kind of visiting card, which has much the same value as a fingerprint or palmprint. If genetic fingerprinting had been known in the 1970s, Bundy would have been convicted as a multiple killer on the evidence of the bloodstains on Carol DaRonch, made during her flight to escape from his car—in which case, presumably, he would have been placed in a maximum security prison, and not allowed to escape to commit more murders. There seems no reason to doubt that the discovery of genetic fingerprinting will prove as great a milestone in the history of crime detection as Henry's discovery of fingerprint classification in the 1890s.

In our present situation, it is tempting to dwell on the sociological causes of crime: boredom, alienation, psychological tensions, and the fact that deprived members of a consumer society feel that they deserve a share of its luxury goods. Seen in this perspective the problem seems insoluble, except in terms of some vague "social revolution." In fact, revolutions leave the problem untouched; they are too wholesale. If this book has taught us anything, it is that the problem has already been solved. It was solved in the eighteenth century, when a new type of "detective" abandoned the old defeatist attitude towards crime, and began to treat the evidence as a witness that could be persuaded to tell its story. That change of attitude was more than a revolution in crime detection; it was a revolution in the history of the human mind.

Postscript

A book on crime detection seems hardly the place for philosophical reflections. But even this grimly practical field can benefit from a wider intellectual perspective.

In the late 1930s, brain physiologists became aware that animal aggression seems to be associated with a part of the brain the amygdala, or amygdaloid nucleus, an almond-shaped structure situated in the limbic system, the part of the brain that plays an important role in emotion and motivation. They discovered that if the amygdala of a highly aggressive ape is removed, it becomes good tempered and docile; when the amygdala of a sweet old lady was electrically stimulated, she became vituperative and aggressive.

But knowing the precise location of the "aggression center" fails to provide any real clue to the control of aggression. For it seems clear that the control of aggression depends largely upon whether a person *wants* to control it. Whether we like it or not, aggression depends, in the last resort, on "free will." Van Vogt says that the "Violent Man" *makes the decision* to be out of control.

This question of decision is an interesting one. Try a simple experiment. Ask a child to stand in the center of the room, then crawl towards him on all fours, making growling noises. His first reaction is amusement. As you get closer, the laughter develops a note of hysteria; at a certain distance, the child will turn and run—it is a good idea to have his mother sitting nearby so he can run into her arms. A more confident child may run at you, as if to prove this is only daddy. Now try the experiment yourself, getting a friend to crawl towards you growling; you will observe that you still feel a certain automatic alarm, which—being adult—you can easily control. It is an interesting demonstration that, although we consider ourselves to be rational creatures, there is still a part of us that stands outside our civilized conditioning.

It can, of course, be controlled. If you went on playing the game for half an hour, you would finally be able to watch your friend's approach without the slightest reaction. Moreover, if someone was rude to you within the next half hour, you would find that you had far less trouble than usual in controlling the rush of irritation.

It operates the other way around. If you respond to irritation by losing your temper, it becomes increasingly difficult to control your temper. The Panzram case is a classic illustration of how a man turns into a violent criminal simply by giving full rein to his resentment. At the same time, Panzram's rational self recognized that he was destroying the specifically human part of himself—after all, we use the word "humanity" to mean decency and kindness.

In an article on aggressive epileptics,* Vernon H. Mark and Robert Neville suggest that brain surgery—on the amygdaloid nucleus—could solve the behavior problems of many violent criminals. They go on to admit that this view will offend many humanitarians, who believe that violence is an expression of free will, and that brain surgery would have a "degrading effect" on human dignity. But they then make the important comment: "This view is particularly inappropriate, not because free will is to be denied, but because the

---

*In *Physiology of Aggression and Implications for Control*, edited by Kenneth Moyer, Raven Press, New York, 1976.

quality of human life is to be prized. Many of the patients who come with focal brain disease associated with violent behavior are so offended by their own actions that they have attempted suicide." (This, of course, is what Panzram did.) They go on to argue that a brain operation could give a patient more rather than less control over his own behavior, and therefore increase his ability to express free will.

Theirs, it seems to me, is the sensible view. Human violence cannot be explained either in terms of free will or of physiological reflexes. It can only be understood as a *combination* of these two. Human evolution depends upon increasing control of the reflexes. This is why "the decision to be out of control" is always a mistake.

If we really wish to understand the issues involved, we must be prepared to consider them from a wider viewpoint than most scientists would allow themselves. In *A Criminal History of Mankind*, I suggested that they should be considered from the point of view of two opposing forces, which I suggest labeling Force T and Force C, the T standing for tension, and C for control. When a man badly wants to urinate, he experiences increasing tension; his heartbeat and blood pressure increase, his temperature rises. When a man becomes deeply interested in some problem, the opposite occurs; he soothes his impatience, focuses his attention, damps down his energies, until he achieves a state of inner calm. Some mystics—Wordsworth, for example—can sink into such deep conditions of calm that they achieve an insight into "unknown modes of being," and seem to grasp the workings of the universe. The criminal, with his tendency to lose control, has abandoned all possibility of such insights.

After publication of *An Encyclopedia of Murder*, many friends—and critics—expressed their perplexity about my interest in crime, which they seemed to feel indicated a streak of morbidity. One day when I was having dinner with the poet Ronald Duncan, and we were both in a pleasant state of alcoholic relaxation, he suddenly asked me: "Why are you *really* interested in murder?" He was obviously hoping that I would admit to a secret compulsion to rape schoolgirls or disembowel animals. When I explained that I saw it as a symbolic representation of everything that is wrong with human consciousness, he shook his head wearily, evidently feeling that I was being evasive. But I was also aware that the fault lay partly in myself, for failing to explain what I meant.

But as I was writing the section on Dan MacDougald in the final chapter of this book, I suddenly became aware that I was succeeding in saying *precisely* why the study of crime seems to me as important as the study of philosophy or religion. It was in the passage where, after explaining that Dickens's Scrooge is an example of what MacDougald calls "negative blocking," I go on:

> Now it is obvious that we are *all* in this condition, to some extent—for, as Wordsworth says, "shades of the prison house" begin to close around us as we learn to "cope" with the complexities of existence. So we are all in the position of the criminal. But criminals do it far more than most people—to such an extent that, when we read of a man like H. H. Holmes, we can suddenly *see* that he was an idiot to waste his own life and that of his victims. As strange as it sounds, studying criminality has much the same effect on most of us that the ghosts of Christmas had on Scrooge—of making us more widely aware of the reality we ignore.

And there, I feel, I have succeeded in putting my finger squarely on the central problem—not only of criminal psychology, but of what I feel to be the essence of the human dilemma. This can be summarized in the statement that although human beings possess free will, they are usually unaware that they possess it. We *become* aware of it whenever we are in moods of happiness and excitement—what Maslow calls the peak experience. But under normal conditions, we are merely aware of the problems of everyday life, and these induce a feeling that we are fighting a purely defensive battle, like a man trying to prevent himself from drowning. Life seems to be an endless struggle, an endless series of problems and obstacles. And this condition produces a dangerous state of "negative feedback." As we contemplate the problems and obstacles, the heart sinks, and we lose all feeling of free will. And if our willpower is undermined, the obstacles seem twice as great. We *allow* the will to sink, until every problem produces a deep sense of discouragement.

On the other hand, when we are doing something we want to do, when we are carrying out some task with a deep sense of motivation, we are clearly aware of our freedom, and of our ability to "summon energy" to surmount obstacles. This has the effect of revitalizing us and recharging our batteries, which in turn deepens our sense of motivation, so that we actually enjoy tackling obstacles. In this state, we often observe that things seem to "go right," that obstacles seem to disappear of their own accord. This may or may not be true, but it certainly increases that feeling of zest and enthusiasm. We experience a kind of "positive feedback."

Now it obviously makes sense, on a purely logical level, to try to achieve these states of "positive feedback." No matter how serious the problems, it is obviously to our advantage to tackle them in a state of enthusiasm and optimism; it cannot possibly be to our advantage to sink into a state of discouragement. Unfortunately, we are not now dealing with a logical reaction, but with a purely instinctive one, like the child's desire to run away when you crawl towards him on all fours. And it is this negative reaction, this tendency to allow the will to collapse, and to seek the solution of the problem on a lower level, that constitutes the essence of criminal psychology.

Here is the paradox: that it is when we experience the feeling of helplessness, the sense that life has turned into a series of unfair frustrations and difficulties, that we are tempted to make "the decision to be out of control," to *restore the sensation of free will* by doing something absurd or violent or even criminal. This is the time when we lose our temper, or give way to a fit of self-pity, or take some dangerous or unjustifiable risk, like overtaking on a bend. Graham Greene has described how, as a teenager, he reacted to depression by playing Russian roulette with his brother's revolver, and how, when there was only a "click" on an empty chamber, he experienced a tremendous surge of joy; he had *become aware of his freedom*.

But this is only half the story. The mechanism can be studied even more clearly in Arthur Koestler's account of how he came to join the Communist Party. In *Arrow in the Blue*, he describes how he lost his money in a poker game, then got drunk at a party and discovered that the car radiator had frozen and the engine block had burst. He accepted the hospitality of a girl he disliked and spent the night in her bed. Waking up beside her with a hangover, he recalled that he had no money and no car, and felt the urge to "do something desperate" which led to the decision to join the Communist Party. Here we can see that his misfortunes had induced a sense of non-freedom that led him to decide to renounce what freedom he felt he had left, and to take refuge in a crowd. (This is, of course, the basic mechanism of "conversion.")

We are all familiar with the same tendency. When our energies are low, our freedom seems non-existent, and everyday tasks and chores seem unutterably tiresome. Then we slip into the vicious circle of boredom and loss of motivation in which it seems self-evident that life is a long-drawn-out defeat. This state of mind tempts us to take "short cuts." And crime, of course, is a short cut. We can study the same mechanism in Carl Panzram, who became a killer after he had betrayed the trust of the prison governor and decided that he was "worthless," and Ted Bundy, who became a Peeping Tom after his girlfriend had jilted him.

In this respect at least, crime is closely related to mental illness. Maslow describes the case of a girl who had sunk into such a state of depression that she had even ceased to menstruate. He discovered that she had been a brilliant student of sociology, who had been forced by the Depression of the 1930s to accept a job in a chewing-gum factory. The boredom of the job had totally eroded her sense of freedom. Maslow advised her to study sociology at night school, and her problems soon vanished; her sense of freedom had been restored. Similarly, William James describes how, during a period of anxiety about his future prospects, he also fell into a state of depression. One day, entering a room at dusk, he recalled the face of an idiot he had seen in a mental home, staring in front of him with blank eyes, and was suddenly overwhelmed by the thought: "If the hour should strike for me as it struck for him, *nothing* I possess could defend me from that fate." "There was . . . such a perception of my own merely momentary discrepancy from him, that it was as if something hitherto solid in my breast gave way, and I became a mass of quivering fear."

We, of course, can see clearly that there was far more than a "momentary discrepancy" between William James and an idiot suffering from catatonia; there was a vast difference in their capacity for freedom. But James had become *blind* to this difference because his depression had narrowed his senses. It is also significant that James began recovering from his period of mental illness when he came across a definition of free will by the philosopher Renouvier: that it is demonstrated by my capacity to *think one thing rather than another*. As soon as he became intellectually convinced that he possessed free will, he began to throw off his depression.

This is a point of central importance. Our free will is normally "invisible" to us, as a candle flame is invisible in the sunlight. We only become aware of it when we are engaged in some purposeful activity. Maslow made the interesting observation that when his students began to discuss peak experiences amongst themselves, and recall past peak experiences, they began having peak experiences all the time. The reason is obvious. The peak experience is a sudden *recognition* that we possess free will. It might be compared to discovering that the candle flame *is* there by putting your finger near it. Once the students became *aware* that they possessed free will, they kept on "recollecting" the fact with a shock of delight—the peak experience—like a man waking up in the middle of the night and remembering that he has inherited a fortune.

But *how* can we fall into this strange state of "unawareness of freedom"? The answer lies in a concept I have called "the robot." We all have a kind of robot in our subconscious minds which makes life a great deal easier. I have to learn new skills—like typing, driving a car, speaking French—patiently and slowly; then the robot takes them over and does it far more quickly than I could do it consciously. The trouble is that the robot not only does the things I want him to do, like typing, but also the things I *don't* want him to do, like enjoying nature, listening to music, even love-making. When we are tired, the robot takes control, and we lose all sense of freedom. We feel that we are merely a part of the physical world, with little or no power to "do." We lose our sense of our own value, and decide that the answer lies in compromise and seeking short cuts.

If we possessed detailed biographies of every criminal, we should almost certainly discover that most of them became criminals after such a crisis of "self-devaluation." But it is also interesting to note that some of the worst criminals—Henry Lee Lucas is an example—undergo religious conversion after they have been caught, as if the attention focused on them has restored their sense of personal value, so that they now become appalled by what they have done.

There is no obvious and simple method of restoring a criminal's sense of personal value, or of preventing him from losing it in the first place. But it may be worth noting the lesson of William James and of Maslow's sociology student: that as soon as the will is put to active use, the sense of personal value returns automatically. I have often daydreamed of the idea of a prison where, instead of receiving remission for good conduct—which is at best a negative virtue—prisoners receive it for creative activity: a month's remission for a good poem or painting, three months for a promising story or article, two years for a novel or symphony... The idea may be unworkable, but I have a feeling that the approach is along the right lines.

These reflections also lead me to the unfashionable view that the social philosophy promulgated by our educational institutions also deserves its share of the blame. The old religious philosophy of earlier centuries was authoritarian and repressive, but at least it assumed that man has an immortal soul, and that our task is to surmount the problems of everyday life by reminding ourselves of that fact. As far as Western civilization is concerned, the great change began after the year 1762, the year Rousseau's *Social Contract* appeared, with its famous words "Man is born free but is everywhere in chains." Unfortunately, this is a half-truth, which can be far more dangerous than a downright lie. Freedom is a quality of consciousness, not another name for a man's political rights. To confuse the two leads to intellectual chaos, which is the reverse of freedom. We all know people who ought to feel free because they have money and leisure, and yet who are miserable and neurotic. We all know people who ought to be miserable because they are poor and overworked, yet who remain remarkably cheerful. The very nature of freedom seems to be paradoxical.

As Rousseau's "Man is born free..." became part of the conventional wisdom, it became a justification for crime. If I believe that I *ought* to be free, and yet I do not feel free, then I look around for someone to blame. And if I allow Rousseau and Marx and Kropotkin to convince me that the blame should be placed squarely on the selfish philosophy of Capitalism, then I have found the ideal excuse for ignoring my own shortcomings and indulging in childish outbursts of self-pity. Lacenaire believed he was combating social injustice by stabbing a "bourgeois" and pushing his body into the river. Charles Manson believed that society is so rotten that it is no crime to murder the "pigs." Carl

Panzram went further and believed that life is so vile that to murder someone is to do him a favor.

We can see that this is merely unbelievably muddled thinking. But when so many academics and philosophers subscribe to it, we can hardly blame the criminals. Sartre is on record as describing the "Free World" as "that hell of misery and blood," and declaring that true progress lies in the attempt of the colored races to liberate themselves through violence. This philosophy inspired Italian terrorists who burst into a university classroom and shot the professor in the legs, alleging that he was guilty of teaching his students to adapt to a fundamentally immoral society. The same philosophy could easily be adapted to defend the activities of the Mafia.

In the Introduction to the *Encyclopedia of Modern Murder,* I pointed out that Albert Camus's book *L'Homme revolté (The Rebel)* was designed as a final refutation of Rousseau. It sets out to demonstrate that all the philosophies of freedom and rebellion, from de Sade to Karl Marx, have led to tyranny and the destruction of freedom. The rising tide of violence in our society demonstrates that Camus was right and Rousseau wrong. And if Rousseau's idea could gain currency because a need for change was so urgent in the late eighteenth century, then the same applies to Camus's idea when there is an even more urgent need for change in the late twentieth century. That observation places the responsibility squarely on the shoulders of our educational institutions and on our "intellectuals." But this analysis of the nature of freedom should have made it clear that this is only part of the solution. The great "metaphysical" problem of the human race is that we possess free will yet are usually unaware of it. We cease to be aware of it the moment we allow tiredness and pessimism to erode our sense of purpose. We *become* aware of it by flinging ourselves into purposeful activity. The real enemy is the pessimism that arises when we contemplate the problems—for example, the serial killers and "motiveless murder"—in a defeatist frame of mind. For, as we have seen, it is that "invisible" element of freedom that spells the difference between failure and success. And since the history of crime detection has been a history of optimism and logic, it would be a total absurdity to abandon our most powerful weapon at this point.

This had been for me the major "lesson" of this book, and my justification in writing it. But I trust I shall not be condemned as too "metaphysical" if I also point out that is the general solution of the problem we all face every morning when we open our eyes. The problem of crime is the problem of human existence.